aaron smith

shanti bloody shanti
an indian odyssey

transit lounge

First Published 2011
Transit Lounge Publishing
95 Stephen Street
Yarraville, Australia 3013
www.transitlounge.com.au
info@transitlounge.com.au

Front cover photograph: Leonid Plotkin   www.leonidfotos.com
Back cover photograph: Kip Scott
Design by Peter Lo

Transit Lounge is a proud member of the A.P.A.(Australian Publishers' Association) and S.P.U.N.C. (Small Press Underground Networking Community)

National Library of Australia
Cataloguing-in-Publication entry

Smith, Aaron.
Shanti bloody shanti : an Indian odyssey / Aaron Smith.
1st ed.

9781921924118 (pbk.)

Smith, Aaron,--Travel--India.

India--Description and travel.
India--Social life and customs.

915.4

'We are all in the gutter but some of us are looking at the stars.' Oscar Wilde

In memory of Leona

CHAPTER 1

The Green Men of Kolkata
March 14 2006 – The first day of the rest of my life.

'Just drive, man,' I say, leaning over towards Garuda from the back seat of his dirty-white Ambassador taxi. I reach past his ear, brushing the edge of his Sergio Leone spaghetti-western bad-guy moustache. Stretching out my green arm, I point to the horizon. It shimmers seductively – sirens and mermaids beckon towards a cruel mirage. I shake my head and blink – this requires focus. It's hot and dry, no mermaids, damn the subconscious. I stare at the bitumen road, the black sticky river undulating like a great serpent. I'm so close to Garuda I can smell the masala in his sweat and the beeswax in his hair. I whisper into his ear, spraying white spittle, 'Just drive, man. Go, man, go.'

Hot dusty air rushes in through the window as the Ambassador picks up speed. It's pungent with diesel, incense, raw sewage, rotting vegetables. An aromatic bouquet to the initiated – an acquired taste, it now smells comforting. To newly-arrived sanitised westerners, the overpowering stench rapes the nostrils. My heightened yet distorted senses are aware of every minuscule detail. I shout, 'We're free! Free to be whatever we want, as long as we stay present in the eternal moment. *Sab kuch milega* (Everything is possible).'

The car speaker blares out radio static, sitars and someone

singing mantras. It's between two stations, a beat mixed by the gods. It works – it's funky. The crackling of the speaker merges with the white noise of the acid hissing in my brain.

The music seems to crescendo and then drop away in unison with the Ambassador as it weaves through the traffic. The tempo slows as Garuda brakes hard behind a line of motorbikes and cars circa 1950, stopping in time with the music. We are suspended in an infinite moment. The lights then flick to green, the music blares out again and we lurch off. Garuda is at one with the purpose of our mission, a mission from God maybe, if there are any gods, even though not another word is uttered. We're communicating on a whole heap of higher levels.

Outside the world flashes past, blending into a mosaic of colours. Soot encrusts the crumbling architecture of the British Raj, the same black gunk I scrape out of my nostrils every few hours. Its sweet metallic taste hits my tongue every time I inhale. Despite this drab background, vibrant colour is splashed everywhere. Every street corner dances in a spasmodic array of rainbows. My perceptual field bleeds, the colours run, the periphery of my senses melts. I grin. Smile lines reach my ears, cracking the salty film of dried tears. Tears of hysteria, laughter and pure joy.

Garuda flies across an intersection splattered on one side with silver and on the other purple. On the left side, people are silver from head to toe and on the right, they are purple. They are totally covered, except for the whites of their eyes and teeth exposed by big smiles. Everyone laughs, jumps up and down and waves at me. Meekly I give the royal wave as we hurtle past.

The scenery flickers, like an over-exposed camera lens. The Ambassador glides. I can't even feel the road anymore.

Through the window I see a motorbike – going fast, it keeps up with the Ambassador. The passenger is a yellow man and the driver a blue man, both are staring at us. Smiling and bobbing their heads, they accept us; without speaking they say, *Mother India welcomes you.*

We're flying now, a random selection of travellers thrown together by fate in the back of a taxi – myself, Munty, Dangerous Dave and Red Man. Nobody speaks, there is no need, everything's been said and anything else would be a cliché. On the dashboard sits a plastic effigy of Shiva, adorned with white flowers, and a mandarin speared with incense sticks. Its LED lights flash on and off, highlighting the beauty and kitschness of everything.

On the potholed road two overloaded Tata trucks approach us, one overtaking the other. Our path is blocked. There is nowhere for us to go. The Hindi music kicks up a notch. I laugh heartily, 'Now this is living!'

Garuda grinds the Ambassador back a gear and accelerates hard towards the oncoming wall of truck. One hand is wrapped tightly around the steering wheel while the other squeezes the butt of his cigarette. There is one more drag left and he intends to smoke it. Unflinching, he steels his gaze to our impending fate.

The exquisite moment, in all its infinite detail, ceases for eternity in the glorious now. Atoms of everything vibrate. Yes, we are all here in the beautiful now. We are free and we are green. We are the green men of Kolkata, except for Red Man. No, he's red, but *same same but different* as they say here.

Or, as they say also here, *Shanti shanti* (peace).

* * *

I awaken uneasily – it's hot, almost too hot to breathe. It's the same heat every day, but something has drawn me out of a restless sleep. Outside it's still dark except for the waning moon. I stare through my mosquito net at the ceiling and watch the overhead fan spinning, its mechanical whirl slowing. Another power failure, a daily occurrence.

Sweat glistens all over my body, trickling into the thin hemp mattress. God knows how much sweat has seeped into it through countless years of sweaty travellers. Dawn fingers its way across the undulating walls, showing the effects of yesterday's acid, charas (Indian hashish) and beer. It all seemed like a good idea at the time. My skin crawls, from either the bedbugs or the poisons in my blood. The temperature continues to rise. At the peak of yesterday's LSD trip, in the back of an Ambassador, I'd had an epiphany. I was free as long as I lived in the eternal moment, the proverbial now.

Today, however, I'm still a thirty-six year old, a recently divorced, slightly depressed guy on the rebound unable to pick up a shag. This is despite countless attempts to appear a wise, ruggedly good-looking, adventurous bronzed Aussie who can wrestle crocodiles. Even so, I don't feel desperately lonely any more, just contentedly alone as I lie in my bed in downtown Kolkata. Right now my life doesn't feel as much of an ordeal as it had.

Then a new sweat forms, a cold sweat. Sharp pain spikes my stomach. I feel the need to fart, badly, but it is only brave men and fools who fart in India. You never know when you are going to follow through with a shart. Groaning and clutching my cramping stomach, I sit up on the edge of my cast-iron bed. The bedsprings creak as I hunch over my knees. A swarm of mosquitoes manifests around my ankles. Too weak to move, I watch them gorge, thinking, *Fuck them and the twenty-two diseases they carry.* Sweat droplets run down my forehead, through my eyebrows and off the bridge of my nose. Glancing over at Dangerous Dave, snoring in his partially collapsed bed, I envy his ability to sleep so soundly.

Now someone is turning a knife in my stomach. My lower intestine starts to spasm. Dizzy, black splotches fill my vision. Nausea rises. I only have moments before everything turns very messy. Lurching off the bed and grabbing my *lungi* (Indian sarong), I stagger out of the room towards the toilet. My mosquito cloud trails behind me.

Acrid gastric juices wash up over my tonsils, and a wave of vomit presses against the back of my mouth and begins seeping out of my nostrils – the gag reflex can no longer be suppressed. I hurl. Clutching the edge of the handbasin, my thumbs sink into the foul custard and I moan. Relieved, I dare a glance into the mirror.

I'm not surprised to see my eyes still dilated and bloodshot, but my long tangled hair and skin are a deep forest green. More than just a hangover, this is the aftermath of one of India's least religious and most popular Hindu holidays: Holi or the festival of colours. I'm green from head to toe – the dye has even soaked through my thin cotton clothing, staining my tattooed body.

Holi, celebrated all over India, is an excuse to run amok and cut loose from usually strict social norms. It unites rich and poor, male and female, and all castes. The legend commemorated by the festival involves Lord Shiva, the god of destruction (one of the big cheeses of Indian mythology), and Madana, the goddess of love. Madana tried to tempt Shiva by appearing before him as a beautiful nymph. Shiva, who was meditating (he did a lot of this), was mightily pissed off at the distraction, so he blasted her with a ball of fire from his third eye, reducing her to ashes. This, and the onset of spring, are the basis of the festival. To celebrate spring and Shiva's great balls of fire, Indians cover each other with coloured dyes in powder and liquid forms, build bonfires in the streets to ward off evil spirits, and act a little unreserved.

Even with this knowledge, I'd felt uncomfortable yesterday seeing a man with rotten teeth running around with no pants on. His family jewels flapped in the breeze as he danced around a bonfire in the middle of the road, shouting, *Bura na mano, Holi hai.* This apparently meant, Please don't be offended, it's Holi.

It had been a long day, we were sunstruck after staggering around the beautiful but ostentatious grounds of the Victoria Monument. This was a marble palace from the height of the British Raj, fronted by a grumpy, pigeonshit-encrusted bronze Queen Victoria and surrounded by acres of English gardens wilting under the Indian sun. We had lain under the banyan trees, asking her majesty, 'What's a nice girl like you doing in a place like this?'

Our very motley crew included Ian, nicknamed the Plastic Bottle Munted Yoga Master, or Munty for short. On any other day he was a respectable Englishman from Bath, balding, slightly overweight, thirty-five and vaguely well-to-do in some IT job. Under the influence of LSD, he had developed a unique balancing act involving a plastic water bottle and an awkward one-footed standing position. Then there was Dangerous Dave, another Englishman, a painter and decorator and cricket fanatic, with a slim build, in his late 20s to early 30s. He was only ever a danger to himself. During our all-night poker sessions he always got cleaned out, and always bought back in to lose again. Every night we asked, 'Dave, do you have a gambling problem?' Smiling like a naughty schoolboy, he always replied with a definitive, 'Yes, I have a gambling problem.'

Dave was a likeable character, with bright blue eyes, sporting a toothy grin and a crop of short brown hair. The sort of guy mothers like. Lastly there was Red Man, whose name we could never remember, a Czech-Republic tour leader, a tall guy in his late 20s, but too thin, with a blond ponytail. He spoke poor English in an accent that sounded like Count Dracula – definitely a man of few words.

We'd been tripping hard since the morning, staggering around Kolkata. Ian, with his T-shirt tied as a bandana and exposing his paunch, crawled on all fours and hid behind what little foliage he could find. He thought the green dye smeared all over his body camouflaged him. Dave wore his shoes on his hands because he said they fitted him better that way. He was also green with pink in his hair. He grinned like an escaped mental patient. Red Man, doused in red, mouth agape with a gormless expression, limped along with only one sandal, the other lost somewhere.

Then there was the taxi-ride through the backstreets, when we made Garuda drive for half an hour in one direction, only to turn around and drive back again. We saw a cross-section of a city of nearly fourteen million people, an endless sprawl of decaying streets. Kolkata was beautiful in its state of decomposition and overwhelming in its enormity.

After falling out of the taxi, back from where we started, I found a playing card in the gutter – the ace of spades – the same image that's tattooed on my inside wrist. I got the tattoo ten years ago. Heroin had nearly destroyed me and when I quit cold turkey I wanted the spade to remind me that if I ever used that hand again, to stick a needle in my arm, I was digging my own grave. It had worked – I hadn't touched junk since. Finding that card on the street felt like an omen; I put it in my pocket for safekeeping.

We tried to buy a soft drink from a stall owner who kept morphing into the 330 million different Hindu gods. Terrified and unable to complete the transaction, we just threw money at him and ran away in hysterics.

Giggling like schoolgirls on prom night, we rambled through the expansive Victoria Park where hundreds of Indians played cricket, a different game every thirty metres or so. A group invited us to play, honoured to have so many nationalities in their presence. Cricket in India is as paramount as religion, and Australia having a reputation of being one of the best teams in the world means that Australians are revered as gods by Indians. A smiling Bengali man shook my hand. 'Yes, Ricky Ponting, Australian captain, very, very good, vorld champion number one. Very much excellent, you must definitely be playing vith us.'

Considering us gods of cricket, the locals were awestruck. But after Dave bowled three wides, I dropped an easy catch and Ian couldn't stop weeping hysterically, we were shunned by all the players in the park. They looked at us with disdain – the village idiots. Smirking to ourselves, we crossed the grounds, inadvertently walking through several games and disrupting play. We apologised profusely for the general public disturbance and Ian's inability to stop crying. Dehydrated, we walked into the setting sun and back to our backpackers' haven. We craved the sanctuary of our temporary home, the Salvation Army YMCA.

It was dark by the time we made it to Sudder Street, and the whole road had been closed off with bonfires. A naked crazy dancing man, accompanied by a giant yellow goat, made me realise how much I had tired of the surreal.

Naked-man took a shine to Ian and did a little dance around him, each circle getting a little closer. He grunted and, in a state of semi-arousal, stamped his feet and wiggled his fingers. Ian stopped laughing and went quiet. Dave, Red Man and I too exhausted to comprehend Ian's predicament abandoned him to the naked man, who was now rocking from side to side, only a foot or so in front of him. Like a giant praying mantis, he had hypnotised Ian. We ducked into a side alley and sat, relieved, resting our aching bodies on the wooden crate bench at the literal cornerstone of Indian culture – the chaiwallah's stall.

Dave rolled a joint as I ordered tea. Found on every street corner in every city, town and village in India, the chaiwallah not only provides sweet milk tea, but also directions, information, even spiritual advice – the East's version of the bartender psychologist. Our chaiwallah couldn't have been more than eight years old but already looked world weary and wise, yet still smiling. He told me how his grandfather and his father had made tea on this same spot for many years and in the future his yet-unborn son would do the same. Beaming, he puffed out his chest. 'I am chaiwallah, this is my duty in this life and I vill do it the very best I can and vith pride. This is my place in the vorld.'

I smiled – his humility and contentment refreshed me. Back home in the West, his equivalent would have told me this was just something he did until bigger, more grandiose dreams were fulfilled. No, this young but wizened Bengali boy already understood the importance of the journey rather than the final destination. The aroma of charas filled the air as Dave passed me the joint. Sipping on my sweet chai, I contemplated the madness of the day. The naked man ran past down the street, arms outstretched, chasing the yellow goat – he must have tired of Ian's unresponsiveness. Maybe he had more chance of getting lucky with the goat. A pale Ian joined our entourage along with other multicoloured, exhausted festival goers. He silently accepted a glass of chai and the joint. On the other side of the wave, the acid began its decline into a subdued finale.

Grinning, I remembered three months earlier, when I'd flown from Sydney to Mumbai, the day before Christmas. I'd wanted to spend Christmas in Bollywood. Why? Because it was the hell out of Australia. I was freshly divorced from Stella, a high-maintenance nightclub diva. Our marriage had been a whirlwind of fighting and fireworks. Then as the fireworks fizzled we just fought until the inevitable end came. A thousand pop songs talk about falling in love but not many mention falling out of love, growing apart until one day there's nothing left in common except the things that annoy each other. She loved clubbing, I'd grown tired of the song that never ended, it had all become so vacuous to me. Ironically we met in a club and broke up over, amongst other things, clubbing. Knowing we didn't have shared interests anymore didn't make the break up any easier, I was relieved the fighting had ended but was left with a hole in my heart. I knew I'd be OK, eventually, but I also knew I'd have to feel crappy for a considerable time.

The whole cliché *go find yourself in India* was as good an option as any. Also a contract put on my life from a jilted cocaine dealer, because of a fling with his girlfriend, was a good motivator. In search of some solace on the rebound, I had opened a Pandora's box of trouble – so I sold all my worldly possessions on eBay and did a runner. During the flight from Australia, I got chatting with an elderly Indian woman. I told her I was going to India to study yoga in the holy town of Rishikesh, bathe in the Ganges river, try to get a break in a Bollywood film and party on New Year's Eve on the beaches of Goa. She smiled and replied, 'Mother India is bottomless. You can go as deep as you like and there vill always be more.'

Those words resonated with me, sitting on that bench in a back alley in Kolkata. Sipping chai, smoking charas and watching the festival's flotsam and jetsam stagger by, I wondered how much deeper I could go. A homeless teenager, filthy with no shoes and dressed in plastic bags, silently approached the chai stand. Stooping low, he touched everyone's feet and then left.

* * *

Staring in the mirror of the YMCA bathroom, I wipe vomit from my lips and mutter, 'Mother India is bottomless.' Suddenly the knife in my stomach twists again, shooting pain down into my bowels. One hand clutching my guts, the other steadying myself on the bathroom wall, I shuffle to the toilet. It's a Western sit-down model, not the usual squat-over-hole variety. Grateful for the seat, I exhale slowly, cautiously releasing my sphincter muscles. What feels like my liquefied internal organs falls out my ass. My stomach turns again. Spying a bucket next to the toilet, I grab it in the nick of time.

Sitting on the porcelain throne, expelling vile fluids from both ends, I have time to reflect. I suspect my current condition is not only due to yesterday's drugs but also to do with yesterday's consumption of so-called pizza in a small establishment called the Super Bar at the opposite end of Sudder Street. I've developed a saying in India: when someone asks me if my food is good or not, I reply, 'Good meal, ha, ask me tomorrow!'

Last night's dinner had obviously not been good despite tasting wholesome. With our appetites rekindled by the joints in the chaiwallah's alley and the dire need to quench a growing thirst, we had been drawn to the Super Bar's flashing neon sign. It looked like an amusement park ride. Instead of the Ghost Train we entered Western World, complete with maroon-clad waiters, cold beer, multi-cuisine food and TVs blaring out a cricket game.

It was packed with both travellers and Bengalis dripping with cheap gold bling-bling. All were overweight, double-chinned with paunches overhanging their belts. To be overweight or at least of generous proportions is considered a sign of high social status in India and not shunned as in the anorexic, oppressed West. Bollywood movie starlets are always on the chunky side from our diet-addicted perspective. A round belly and some thunder on the thighs are considered positively sexy.

It was the closing minutes of a legendary game. Australia vainly tried to overturn South Africa. I was soon absorbed into a group of excited Indians and being Australian automatically qualified me to be the ambassador of Australian cricket. Each time the South Africans smacked the ball around the field, our party of Indians turned to me to gauge my reaction. A large Indian man hugged me with his ample arm, his sweaty armpit pressed against my shoulder as he jeered, 'Yes, yes, Australia is most definitely being in trouble. Do you think you can possibly vin? You are the vorld champions, vhat must your captain be feeling at this very moment?'

'Yes, yes, Ricky Ponting, Australia's captain,' proclaimed another Indian as he jumped up and down, spilling half of his beer.

As pizza and pitchers of the popular Indian beer Kingfisher arrived at our table, Ian was still quiet and not enjoying the frivolities. Looking disturbed, he frowned at me. 'Can I talk to you, in private, outside?'

I escorted Ian outside with a piece of pizza in one hand and half a pitcher of beer in the other. 'Step into my office.' Standing there in the street as a rickshaw rattled past, Ian looked like a sad clown, limp shouldered and green. Staring at the ground, he shuffled his feet and stammered, 'Look, this may sound strange, but I keep having déjà vus.'

This had definitely come out of left field, I tried to look concerned while I munched on my pizza. He continued, looking even more perplexed. 'The taxi ride, the yellow goat, the naked crazy man, the cricket on TV and even that rickshaw that just passed – I knew it would all happen. At first it was only every now and then, so I didn't think much of it. But then it started happening every few minutes, and now every few seconds. What's next? What happens when the points of time unite, when the moment before joins with the moment after?'

OK, this could've been a dicey situation. An acid freak-out casualty. Was Ian about to become part of the flotsam and jetsam in the gutters of India, left behind by the receding tide of his own mind? He wouldn't be the first or the last victim, and he fitted the profile – an escapee from a high stress job, a string of failed relationships, and in dire need of spiritual growth to fill the void inside. Like myself and many other earnest travellers drawn to the subcontinent – like moths to a candle or flies to shit – he was in search of something, anything. We were soldiers of misfortune in search of truth, armed only with our *Lonely Planet* guidebooks and backpacks – jetset vagabonds with nothing to our names but travel-insurance self-assurance.

Every battle has its casualties and Ian was dangerously close to the edge of the abyss. He was teetering on the precipice – painted green, sweating profusely, his T-shirt tied around his head, his Buddha belly hanging over his tattered Thai fisherman pants and on the wrong end of an acid trip in a Kolkata alley. I had to act fast. Putting my arm around his shoulders I started to walk him down Sudder Street. 'Munty, my good man, do you know what a déjà vu actually is, in scientific terms?'

His bottom lip quivered. 'No, not really.'

'OK, It's to do with the right and the left hemispheres of the brain. Memory is stored in the left analytical half, while new experience is dealt with by the creative right side.'

Ian hung onto my every word. I continued, 'Now, in normal experience, information from our five senses goes first to the right side of the brain. The right side then sends this data to the left side, where it is stored as memory.' For extra impact I stopped walking and turned to face him. 'Are you following me so far, Munty?'

Eyes wide like a scared child, he replied, 'I think so.'

'Alright then, what happens with a déjà vu is that this incoming information goes straight to the left, memory side of the brain a millisecond before the right side sends the information across. So, when the left side receives the data again from the right side, it goes hey, we already have a recorded memory of this. So your mind is fooled into believing it happened before. So that's all it is, just a trick of the mind.'

Ian paused, then his voice wavered. 'Thing is, see, I'm positive that when the two points of time finally meet, the near past with the near future, I'll die. This is my death. I'm witnessing my own end.'

I sighed and he continued, 'It's like what you keep saying about being in the now. That there is only the now and all that. Well, this is my now and I think I'm only moments away from my death. This is the last day of my life.'

Was this the aftermath of my having read too many self-help books big on being present in the moment? I'd been fervently digesting this material to keep away feelings of self-destruction and lift myself out of a pit of depression. I'd been pontificating a lot about the now during our all-night poker games.

I decided to try a different approach. I smiled. 'Ian, you're just tripping, mate, OK? Go home and hit the hay. I personally guarantee you won't die and you'll be fine in the morning.'

For the first time since the episode with the naked dancing man, Ian smiled. He inhaled deeply and straightened up. 'Right, yes. OK, will do, thanks for that little pep talk. Look, sorry, um, can we keep this under wraps? Wouldn't want the lads getting the wrong impression and all.'

'No worries, Munty.' I gave Ian a brotherly hug. He froze up, uncomfortable with the physical contact. Maybe it was because of the episode with the naked dancing man, or maybe just stiff upper lip, anal Britishness. He stepped backwards, mumbling, 'Really, I'm fine now, honestly. Think I'll go and sleep it off. Right then, see you in the morning.'

* * *

Sitting here now on the YMCA toilet, I stare into the bucket. I see pieces of what looks like sweetcorn, but I haven't eaten corn for months. I reflect on why I get myself into these situations. Some would say it's my karma. Others would just say it serves me right. This is actually the first time I've been sick in India. Until now, I thought I had a cast-iron stomach while my fellow travellers fell by the wayside. Ian, especially, had been complaining of stomach upsets for the whole month I'd known him.

It's amazing. Only somewhere like India can you meet a traveller, someone you have never met previously, and within minutes be talking in detail about your bowel movements – their consistency, colour and looseness. This is a country where it's considered provocative for a woman to show an ankle or upper arm, or for straight couples to hold hands. It is, however, completely OK to defecate and urinate in public. Some Indian men never see their own wives naked, Indian couples go steady for five years without kissing, and foreigners have been extradited and even jailed for showing affection in public. Yet people don't bat an eyelid at someone dropping their drawers and shitting on the footpath, the beach or anywhere the urge takes them.

Seeing the body as a temple for the soul, Indians are obsessed with expelling all waste from this shrine at every available minute. It's all part of the nirvanic purification every multiple-god-fearing Indian Hindu is encouraged to aspire to. So it's common to see bright-eyed children beaming proud smiles as they shit in the street. Mothers hold naked babies in outstretched arms as they wee. On the beaches in southern India in the mornings, or in the rice paddies along railway lines in the evenings, the whole village bares asses and strains towards purification. Crapping is a social act that many Indians revel in. I, on the other hand (call me a prude), like to strain towards my nirvana in private and without an audience.

Cradling my head, which aches from dehydration, I ask myself again, why the acid trip, and in Kolkata of all places? It was delivered by the gods of fortuity the day before Holi by a strange Lithuanian chemist at the chai stall. We had struck up a conversation, deliberately avoiding the usual *Where do you come from? Where are you going? How long have you been travelling?* No, we started on the subject of drug use as a modern rite of passage. The Lithuanian finished his chai, smashed the disposable clay cup on the ground and lit a cigarette. 'I need to get out of zis fucking city, ze pollution, ze crowds, it's too fucking much, man. I need somewhere fucking shanti shanti. I'm thinking of going to ze Andaman Islands.'

My eyes lit up, having arrived from the Andaman Islands the previous day with Ian, Dave, Red Man and other newly-made travel friends. 'My man, get your little black book out. I'm going to give you some pointers that'll make your trip easy.'

The Andaman Islands, once a British Raj penal colony, are a thousand kilometres off the east coast of India. Many of the islands are uninhabited, and others are sparsely populated by indigenous tribes who have never seen white people. Remote and underdeveloped – it's a paradise. I told him about the best guesthouses and beaches. Afterwards the Lithuanian rummaged through a leather pouch and handed me a small package wrapped in silver foil. 'Energy for energy, man. This is special fucking recipe, very fucking strong, I make myself.'

It was obviously a sign. My old friend Frankie was due to turn up for Holi and this dose of acid was perfect for our reunion.

I met Frankie when we were both eighteen. We had been working in an orchard in rural Australia. A real gypsy by then, he'd grown up in an old school bus travelling around Australia with his mum, little brother and ex-biker stepfather. When Frankie got sacked for arguing with the orchard farmer, I got sacked for being his friend. So we set off together and hitchhiked around Australia. It was a real coming-of-age journey for both of us. Now, eighteen years later, we were doing the sequel, but after a small falling out, decided to travel solo for a couple of weeks.

Frankie, to say the least, is an eccentric character. He's the same height as me, 6'2", with a wiry build, short black hair and a moustache-less beard that often gets him mistaken for a Muslim and occasionally even Osama Bin Laden. He encourages this with his disregard of authority and contempt for middle Australia. He's an artist, painter and musician convinced he's not from this galaxy, but from the Pleiades constellation.

Our relationship has at times been contentious, and sometimes we haven't seen eye-to-eye, but we've always managed to stay friends. We've even been blackmarket business partners – contraband couriers for pizza-shop mafia dons and biker gangs. Frankie often returned without the cash we needed to pay our creditors but with an array of bargains that had been too good to resist. He was like Jack and the beanstalk with his magic beans. One time he returned with – and I quote – 'a classic vintage 70s hang glider'. Not to mention the dune buggy that only needed a bit of work, a variety of obscure musical instruments and an extremely rare and exotic breed of cat. In more recent years we drifted from two-bit grifting to working demeaning jobs, but our philosophical conversations remained stimulating and would have given Jung or Descartes a run for their money – well, on one of their bad days, maybe.

But Frankie didn't show up. Every day he emailed saying he'd be there for Holi, but he never appeared. So I got the backup Andaman crew together, the Fabulous Four – Munty, Dave, Red Man and me – and the rest is history.

CHAPTER 2

Christmas in Bollywood

I first flew into India to Mumbai (formerly Bombay) late on Christmas Eve 2005. On the northwest coast of the Arabian Sea, Mumbai is an expansive metropolis of around fourteen million people and represents India's most populous city. Located at the fat edge of the wedge of the subcontinent, Mumbai sits on a land reclamation of what was once the seven islands of Bombay. Through the plane's window I could make out the lights of the endless lattice of city streets shimmering to the dark horizon. Passing through customs and stepping into a humidity so thick you could carve it with a knife, I was shellshocked from culture overload and wasn't sure if I was doing the right thing. Sitting in the back of my first Ambassador taxi, which looked like it was made in the early 60s, I watched as we passed through blocks of slums, destitute shantytowns built from pieces of plastic, scraps of metal and whatever refuse could be salvaged from the streets. Overhead, masses of tangled powerlines were illegally tapped from the city grid. Even with the overwhelming poverty, I was surprised by the number of earthen-floored shacks with nothing inside but a widescreen TV.

Mothers washed children in buckets on the side of the road as my taxi crawled along, bumper to bumper with other cars caught in the endless gridlock. Everybody blasted their horns as rickshaws squeezed through impossibly small gaps. A teenager rode past my window with a block of ice strapped to the back of his bone-shaking pushbike. So this was India. Masses of people everywhere, thin, brown, with eyes wide open – all staring.

As I struggled to breathe, we pulled up at the Green Palace Hotel. It had looked a lot nicer on the internet. The Green Palace was no palace, but it was green in a mildewy way. It was a rat and louse infested brothel with dirty sheets, blood spots on the walls and jaded-looking staff. Worst of all, there was no sign of Frankie who had left for India a couple of weeks before me. In fact, I hadn't heard anything from him since he'd left, apart from one email that he was drowning in people and was getting the hell out of town. He was meant to meet me at the hotel. But Frankie never was one for either convention or timeframes.

So I went to bed that night wondering if I was about to venture into the madness of India alone. I downed a handful of valium that my doctor had prescribed for my divorce-fuelled insomnia. Alone in an alien world, I listened to the rats scuttling in the walls and the bustle of Mumbai outside. Already I started to regret leaving Australia. Humming *Jingle Bells* to myself as I waited for the valium to kick in, I mulled over the conversation with Frankie that had inspired the perhaps rash decision to come to India.

It was at an arty bohemian café in Sydney's inner city a couple of months before Christmas. Staring into my latte, I'd confessed to him that I may have been having a premature midlife crisis – with my divorce, and subsequent disintegration of the great Australian 2.5 children, white-picket fence, suburban wet dream, my failed grunge-rock and bit-part acting careers, all topped off with an existential questioning of what I was doing with my life. Raised a strict atheist, dare I say I was seeking God? All I knew for sure was that the only things keeping me sane at that point were my yoga class at the local gym and lattes with Frankie.

Spooning milk foam around my glass I looked up at Frankie, 'I mean, is this it? Frankie, fuck, there's gotta be more to life. Am I destined to always be a chronic underachiever? It's like I've been searching for something my whole life, but nothing's ever worked out, it's no wonder I used to be a drug addict.'

Frankie nodded slowly then gazed out the window as rain drizzled down the glass. 'It's like nobody understands us here. It's even tougher for me dude, try being Pleiadian in this country. I got called gay the other day. Just because of my fine bone structure, you know, coz the atmosphere on my home planet is much thinner.' Frankie sighed, 'Not that there's anything wrong with being gay, I just haven't had a girlfriend for a while – it's not easy to meet girls 500 light years from home. Anyway I don't care – sex just drains my vitality and meditation powers.'

I ran my hands through my hair. 'Yeah, right, I hear ya Frankie. Look, what's the common denominator here?' I stared at him intently, 'We're both seeking something, right?'

Frankie's eyes lit up. 'I know, let's split, let's just leave. Let's like go to India man, meditate, do yoga, escape the distractions of women. You know, like transcend this illusion.'

And that was it. We vowed to flee to the subcontinent together. But then I met a girl. Amber, a twenty-two year old Ghanaian girl with an English accent, was drop-dead gorgeous, witty and great fun. I'd met her at a nightclub. A party girl, she was the girlfriend of a cocaine dealer. Incidentally the same coke dealer I'd stolen Stella away from several years earlier; it felt like old patterns repeating.

Amber and I had hit it off instantly. The chemistry was electric, and she made me feel young and alive again with her carefree spirit. One time we'd pretended to be millionaires and test-drove a new Mercedes convertible, before ordering a burger buck naked at a McDonald's drive-through. She'd tell her boyfriend she was out of town visiting family, and then stay with me for week-long sex marathons that were fuelled by handfuls of zinc tablets, home-delivered pizza and jars of peanut butter. It was just the boost my shattered ego needed after the castration of divorce. But I knew I was playing with fire. What with my shared history with the coke dealer and his predilection for violence. To top it all off I started to fall in love with Amber. She represented the last turnpike before the highway to middle-agedom and all its crises. I was in denial and on the rebound.

Frankie had kept calling, asking when we were going to leave. He'd had all his shots, packed his bag and was waiting with bated breath. He had already sold his only worldly possession, an early 70s VW Kombi van. I'd kept stalling him. I'd told him the divorce was taking longer than expected. Days had turned into weeks and as Christmas quickly approached Frankie grew increasingly impatient. So we'd agreed he'd leave a couple of weeks before me, while I pretended to finalise the divorce. I'd procrastinated and avoided booking my plane ticket. Frankie pressured me one last time on the phone moments before he boarded his flight. 'Man, you could stay here with this new girl, but in your heart you know you need this journey. If ya don't go now, you'll never face yourself. Don't stay coz of a girl, dude – get out of the country!'

It was the phone call from Amber that clinched it, 'Um, my boyfriend kinda found out about us and he kinda has a contract out on you now. I am so sorry.'

I thought she was being metaphorical, 'So he's pissed then?'

'Well at first, but now he's calm, now he's paid the guy to do the hit, said it felt like closure.'

Running into a travel agency on the last business day before Christmas I announced, 'I want a ticket to India.'

'Sir, we close in ten minutes.'

I slammed a wad of cash down on her desk. She stared at the money for a moment, then started tapping away on her keyboard. 'OK, sir, right away.'

After a few minutes she stopped. 'Well, there's only one seat available – it leaves Christmas Eve. Everything else is fully booked till February.'

'I'll take it.'

'Look, this ticket's going to be expensive. However, for a fraction more you can upgrade to a round-the-world flight. The only problem is you have to book it now, with all the destinations, as we're about to close and the system will be locked down for Christmas. You only have five minutes to decide. What do you think?'

She was trying to upsell me, super-size my ticket. Feeling reckless, I answered, 'What the hell. Let's do it.'

Typing, not looking up from her keyboard, 'So where to? You can pick three continents. You're already in Asia, so that's one. You can squeeze in one more stopover, how's Thailand sound. Remember, the clock is ticking.'

'Um, OK I guess.'

Still typing, 'Done. Now you can pick Europe or Africa, but we only have three minutes.'

At a loss, I looked around the office. There was a client picking up his ticket. 'Excuse me mate, where are you going?'

The guy looked surprised. 'Err, Greece.'

'Is it nice there?'

'Yeah, well, I am Greek.'

Yelling over my shoulder, 'Lock it in.'

The travel agent stopped, stretched her fingers and wiped her forehead. 'One continent to go, North or South America, in less than two minutes. You can choose New York or Brazil.'

'I'll flip for it.' Pulling a coin from my jeans, I threw it into the air and slapped it down on the back of my hand. 'Heads, Broadway and pretzels, tails, samba and the Amazon.' Lifting my hand, I looked. 'Brazil it is.'

The travel agent finished typing. 'It's now or never, once I hit Enter it's in the system and can't be changed. Any last-minute doubts?'

'Do it.'

In four minutes flat, I'd decided my fate for the next year of my life. Then, some twenty-four hours later, in what felt then like the ass end of the world I was uncertain I'd done the right thing. On Christmas Eve in the Green Palace Hotel in downtown Mumbai my last thoughts as the valium swallowed my consciousness were, *This is not what I expected at all. India looked much nicer in the brochures.*

* * *

I was awoken suddenly from a nightmare by a tapping on my door – I had dreamt my ex, Stella, was a giant insect pulling my legs off. Still groggy, I got up and opened it.

'Namaste, Babaji.' Namaste is a Hindi all-purpose greeting, and *Babaji* is a respectful term for 'important uncle'. Frankie stood there, bright-eyed and bushy-tailed. I hugged him. 'Man, I was worried when you weren't here last night and no

email for weeks. I thought you'd disappeared off the face of the earth. Thought I'd be flying solo. Shit, dude, it's good to see ya.'

He smiled. 'Hey, Merry Christmas, ya fucker, good to see you too.' He thrust a book into my hands, *Freedom from the Known* by Krishnamurti. Frankie, a big fan of this guru or anti-guru as he called him, always spouted his quotes. 'Hope this starts you on your spiritual quest in India, man. Hey, I have a friend to introduce you to.'

Over Frankie's shoulder I saw a short smiling middle-aged hotel worker grinning back at me. I stared at Frankie. He laughed. 'No, man, not him. Her.'

A pretty petite girl with short blonde hair, maybe late 20s, stepped out from behind him, waved self-consciously and in a French accent squeaked, 'Bonjour.'

'Aaron, this is Monique. Monique this is Aaron. She's French, she's a professional photographer.' Frankie beamed with pride.

I was in shock for the second time in twenty-four hours, as Frankie had been a self-confessed monk. But now the bastard had a girlfriend! Stunned, I replied, 'G'day, Monique.'

Frankie continued, 'Yeah, man, you wouldn't believe it. We met in this little village in the hills outside the city. The guesthouse had double booked my room, the fuckers. So we had to share it. I was suffering really bad food poisoning from a bad chicken tikka masala – actually nearly died (I doubted this, Frankie was always a hypochondriac). I spent two days on the toilet floor throwing my guts up, really, I nearly died, didn't I, Monique? Yeah, there I was in the foetal position and Monique brought me water and changed my buckets. Then, ya know, one thing led to another.'

'Sounds romantic.'

Frankie spoke very quickly. I suspected he was nervous about how I would react. 'You don't mind if Monique tags along with us, yeah? I told her you wouldn't mind.'

What could I say? I hadn't expected this. Sure I minded. Especially considering Frankie had pressured me to go to India after I'd just met Amber. As I looked at Frankie, smiling nervously in my doorway, the word 'hypocrite' came to mind. I forced a smile. 'Of course I don't mind if Monique comes, the more the merrier.'

* * *

I spent a couple of nauseating days with Frankie and Monique in Mumbai. Suffering from culture shock, I followed them about like a stray puppy. Mumbai's endless layers of living history engulfed me, a city that was constantly eating and re-birthing itself, its side streets swelling with vendors selling strange herbs, cheap electric gizmos, polyester socks and effigies of bizarre gods. The smells curdled my stomach – kerosene blended with incense and shit. Seeing Frankie and Monique happy together reminded me I missed Amber. Monique didn't like big cities, so we jumped on a sleeper bus and headed south down the coast to neighbouring Goa, to the quiet and romantic Colva Beach in the southern end of the state. Once a Portuguese colony, Goa was a small Indian province that represented the epicentre of beach and nightlife culture for tourists in India, where beer and bikinis were tolerated, bars blasted Bob Marley and even the locals said 'cool'. Monique didn't want to be around all the noisy partygoers of north Goa and Frankie, who was by then Monique's little lap dog, agreed. I figured, at least it was a beach.

'Sleeper bus' is at best a colloquial expression, more

realistically wishful thinking. It was eighteen harrowing hours to travel a mere 600 kilometres on a bus where the driver continually drank Indian whiskey. He drove at breakneck speed, swerving randomly, sporadically accelerating and braking hard, bouncing all the passengers around. It was an effort just to stay in my seat, let alone sleep. I'd heard that in India bus drivers only get fired if they have five traffic accidents that cause fatalities. Not just five accidents or driving under the influence, but five fatal accidents. So if an Indian bus driver only has four accidents that kill people during his career, does that mean he's a fairly good driver? Needless to say, it was a long and arduous journey.

* * *

Colva Beach was a tourist town populated by courting couples and old European retirees drinking odd-tasting pina coladas under coconut trees. A dirty green Arabian Sea lapped against the beach, where rickshawallahs tried to sell the sexual services of their sisters. After a couple of days, I decided to leave Frankie and Monique to whisper their sweet nothings and bused north back up the coast an hour to Goa's infamous party beaches. I arranged to meet Frankie in a couple of weeks after Monique returned to France.

It was the day before New Year's Eve when I arrived at the popular party town of Vagator, a fishbowl of lost souls, the lonely, the misguided and the deranged. Throngs of burntouts, dropouts and freaks in beachwear milled around as I tried to find a hotel, but everywhere was booked out. Feeling vulnerable and depressed, I wondered why I had come to India. I had left Australia partly because of misplaced loyalty to a friend who had himself deserted me for a girl.

On the verge of tears, my whole life was a mess – no partner, no friends, no home and no future in a foreign country I wasn't even sure I wanted to be in. I wanted to call Amber and whine like a baby and tell her I was coming back to her, but that wouldn't have been cool, no, not twice in one day. Besides with a price on my head I had little choice but to stay put. In my heart though, I knew that – apart from being literally a potentially fatal attraction – what I yearned for with Amber was something not based in reality. She was young and full of beans, she wanted to start doing all the things I was already tired of, another night club diva in the making. I had been lying to myself pretending I could do it all again. I sighed and looked about Goa. It was at that moment I accepted that I had to stay and make this journey work as best I could.

Just then a young Indian guy pulled up on a motorbike. 'Hello, sir, are you in needing of a room?'

Sweating in the afternoon sun and straining under the weight of my backpack, I sighed. 'Yes.'

'Vell, you are very most velcome to be staying in my village – my uncle is having a room. It is possible, but as you like.' His white teeth shone as he smiled and his head wobbled.

'I like, I like.'

He took me on his motorbike ten minutes down a dirt track to a small village. Kids chased dogs that chased chickens in and around small mudbrick huts, while an old toothless blind man showed me to my room. The toilet was a hole in the ground and the shower was a rusty drum of water with a ladle, surrounded by a one-metre wall. He threw in a moped scooter to seal the deal.

After settling in, I ventured back into town, sat in a bamboo hut café and started on the first of many Kingfisher beers, trying to wash away my depression. I watched the endless circus of shady sadhus, shifty merchants and other panhandlers meandering through the shantytown, dodging motorbikes and cows as they plied their trade. Racks of fresh, nubile gap-year innocents were lambs to the slaughter for the platitude-spouting spiritual pimps, guru conmen and tantric sex predators – it was a feeding frenzy.

North Goa isn't really India, it's a cross between Amsterdam and Ibiza. Every drug under the sun is available in Goa: Special K, speed, morphine, valium and viagra, and that's just from the pharmacy. Stoned dreadlocked society-fringe dwellers, 60s castaways and sunken-eyed skeletal junkies walked into these places with shopping lists and the pharmacist handed it all over without enquiry. I mean, what possible reason could these characters give for needing horse tranquilisers?

After a while, a beefy Englishman named Chris came up to me. He was built like a brick shithouse, with a crew cut, looked like an ex-rugby player, and was about my age. 'Mind if I join you, mate?' He made himself comfortable at my table. He had the tact of a geezer bullyboy.

Not the usual company I'd keep but being a lonely pathetic wreck I actually appreciated some conversation. It turned out Chris worked in Delhi, managing some English software company that outsourced its workforce to India. 'Delhi is the Devil's asshole, mate. Nothing there – can't get a fucking steak anywhere. Full of bloody Indians. No, to be honest, they're alright. Couldn't stand the little bastards when I was home in England, but now I'm here, I've kind of got used to them, have to, really.'

I eyed Chris suspiciously. 'Well, it is their country, mate.'

'True enough, but I don't like the men holding hands, won't allow it in my office. They're all bloody poofs you know, but apart from that they're actually alright.'

'I'm sure they're not all gay, Chris.'

'No, mate, all the guys are fucking fairies, seriously.' The beer flowed faster. I started questioning the integrity of my drinking partner. 'No, really, the poor sods never get any pussy. They're so bloody segregated, they don't get to go near the girls till they're fucking married. They're all doing each other up the batty. You ever heard of the tittie tourists?'

'No.'

'Busloads of horny single Indian guys paying a fortune to come down here and look at the Western girls on the beach and take photos of them. Poor bastards are horny as hell. They didn't even get porn till the internet arrived. That's why you get all these internet shops with private booths and sticky keyboards.'

'Jesus, that's got to be bullshit, doesn't it?' I was astonished.

It's true that a lot of Indian men are very physical with each other, holding hands, walking arm-in-arm, resting on each other, always in close proximity. But I doubted if Chris's theory was true and suspected he was a homophobe, not to mention a bigoted racist redneck. Chris suddenly changed the subject, 'So, what the fuck are you doing in India? I have to be here, no choice, it's my job.'

'Well, I ...'

'You're not a fucking hippy, are you?'

'No. It's a long story, basically I got divorced recently and needed a change of scenery.'

'Came to India to find yourself, eh?'

'Kind of, also want to study yoga.'

'Christ, you are a fucking hippy. Yoga – isn't that what poofs do?'

'No,' I was struggling for a witty response, 'but there're plenty of fit chicks who do it.'

'So that's why you came to India?'

'I don't know.'

'Fuck, mate, if I got divorced I'd go to Thailand and have a sex holiday, not come here, for Christ's sake.'

I was feeling self-conscious and wishing Chris would go away, when an explosion of noise overwhelmed us. The thunder of a dozen or so motorbikes roared past like hippy versions of the Hell's Angels – long hair, dreadlocks and tattoos. Sexy bikini-clad girls were riding pillion. They all rode Royal Enfields, chunky four-stroke bikes. The Enfield, originally an English motorbike, was now only produced in India. It had become the iconic symbol of motorcycle lifestyle on the subcontinent, affectionately referred to as the Indian Harley. These were splendid examples, with leather tassels on the ends of the handlebars, leopard-skin print on the seats and the three-pronged staff of Shiva protruding from the back seat-rests. An old but tough-looking man in his sixties with long silver hair led the group.

Chris bellowed over the top of the noise. 'These guys fucking have it made. They just cruise around India all year. They start down here and make their way north as it gets too hot. Then they hang in the hills in Manali and Parvati valleys, in all the dope plantations. Always have the best drugs and the hottest chicks and they do it all on someone else's money.'

'What do you mean?'

'The lucky fuckers get sponsored to cruise around India by rich hippies who are too old or fucked-up to do the trip themselves. All they have to do is send them photos and emails saying how much fun they're having with their fucking cash.'

'Fuck!'

'It's a fucking hippy wet dream, pretentious wankers if you ask me. They call themselves the Shiva Riders. Can you believe that shit?'

'Yeah, what wankers.' I secretly thought it sounded pretty cool.

Chris insisted on more and more rounds of beer and we continued drinking through the night until we ended up in a nightclub called Paradisio. By sunrise the music was as obnoxious as the clientele. Feeling seedy, I left, reluctantly agreeing to meet Chris later that night for dinner and to celebrate New Year's Eve. Despite the fact he was a misogynist, tactless, a bit of a bully and had nothing in common with me, Chris had a certain quality that was comforting in a round about sort of way. I wouldn't go as far as to say he had a charm, not by a long shot, but he had a brawny, beery, no bullshit boy's own adventurousness about him that may have been just what I needed to blow away my dark clouds. Anyway, unless I wanted to spend NYE completely alone, he represented my only option.

Dinner later that night consisted of half a dozen Kingfishers and a plate of pappadams. The medicinal hair of the dog cured our hangovers and like Easy Rider on scooters we hit the road. I fancied myself as Dennis Hopper and Chris was a large Peter Fonda. They weren't exactly Enfields and we weren't exactly the Shiva Riders. Chris called them jet skis. 'Mate, they're not real bikes, just point and shoot. Easy as piss.'

We went bar-hopping. I let myself go, attempting spiritual suicide, chemical hara kiri under the guise of having fun, hoping to cauterise the hole in my heart. In one club a girl gave us some ecstasy, in the next a hippy gave us speed pills and in yet another club, a very intense Italian with veins swollen to bursting point on his forehead gave us MDA powder.

Ecstasy always struck me as a cop out sort of drug: the cost of the warm fuzzy feeling and artificial connectivity is a hole fried in your head the next day. After years of being around the E sub-culture, I realised there's no genuine bond, just a lot of white noise fizzing out of empty skulls. The last couple of generations of human guinea pigs will no doubt show the real cost of the party in years to come. A couple of million burnt out brain cells, just to tell your friends (and some complete strangers) you love them. It was one of the dividing points in my marriage, Stella thought ecstasy was a fast track to happiness, I didn't, not anymore, the dis-euphoric Tuesdays after the weekend bender had become an unbearable burden. Don't get me wrong, I was no monk and as my drug-taking, whiskey-drinking Sri Lankan Buddhist poker buddy back in Australia always said with a ciggie hanging out of his mouth, 'As us Buddhists say, mate, everything in moderation, including moderation.'

We ended up at a big outdoor psy-trance party. Everyone was dancing to the throbbing beat from massive speakers. All the uber-feral dreadlocked elite were there, complete with silver and turquoise bling-bling and chic custom-made leather bumbags, fluorescent green and orange furry-flared pants, sequined miniskirts and sunglasses at night. Sweat glistened on masses of tattooed skin. The jet set poor and international misfits. The dance floor writhed with group sensuality, everybody dancing with everybody but nobody dancing with anybody.

Harems of sexy Israeli girls in tiger-print bikinis and knee-high leather boots adorned the arms of grey-haired acid-smuggling mafia. The aloof Shiva Riders wove through the dance floor like sharks, doing secret Masonic Lodge-like handshakes with the other Goan royalty. Barefoot neoflower-power hippy chicks, eyes closed, swayed back and forth, the Goa kiss on many ankles (the small burn mark from motorbike exhaust pipes as a result of being driven by stoned boyfriends). We all danced like lunatics through the night. The beat reached a crescendo as the sun rose. Red dust clung to our perspiring bodies; possessed, we stomped our feet harder into the dirt.

The dancing continued throughout the day, people periodically retreating from the sun to take refuge under the trees that surrounded the dance floor. By early afternoon I was resting, drenched in sweat, in the shade. A middle-aged dreadlocked Indian in a multicoloured top hat approached me. Like a demented Cat in the Hat from Dr Seuss, he introduced himself as Baba Rainbow and enquired, 'Chillum?'

The question obviously rhetorical, he produced a small chillum from a cloth pouch attached to his belt like a Wild West gunslinger. A chillum is a ceramic tube-like pipe about six inches long that tapers from a wide to a narrow end. A stone is placed halfway down the hole and it is filled with a mixture of tobacco and charas. A small piece of cotton cloth is then held over the narrow end of the chillum in a closed fist and the other end is ignited. It has quasi-religious significance in India, being one of the few possessions of the Indian holy men, the sadhus.

Sadhus practise yoga and surrender the pursuit of pleasure, wealth and duty. They are solely dedicated to achieving liberation through meditation and the contemplation of God (either Shiva or Krishna) and are the oldest continuous monk tradition in the world. They are often referred to as *baba* or *babaji* as a sign of respect. Many sadhus are in the *Guinness Book of Records* for feats of marathon endurance in their quest for liberation, including not sitting down or standing on one leg for years, crawling thousands of kilometres and keeping a vow of silence for decades. They fast, rise early and take cold baths – it is not a path for the faint-hearted.

Sadhus believe smoking cannabis is a sacred act that allows them to attain a meditative state similar to that of Lord Shiva. They also believe it furthers a sense of dispassion and separation from mainstream culture with all its temptations and distractions. Chillums are very popular with the stoner traveller in India, as they legitimise their hedonistic state as a spiritual quest. Whether my new friend Baba Rainbow was really a sadhu or just called himself one was a mystery.

Rainbow passed me the freshly-packed chillum. 'Manali cream. I bring down one kilo every year for selling to help my village in the mountains. This smoke is for karma and to thank the gods for you *gora* (white tourists) for spending your monies here.'

Standing above me, he held a flame to the top of the pipe as I inhaled. The rush of sweet charas filled my lungs, the ground spun beneath me and my head went light. With tunnel vision I passed the smouldering pipe to Rainbow. He sucked deeply on the pipe, and the top of the chillum glowed crimson as the mix burned. He exhaled a plume of white smoke, followed by a rasping phlegm-rich cough. Holding the chillum to his forehead, he recited a blessing to Shiva, one that all sadhus and consequently lots of stoners perform:

Alakh, alakh boom
Alakh, alakh boom, boom
Alakh Shiva Shambo
Kailash Ke Raja
Shiva Boleh
Boom, Boom, Bholenath

Rainbow tapped the pipe into the palm of his hand and removed the ash and the stone. Then he twisted the piece of cotton rag into a rough thread and fed it through the chillum. Pulling the rag back and forth, he cleaned and returned it to the holster on his belt. He then rested his arm casually on my shoulder, '*Hits shay hagase nu dai che khkari.*'

I tilted my head and shrugged.

Rainbow smiled, 'Nothing is what it seems. This place is not the real India my friend, you must be looking between the cracks to be really seeing her.'

He winked at me and disappeared back onto the dance floor. Moments later I drifted off to sleep in the red dust, serenaded by the rhythmic thumping of the music. What felt like only seconds later, I was abruptly awakened,

'Fucking, lightweight Australian wanker! What ya doin' fuckin' sleeping?' Chris shook me violently. I rubbed my eyes, regaining consciousness. As I sat up, he shoved an ecstasy pill into my mouth and slapped me on the back, making me swallow it with a gasp. 'Been looking for you for hours. You fucking lightweight.'

Chris was a mess, wired, red-faced and sweating. Groaning, I reluctantly rose to my feet. Dusk had settled as the party powered on. The music increased in tempo as the night crept in, raising the energy of the dance floor. Chris snarled at me. 'Let's get the fuck out of here. Too many fucking hippy chicks, all these bitches are fucking frigid.'

I looked at Chris – sunburnt, with bloodshot eyes, sweating, reeking of BO and with white spittle encrusted at the corners of his lips, he was totally yangin' (as opposed to yingin' and the whole Zen balance thing). I wasn't surprised he wasn't having any luck with the ladies.

'Let's fuck off and find a different club.'

We rode around aimlessly on our mopeds, until we stumbled across a club called the Matrix. The sign out front boasted *India's only underwater nightclub*. It was a circular building in the middle of an artificial lake, a footbridge the only entrance. Chris and I staggered up the overpass to the door. He slurred to the door staff, leaning heavily on the handrail, 'Is this place fucking happening or what?' The smiling Indian behind the counter bobbed his head as he responded in a clichéd manner, 'Oh yes, sir, the place is most definitely very much happening.'

Inside it stank like a public toilet. Loud 80s euro-techno blasted out of the overdriven sound system. My temples started to constrict, the beginning of a new hangover and the cerebral burn of the fresh ecstasy. Three drunken Western girls danced, surrounded by about twenty over-stimulated Indian guys. Each of them tried to shimmy his way in front of the others to gain the best position beside the wasted girls. Chris bellowed, 'This place is a fucking shit-hole, let's get a drink.'

He looked increasingly unsteady as he lurched towards the bar and slumped onto a barstool. 'Two fucking mojitos and keep 'em coming.'

After a few rounds Chris was face down on the bar, clutching a mojito in one hand and his moped keys in the other. I paid the tab and wrote on the bill, 'English lightweight'. I slipped the note into his clenched paw, staggered out of the underground toilet of a nightclub and rode off on my jet ski. Time for Chris the British bulldog in a china shop and me to part ways.

I got lost on my way back and ended up riding through the deserted stalls of Anjuna Market, a hippy flea bazaar that overflowed with trinket-seeking shoppers during the day, but at night was a vacant ghost town. A pack of rabid dogs chased me as I wound my little moped up to full capacity, speeding through the market with only inches of clearance between the ends of my handlebars and the empty stalls. Rabies was present all over India and packs of stray dogs that wandered at their whim were one of the main carriers. Travelling at breakneck speed with the dogs, mangy and foaming at the mouth snapping at my heels, I remembered a story told to me days before. An Irish guy had recently died in Goa from a rabid dog bite. He, like me, had never had his vaccine shots. Through the cracks of *gora* Goa's stoned veneer, the real India wanted to tear me to shreds.

I was a mental wreck the next day, suffering a self-induced lobotomy. I lost my camera on the beach and nearly lost my mind. More wretched and lonely than ever, I spent most of my time in internet cafes telling friends about the amazing time I was having, hoping someone would reply. Only mum wrote, worried I wasn't eating properly and warning me of the imminent dangers of bird flu outbreaks. I knew I needed to take time out and be alone, no matter how terrifying it seemed. I just didn't think I would be that alone. I thought I was going to be alone with my buddy Frankie. Funny how things turn out, but I wasn't laughing.

CHAPTER 3

Looking for My Own Utopia

Managing to escape Goa a few days after NYE, I caught a sleeper bus 300 kilometres southeast inland into the next state and to the small town of Hampi. Hampi was apparently a very spiritual place with some of India's most renowned temples. It was also where Frankie and Monique were heading after Colva Beach. Black monkeys ran across tin rooftops stealing food from windows, while endless streams of cows and pilgrims meandered through the narrow lanes below. The scorchingly hot landscape with its crimson desert sand reminded me of the Australian interior. Unusual spherical rock formations littered the landscape like an ancient god's game of marbles.

Apart from an amazing sunset and being blessed by an elephant, which I had to pay for afterwards, I didn't see much of Hampi. I did see a sadhu who, meant to own nothing, was talking on his mobile phone. That's pilgrimage, twenty-first century style. No, all I really saw of Hampi was the inside of my windowless room for two nights. I locked myself in not wanting to face the world. Wretched and lonely I listened to Johnny Cash on my MP3 player – his black melancholy fitted my mood like a glove. The coupled effect of the dysphoria of my NYE drug binge and the existential crisis that originally brought me to India made my life feel like a country and western song – lost, lonely, down and out.

I was filled with fear. Fear of what, I wasn't exactly sure. I had spent most of my life rushing around, feeling afraid – afraid of acceptance, afraid of not being loved, and afraid of being alone. I looked at a poster on the wall of my room, two peacocks sitting on a flowering branch, staring at each other. A quote read, *Joy is not in things but in us.*

I had always sought happiness in something or someone else, when it actually had to be found within myself. Lying in my room I hit emotional rock bottom. The burnout of the divorce and everything else in my life took me the closest I've ever been to feeling suicidal. I opened the book Frankie gave me for Christmas to the first page. Inside the cover his inscription read, *May this begin your spiritual journey. Always your friend, Frankie.*

Flipping through the book, I stopped on a page talking about how if one allows the mind to die every day to the memories of yesterday then one's mind is fresh and innocent and has no age. Unburdened by the traumas of the past, the mind is free. This appealed to me, the idea of a trouble-free mind. I continued to read Krishnamurti. He explained that one should not be afraid to die every moment, every day. Die to the agony of heartache, loneliness, the relationships we cling to, even to the way society defines us. Freedom can only be found in the continual death of all these definitions. It reminded me of an old saying: *The past is history, the future is a mystery and today is a gift and that's why it's called the present.*

The only problem was that my gift of the now felt, at that point, kind of crappy. I finally got an email from Frankie.

```
Hey Bro,
Have a good NYE? Hampi was cool, very relaxed
hippy vibe. We are going to Gokarna now, chill
```

out at OM beach, why don't u meet us there?
Frank

Determined to break the downward spiral I caught another sleeper bus southwest back to the Arabian Coast, to Gokarna, a sleepy village with winding lanes shouldered by tin roof shacks and crumbling stone temples adorned with flowers. At the bus station, in the shade of a stand of eucalypt trees, an Indian man tinkered under the bonnet of a flat-tray truck in the back of which stood an orange-painted, cud-chewing cow. It had a fifth leg growing from its rump. The Indian, oil smeared across his brow, looked up from the engine and smiled. 'It is a lucky cow, please kiss the magic leg and be making a vish.' I wondered how lucky it could be if his truck had broken down but, figuring I had nothing to lose and everything to gain, I leaned over and tentatively kissed the magic deformed leg. Apart from wishing not to get sick from kissing a cow, I wished for happiness. With still no sign of Frankie, it began to feel like a game of *Where's Wally*? Or searching for Kurtz from *Apocalypse Now*. I finally got another email.

Bro, Where r u??? Monique has gone home and I am
feeling a bit lost. Man, made a cool connection
then she has to go back home. It's fucked up.
Feel lonely now, got a toothache too, think it's
serious, maybe an abscess. I think u can die from
those. Didn't make Gokarna, catching a train to
Pondicherry on the other side India, come meet
me there. Frankie

Why should I drop everything and go running to him again? But I did just that. I hadn't spoken to anyone for days, other than, 'How much for a room?' or 'Can I have the chicken masala, please?' and 'Bill, please.'

So I hitched a ride on a motorbike to the station, and then caught an overnight train across to the interior of southern India to the east coast and to the country's fourth biggest city, Chennai (formerly Madras). We crossed arid plains, passing village after village scattered in the red dust of dry rice paddy fields. Potholed roads criss-crossed the landscape where oxen hauled farmers' carts laden with crops. Occasionally we stopped at larger towns where streams of commuters filed past my window – nobody on the train talked to me – it was like I didn't exist. The only exception was a happy-faced Indian sitting opposite me. We had the standard Indian/Westerner conversation.

'Vhat is your good name, sir?'

'Aaron.'

'Vhere are you from?'

'Australia.'

'Ah, Australia, cricket vorld champions, Ricky Ponting a most excellent captain.'

'Thank you.'

'Vhat is your job?'

'I don't have one.'

'Oh, are you married?'

'No.'

'Vhat is your age?'

'Thirty-six.'

'And you are not married?'

'No.'

'Oh …'

The conversation then ended abruptly. It made me feel more desperately alone than ever. Arriving in Chennai, I sensed

I was really in India again for the first time since Mumbai. A city of some 6.5 million people, it was magnificently dilapidated, its congested centre in a sea of slums. Sitting on a delta plain, sandwiched between two rivers and on the coast of the Indian Ocean, Chennai was awash in a haze of pollution – it's the industrial heartland of southern India, brimming with factories and a bustling seaport. As soon as I stepped off the train I started to suffocate in the crowds of people. A leper approached me, making gurgling noises. His arms outstretched, he looked so wretched I gave him a handful of coins, but he had no hands. So I sort of balanced them on one of his stumps. He looked at me like he was thinking, *Great, now what am I meant to do?*

'Sorry,' I muttered, backing away. As soon as he moved the coins fell to the ground, then other beggars, laughing at him, picked them up. Claustrophobic, I needed to find the bus terminal to continue south down the east coast another hundred odd kilometres to Pondicherry. Outside the station a taxi driver laughed at me as a street kid tried to pick my pockets, his eyes and teeth scarlet from chewing the narcotic palm seed betel nut. Dazed by it all, I jumped into a rickshaw.

'Bus station, please.'.

Exhausted, I endured another nail-biting three-hour bus journey by watching a nonsensical Bollywood film. The story went something like this. Boy and girl are born on the same day. They meet by chance as infants, then again at university. Then it becomes a little hazy – both become pop stars and start to fall in love, until the girl catches the boy almost having it off with some promiscuous whore (by Indian standards at least, you could see her upper arms). Then the boy has a big slow-motion kung fu fight with ten bad guys (obviously bad because they are all uglier than the star and have big moustaches). Boy and girl then do song and dance numbers at famous locations all around the world, climaxing with them getting married.

By the time I reached Pondicherry it was dark, and everything looked ominous. This was definitely the 'real' India and I didn't like it at all. I wanted to go home. I had been travelling for over twenty-four hours with barely any sleep across the breadth of southern India. I had no idea where Frankie was. Then, as I checked into a hotel, he just happened to swan into the foyer wearing a lungi, a very Indian-looking loose cotton shirt, and a hippy manbag slung over his shoulder. Behind him stood a different young girl.

'Hey, Baba Aaron, nice to see you.'

Obviously over his crisis, he had transformed himself into a seasoned Indian traveller sage-like dude.

'Frankie, are you staying here, man? What a coincidence!'

Frankie raised his hand like Sitting Bull. 'No, it's synchronicity. Universal connection and don't call me Frankie.'

'Why?'

'I've changed my name to the Kobra, spelt with a K.'

'What?'

'It represents my newly-awakened kundalini power.' He turned to the girl behind him. 'Star Child, go to our room and I'll join you soon.'

I couldn't believe this, another girl! She scurried off obediently. Frankie looked at me. 'Can you believe this?'

'What the fuck's this Kobra and Star Child bullshit?'

'Man, I met her at this ashram, you gotta check it out. I just spout all this philosophical stuff, play the guru line. I called her Star Child. Her name's actually Beatrice from Belgium. You should try it – works a treat. Monique Kama Sutra'ed me, man, I'm all Tantric now. These chicks are just drawn to me.'

Too tired to listen to this, I stared at him blankly. 'Man,

I need sleep. I'll see ya in the morning.' After a cold shower I fell into a bed that had a faint scent of masala spice and mildew and was serenaded to sleep by a squeaky overhead fan, dripping faucets and the rattle of rickshaws on the street outside.

The next day, Frankie the Kobra showed me around Pondicherry like he owned the place. Its French colonial heritage was apparent from the architecture and orderly streets. By the light of day it wasn't nearly as ominous. The boulevard hugged the rocky shore and passed a statue of Gandhi and an archaic English-styled seaside fairground. The Ferris wheel looked like it was made from the bodies of rickshaws and creaked as it spun too fast. Vendors sold masala flavoured popcorn to throngs of Indian families, while others sat grinning in ice-cream parlours on the opposite side of the street. At one end the boulevard abutted a naval base, while the other terminated in the slums of the fishermen – longboats lay tilted on their flanks on small sandy beaches, fishing nets billowing in the breeze as stray dogs and seagulls picked through rubbish. It still didn't feel like I imagined the real India to be, but it seemed a lot closer to that than Goa. It did have cows standing in the middle of the road and the occasional child shitting in the street. Frankie, keen to pursue his new Kobra powers, convinced me that we should check into the Sri Aurobindo Ashram, hoping some enlightenment would rub off on us.

The ashram, two blocks back from the boulevard, felt more like a halfway house. A high stone wall enveloped a whitewashed courtyard; the centrepiece was the graves of the founding guru Sri Aurobindo, an Oxford scholar Brahman and his protégé known affectionately as the Mother who died some twenty years after him in the 1970s. The ashramites looked gaunt, anaemic and malnourished as they queued for plates of what can only be described as gruel. Every meal was the same, day in, day out. Everyone looked like a lobotomy patient. They were trudging along like a conveyer belt to receive their yellowy tasteless slops. It depressed me, like a spiritual prison. Disturbingly even the sign on the wall said, *All inmates must be silent at all times.*

I attempted to digest as much of the ashram food, philosophical reading and *satsangs* (lectures) as possible, but it was all hard to swallow. Clearly my mind was not of the disciplined calibre required for such lofty concepts. After a few days of struggle, I gave up. Subversively I started reading the autobiography of Lemmy Killmaster, the frontman of my all-time favourite heavy-rock band, Motorhead; maybe that was closer to my nirvana. Instead of going to talks on karma, meditation and reincarnation I spent the afternoons jumping around on my bed, playing air guitar and listening to Motorhead.

To break the monotony of the food I smuggled in a jar of hot lime pickle. But when I couldn't fit the spoon into the jar it broke me – I gave up on the ashram soup kitchen for the spiritually destitute. Eating gruel, being seriously serene and wearing lots of white just didn't cut it for me. Then, when Frankie got into a passive-aggressive fight with a fellow inmate over how to stack the dishes and Beatrice from Belgium, or Star Child, got tired of his metaphysical rhetoric and left, we both decided it was also time to move on. We snuck into town and gorged ourselves on chicken tikka. Absolutely divine, the pleasures of the flesh.

Frankie the Kobra, the great white hippy-chick hunter, insisted we head to Auroville, a commune about five kilometres down the coast road south of Pondicherry. Auroville was a concept created by the Sri Aurobindo Ashram in the late 60s in conjunction with the Indian government, UNESCO and the Mother. The Mother spearheaded a campaign to realise Aurobindo's dream after his death. It started with the heady ideals of creating an international community that belonged to no single country, but to everyone. Neglected and overgrown by weeds, the Age of Aquarius architecture of much of Auroville looked like a forgotten set from *Hair*.

In the middle of the commune's vast acreage of eucalypt woodlands was the *Matrimandir*, a temple that was the supposed soul of the city. It was meant to represent the birth of a new consciousness that was expected to arise in the new millennium. This mysterious giant golden orb, dome-like structure was fenced off and under constant guard by serious commando-style vegans who prevented non-Aurovillians from entering. Rumour was it contained an enormous amethyst crystal, a metaphysical supercomputer, and it had the vibe of some sort of secret spiritual military intelligence base.

Finding digs in Auroville was a wild goose chase. We scuttled around on mopeds from one overpriced MasterCard commune to the next. By late afternoon we'd stopped for chai at a roadside stall and resigned ourselves to sleeping on the beach. I was doodling with a stick in the dust at my feet, a bit melancholy and 'poor me', waiting for Frankie to return from his urgent toilet mission. A huge French guy with long hair, tattoos and a biker beard, started talking to me in an alarmingly high-pitched voice like an altar boy or a Disney chipmunk. It didn't match his imposing appearance at all. 'What's wrong, brother?'

I looked up at him, afraid that if I laughed he would pulverise me. 'Can't find anywhere to stay.'

He patted me on the shoulder, 'Have no fear, brother, the universe always provides.'

With that he walked off into the sunset like a cartoon apparition. Moments later a previously grumpy Frankie returned, smiling, his brown eyes sparkling mischievously as he thrust a cup of steaming hot chai into my hand.

'I got a room.'

'What?'

'Yeah, I got a room, but there's only space for me, sorry, dude.'

He smiled like a spoilt child, holding the pause. 'Ha, just kidding, man. I got an apartment, two bedrooms, fully furnished for three bucks a day.'

'You bullshitting me?'

'Nope.'

He explained how, on his toilet mission, he'd had a frustrating conversation with the chaiwallah. He'd kept pointing to a sign that said *Tolet*, asking where it was, and the chaiwallah kept answering, 'No, no, no toilet.'

He'd persisted, insisting there must be a toilet, until the chaiwallah managed to explain in broken English that the sign actually said *To let* and referred to an apartment. I chuckled to myself as I thought *Yes, the universe certainly does provide*.

Soon after settling in, I discovered a place to study yoga in a nearby village with a Dr Mohanti, Doctor of ayurvedic medicine, natural therapies and hatha yoga. Dr Mohanti lived with his wife and mother in a small but relatively well-to-do apartment. He was petite, with black hair and a large Tom Selleck moustache, and his eyes shone. Speaking excellent English with a deep Bengali accent, he taught me the *Surya Namaskar* on the rooftop of his apartment building.

He explained that Surya Namaskar, meaning sun

salutation, was a meditative series of twelve asanas or stretches that consisted of posture, vital energy or prana and rhythm, connecting breath with movement. Vedantic philosophy purports that doing the Surya Namaskar helps maintain the five onion skin-like layers or 'subtle bodies' that constitute our reality. Each of these psycho-spiritual layers corresponds to different planes of existence that make up the subjective experience of being alive. From the lowest, densest level of the physical, up through the finer subtle bodies of emotions and ego, all the way to the highest layer where the boundaries between the individual and the universe dissolve.

Dr Mohanti started the class by chanting a mantra, *'Surya Dev, Mera Pranaam sweekar karen, samasta Bhaagya Jankaton Se meri raksha.'* (Lord Sun, Salutation to you. Bless me from all ill fortunes fate has destined for me).

For some reason I found myself responding with 'Amen'. The cycle of asanas or positions always started and finished with the same pose: standing feet together, hands in front of the chest in prayer. Each time I worked through the sequence Dr Mohanti fine-tuned me by making adjustments to each posture. At the end of the class I lay there in the glow of the setting sun and cool sea breeze. Above me scores of ravens spiralled, riding thermals. I was both energised and tranquil – a momentary balance in the frenetic madness of life. I felt my first taste of living in the now.

It's amazing how soon after establishing any sort of routine, even in the most exotic of locations, it can become the new normal. After a few days of my daily commute to Dr Mohanti's rooftop yoga class it felt like I had been doing it forever. Then, one day, I found myself in a traffic jam, wedged between an elephant and a parade float with a meditating yogi. It was the Pongal festival, which worships Surya, the sun god. Symbolically it is all about letting the light into your life. For three days there is feasting, celebrating in the streets and painting cows. At first I found myself feeling agitated, like a commuter caught in peak-hour traffic on the way home from some demeaning job. Then I stopped. I breathed, took a reality check and let some of that light in. The elephant was ornately painted, and the yogi deep in his meditation on a bed of flowers. I stood shoulder to shoulder with the locals, all smiling and laughing, and the scent of incense and flowers filled my nostrils. How could I take this for granted?

I continued to observe, laughing to myself. A marching band bashed drums and blasted unusual wind instruments. On a side street a young girl walked a tightrope, rhythmically swinging the thread from side to side with her toes. At the main intersection the parade converged with a wedding party coming down another road. A collision of colour, sound, smells and activity ensued – a cacophony for the senses. Weddings go for days in India. The bride and groom, who had probably only just met, were sitting side by side in their wedding finery, after being admired and doted on by hundreds of anxious and proud relatives. The couple smiled nervously up on their podium as they were towed through the streets.

The separate marching bands of the festival and the wedding melted together, each trying to maintain their individual composition in a clanging of rhythm and sound. Nobody seemed to mind. The festival revellers catcalled to the wedding guests, who in turn showered them with flower petals. The dancing transvestites or *hijiras*, who always accompany weddings uninvited, continued their seductive yet strange dances to ensure that the relatives kept paying them. (*Hijiras* are not actually paid to dance, but rather to not expose their mutilated genitals and consequently disgrace the occasion.) Young street kids giggled as they snaked through the confusion, picking pockets and rejoicing in the cover of the mayhem. I laughed out loud. It was overwhelming. It was beautiful. It was chaos and harmony and it was almost too much. It was India.

The daily commute to Dr Mohanti's yoga class made Auroville's artificial world starkly apparent, particularly when seen against the real India. I started to see through the cracks. The concept of Auroville had begun with high ideals but had decayed into a European hippy Club Med with lots of middle-aged French guys getting around in tie-dyed T-shirts and Speedos, those tight swimming bathers that in Australia we call 'budgie smugglers' or 'dick stickers'. One day I heard them all talking about the wonderful health benefits of drinking your own urine; I interjected and said that eating shit was great for the skin. I was just trying to make a joke but they didn't appreciate it, making a point of ignoring me after that. I would've loved to see Chris the British bulldog with this mob – a cat amongst vegan pigeons.

It all seemed like a bit of a wank to me and Frankie the Kobra, who appeared to be in his element, started to get pissed off at my general disdain for the Aurovillians. If it hadn't been for Dr Mohanti's yoga class keeping me grounded, I might have slid into the India Syndrome, and gotten lost in a world of hippy rhetoric and quasi-Eastern mysticism.

I stagnated. Had I come to India for unclear reasons? To reinvent myself? It sure wasn't happening for me in Auroville. I felt wretched. I just couldn't fit into the clique of Auroville and the hippy elite Aurovillians. Maybe if I started drinking my own piss I'd make more friends, but I figured they were friends I didn't really need.

That said, Auroville had some positive aspects. I went

to a very interesting talk on meditation. When we entered the venue for the satsang, the place was empty apart from one well-dressed, elderly Indian man sitting behind a desk. Frankie asked about the lecture. Speaking in perfect English, he replied jovially, 'Ah yes, the discussion on meditation. So good of you to come. Please allow me to introduce myself. My name is Janardan and I run the facility here.'

He stood and shook both our hands, then gestured towards the door. 'Please, if you would like to come this way, we will commence the discussion.'

He glided past us, out of the door and past an auditorium filled with Europeans in white kaftans standing in a circle and humming, 'Ommmm.'

Frankie winked at me as he scanned the group for potential nubiles. I rolled my eyes. Janardan walked out into a beautiful garden that extended for at least a couple of acres through the grounds. After a couple of minutes we arrived at a small clearing with three plastic chairs placed in the shade of a tree. Frankie and I looked at each other. It was all a bit surreal, three chairs; how the hell had he known only two people were coming? Janardan pointed to the seats. 'Please make yourself comfortable.'

We sat there for a few moments admiring the garden. Janardan, smiling, with his hands across his round belly, started to chuckle to himself but didn't say anything. More moments passed. Frankie started to become agitated. An awkward silence built, until finally Frankie couldn't take it.

'So, um, which aspects, exactly, of meditation are you going to discuss?'

'Ah yes, meditation. What a wonderful thing it is. A lot can be said of meditation.'

Another awkward silence followed. Frankie interrupted it

again. 'So, ah, I've read a lot of Krishnamurti recently, and he talks about being in the moment, allowing yourself to die to every second, focusing on just the now.'

'Yes, Krishnamurti. I have read much of him and many, many more books. We could talk for many hours on the matter. But none of this will actually develop an ability to meditate.'

He continued to laugh gently to himself and slowly rubbed his belly. 'All talk is essentially nonsense. Take, for example, these two analogies to illustrate my point. Firstly, if a man studies the entire contents of milk, the two thousand components that make up its composition, he has still not experienced the milk – only analysed it. To experience the milk he would have to drink it. This demonstrates that meditation is experiencing. Books and discussions can only inspire one to meditate, but will not actually induce the experience. Secondly, if you have two pieces of ice, one in each hand, they are separate. Then the ice melts and you have a single puddle of water at your feet. This illustrates the oneness of everything – nature does not differentiate between me and a tree or anything else.'

He smiled, letting this sink in. 'We desire material wants, which create our reality. This reality is essentially incongruent with the reality of nature. We all start and finish as dust. We are all the same. We have a saying here in India: I was never born, I will never die, I will always be. To just be is the essence of meditation. Look around yourselves here, in this beautiful garden. It was Krishnamurti who once said that being surrounded by nature was one of the easiest ways to induce meditation. So, we can sit around and discuss the merits and benefits of meditation or, instead, we can actually meditate amongst nature now. Shall we say, for fifteen minutes?'

So, smiling, we all sat together there in the garden. Then I had a breakthrough, my first real taste of any sort of inner peace. I realised I didn't have to come halfway around the globe to find myself. Meditation didn't have to involve checking into an ashram or commune. No, meditation could be achieved anywhere, it didn't depend on anything or anyone other than myself. I also realised it was time to leave Frankie in his hippy utopian playground and venture out on my own again.

Flicking through my *Lonely Planet*, I decided on a whim to leave for the Andaman Islands, remote, tropical islands four days' sail east of India. It sounded like a perfect, quiet vacation from the craziness of my journey. So I left Frankie the next day, promising to meet up in a couple of weeks. I jumped on a bus back to Chennai. On arrival, I managed to place my foot into the middle of what I only hoped was a pile of cowshit. I grumbled under my breath as the steaming mass oozed over my sandals and between my toes, 'Welcome back to the real India.'

By fate or fortune, the next boat to the Andaman Islands was leaving that evening. Hungry, with a few hours to kill before the boat departed, I headed to the nearest *dhaba*. A dhaba is a local Indian eatery usually specialising in *thalis*, all-in-one plates which consist of *sabji* or curried vegetables, dhal, rice, chapatti and curd. It is eaten with your right hand only, no fork, just your fingers. The left hand is never used, as that is the hand used to wipe your ass. Your plate is refilled as often as you like. It's the original all-you-can-eat buffet. Sitting there munching on my thali, I noticed a small boy observing me. That's all he needed, eye contact. In a flash he appeared at my side, grinning. 'Hello, sir.'

'Namaste.'

'Vhere are you from?'

'Australia.'

'Ah, Australia, cricket vorld champions ...'

I cut him off quickly. 'Yes, Ricky Ponting.'

'Yes, Ricky Ponting number one.'

There was a silence and he looked at me inquisitively.

'My name is Ajay.'

'Namaste, Ajay.'

Another uncomfortable silence. 'How long you stay in Chennai?'

'I'm not staying. I'm leaving tonight.'

Ignoring my response Ajay continued, 'I can be your guide.'

'I don't need a guide, thank you.'

'I can take you to the very best guesthouse.'

'I don't want a guesthouse.'

'And the bazaar, I can help you get the very best bargains.'

'Look, I'm leaving in a couple of hours, I don't have time for sightseeing. Thanks anyway.'

Ajay was starting to annoy me. Finishing my thali, I struggled to put on my backpack and lumbered back out into the heat, Ajay close on my heels. 'Where are you going?'

'This way.'

'I can be your guide.'

'Look, matey, I really don't need a guide. I'm only going to an internet café, OK? But thanks anyway.'

'Ah, internet.'

Ajay gave me a knowing wink. 'Yes, I know the very best sexy internet. Yes, that is right, this way.'

He pointed down the street I'd already started walking down. 'Thanks, Ajay, but I can find it on my own.'

'No, no, sir, no problem at all. I vill guide you there.'

After walking for five minutes we reached an internet café.

'OK then, thank you, bye now.'

'I vill vait for you here.'

'No, really, I don't want you to wait for me, OK?'

I entered, heading straight into a private booth, checking to see whether the keyboard was sticky. Chris's story had made me paranoid. As I left an hour later, Ajay jumped up from his haunches. 'Yes, yes, I am here, Ajay, your guide.'

'Look, you're not my guide, OK?'

'But I guide you here.'

'I was walking this way anyway. I would've found this place on my own.'

'OK, as you vish, pay me and I vill go.'

Too tired to argue, I pulled out a crumpled ten-rupee note and thrust it into his outstretched palm. He looked at me incredulously, like I'd just spat on him. 'Ten rupee for a guide, no, no, no, sir, my fee is being one hundred rupees.'

I'd had enough. 'Look, buddy, I didn't want your bloody help in the first place, so please just leave me alone.'

Ajay seethed, murder in his young eyes. Slowly raising his arm, he pointed his finger at me. 'You are very bad man. I put a curse on your karma. You must be very careful in India now. You cursed.'

I backed away, lost for words. Great, now my karma was cursed. Heading back to the ferry terminal, a policeman on an old rusty pushbike pulled up next to me. The bike creaked every time he pushed down on the pedals. He smiled. *'Baksheesh.'*

'What?' I stopped and looked at him. His uniform was grimy and the seams were beginning to split. He grinned cheekily, a man with a light build, not more than five foot tall, armed with nothing more than the standard issue, short bamboo stick stuck in his belt. 'Baksheesh, baksheesh, you must pay baksheesh.'

Baksheesh, meaning 'bribe,' is used to grease the wheels of the corrupt Indian bureaucratic system. I glared at him. 'Baksheesh? Why?'

He looked surprised. 'I policeman.'

'No.'

'I am policeman, baksheesh now, two hundred rupees.'

Hot, sweaty, with dried cowshit between my toes, apparently cursed and now being ordered to pay baksheesh, I snapped. 'I don't give a flying fuck if you're best buddies with Gandhi, mate. I ain't paying. I'm cursed, you hear me, my karma is cursed. Hit me with your little bamboo stick if you like, I don't care.'

Stunned, he looked me up and down, realising I was at my wit's end and probably more trouble than I was worth. He rode off muttering in Tamil under his breath. Relieved, I finally boarded the boat.

* * *

The boat to the Andamans was definitely no QE2. Covered in rust, the old ocean liner obviously hadn't been painted in years. The pool was dry and fenced off with wire mesh. A dead bird lay in the bottom. Half the toilets didn't work and the ones that did were filthy. Cockroaches and rats scurried in the shadows. The entertainment room's seating faced a blank wall, where a TV may once have stood. The decor was faded, styled in the early 80s, with torn and stained upholstery and grubby brass fittings. The boat looked older than the plaque announced: *Nancowry, Poland 1982*. Oddly, a sign on the outside deck said *No spitting. Fine 500 rupees,* while inside the diningroom a different sign read *No spitting. Fine 50 rupees.*

With the salty breeze on my face, next to the empty pool, I watched the sun set over Chennai. The evening light diffused through a red haze of pollution. A wave of inner peace washed over me, like the one I'd had with Janardan in the Auroville meditation centre's gardens. I'd made the right decision. Peeling a mandarin, I offered some to the guy sitting next to me. About my age, his pasty white skin gave him away – he obviously hadn't been in India for long. Balding with close-cropped hair, he was slightly overweight and seemed to be alone. 'Like a piece, mate?'

'Yes, cheers, thank you.' We sat silently watching the sunset. He wiped his hand on his new khaki shorts and extended it to me. 'Hi, the name's Ian – England.'

'It's a pleasure, Ian. Aaron – Australia.'

Ian passed me the front page of an Indian newspaper. The headline reported an earthquake on the Andaman Islands. He rolled his eyes at me, like he was saying *Great, just as I was heading there.*

After Ian, it wasn't long before I befriended Red Man and Dangerous Dave. I met Dangerous Dave with a twenty-four year old Japanese hippy chick called Suz. On first appearances Suz seemed a stereotypical Japanese girl – long black hair and all coy and demure. That is until she opened her mouth and started talking. Speaking in a broad Australian accent she seemed 'true blue' (very Australian). Suz had learnt to speak English from her Australian ex-boyfriend in London. She introduced herself as 'Suz the Nip. No shit mate, aye. Never been to Aus meself, it'd be grouse to go there but.'

I overheard Suz and Dave having a discussion, trying to decide whether the word 'diarrhea' had the letter 'o' in it. I couldn't help interjecting and in no time we had formed the poker dream team – Ian, Dangerous Dave, Suz the Nip and me. We played from the first night on the boat until the last. All of us were seasoned players other than Suz. But being a gutsy chick, she was *pukka* (genuine) to learn. We took all her money in a couple of hours, but she didn't flinch. She just gritted her teeth and bought back, and over the following hours cleaned us all out. From that point on she was officially one of the boys. We played Texas hold 'em in the restaurant after dinner, late into the night, under a sign that said, *No gambling*.

Then there was Carlitos, a tall thickset Spaniard thirty-three, with shaggy black hair, cropped beard and friendly eyes. He tried to chat up as many girls as possible, offering free massages. Obsessed about becoming a father, he felt the lack of a mate. A seasoned traveller to India, Carlitos made his living selling cheap jewellry, lungis and other paraphernalia on the European festival circuit every summer. He always wanted to wrestle me like a big playful bear, saying it showed off our virility to the girls. We knocked over tables and chairs throwing each other about.

Nights on the boat were long and fun, but mornings were a different story. The Indian passengers started the day by turning on every light and talking loudly, an hour before sunrise. I couldn't fathom why. There was nowhere to go and nothing to do. For people who no doubt usually had to rise early to do some backbreaking job, this was the perfect opportunity to have a good sleep in. Perhaps 4:30 am was sleeping in for them, because that's the time they got up. Then they all queued for the bathrooms, for their morning purification ritual. Good old temple cleansing – the loudest being the expelling of all phlegm from the throat, nose and sinuses.

They took turns hacking up phlegm, coughing, snorting

and spitting until they made themselves retch. Continuous sounds of people being sick, spitting and nose-blowing filled our mornings. Not with a hanky, I may add, they just performed the 'bushman's blowie', where one blocks one nostril with a thumb and blows out the other nostril hard, clearing it.

There was only a very limited time to get a breakfast of *iddly*, a small doughy savoury pancake in a spicy masala sauce (everything is masala-flavoured in India) and a cup of hot chai, so timing was vital. Being late, if only by minutes, meant the guy behind the counter refused you anything. He reminded me of the Soup Nazi from the sitcom *Seinfeld*. 'No, no chai. No chai for you, go away.'

On the third morning, after another big night of cards, I realised my mobile phone had been stolen. Already suffering from sleep deprivation, I was furious. I rashly accused the Indian guy in the next bunk of the theft. He and his buddy were laughing at me.

'OK, where is it?'

'Vhere is vhat?' He smiled, giggling to his friend.

'Where's my mobile phone? It was in my bag when I went to sleep and now it's fucking gone and I reckon you stole it. No one else could've reached it.'

'I never taking anything from you, fucking.'

I insisted on searching his bag but found nothing. Carlitos heard the commotion and came over to my side. 'Wha' is wrong, amigo, you look very very angry, why de shouting?'

'This fucker ripped me off.'

'I did not fucking.'

Carlitos scratched his balls through his lungi and considered my predicament. With no hope of getting my phone back, I saw the futility of my situation. As my anger cooled, I realised my Indian neighbour may have had nothing to do with it. Carlitos, however, looked resolute, hitting his fist into his palm. 'We mus' group together, we mus' defend ourselves; we can make a search party.'

Carlitos began searching all the Indians in our dorm. None of them resisted the bear-sized Spaniard. Dumbstruck, they didn't know how to react. I felt guilty about Carlitos's overzealous attempt to help me. He didn't search the tourists because we assumed it was an Indian passenger. Uncomfortably I watched Carlitos steam ahead, ploughing through bags like a one-man Spanish Inquisition. When he'd finished, he decided on a different tack. 'We mus' make de dorm secure, guard our half.'

Dropping to his knees, he tied a piece of string at ankle height across the corridor between the bunks. 'De robber will trip on dis string and fall down. He will make de noise ouch when he hit de floor, den we jump on him and catch him.'

I looked at Carlitos, bemused at his hare-brained plan. I questioned his sanity but at the same time was touched by his concern. India was like that, you met weird people who were some sort of damaged goods with baggage, me included. You didn't come to India to lie on a beach and go clubbing, no – most travellers here had the 'finding themselves' thing going on.

I justified the loss of my phone as a process of material shedding; first the camera, then the phone. Maybe it was inevitable, losing everything of value. It almost appealed, this kind of freedom in having nothing, just walking the earth and being at the mercy of the universe.

By the fourth day on the boat, everyone was relieved to see the Andaman Islands on the horizon. White beaches rimmed hinterland obscured by jungle. Armed with MP3 players, trashy novels and beach towels, an excited buzz permeated the air as we disembarked and checked into customs for our thirty-day visas. It had that real islander vibe, relaxed. Even the custom officials made jokes when Suz the Nip showed them her passport. One of them started singing, 'Hey there, little Suzie …' The others joined in as impromptu backup singers. 'Do up da do up …'

After passing through the singing customs, Carlitos, Ian, Dangerous Dave, Suz the Nip and I piled into an Ambassador taxi and rode into the so-called capital of the islands, Port Blair. It was no more than a provincial town comprised of ramshackle buildings, open-air markets and a military outpost, the only place in the region with access to the internet, semi-permanent power, an ATM and a hospital. It was also the only place to access the rest of the islands, including Havelock Island, the beachbum mecca with legendary beaches, coral reefs and crystal-clear tepid water. Our party's final destination, it required us to spend the night in Port Blair and catch a very early local ferry the following morning.

Accommodation was tight, and we could only find two rooms in one hotel in the whole town. Suz took the single room, and we boys took the other room with two double beds. Carlitos sat on one of the double beds, naked and wrapped in a towel. Intently focused, he was rubbing a bamboo flute with a rag. I bee-lined for the other bed, preferring to take my chances with Dave. As I watched my curiosity grew, and as Ian came out of the bathroom I had to ask, 'Hey, Carlitos, what're you doing?'

'I am greasing my flute; it's good to keep it oily.'

Ian realised the only available bed was sharing with Carlitos. 'Right, so the Spaniard is greasing his flute and this would be my bed, I presume?'

I grinned at him. 'You could be in for a long night, mate.'

'Yes, quite.'

Dave sat up smirking. 'Well, at least he's lubricating it for you, that's considerate.'

'Yes, OK, very funny.'

Ian sat on the edge of the bed, looking suspiciously over his shoulder. Carlitos rubbed his flute with even greater concentration. 'It will sound much better when it is oiled.'

Laughing, I jeered, 'Mate, if I hear *Three blind mice* being played in the middle of the night, I promise I won't turn on the light.'

Dave continued the stir. 'Yeah, I really don't want to see Ian playing Carlitos's flute.'

Ian rolled his eyes and sighed, 'Good god, grow up.'

Carlitos scratched his head and looked at the flute. 'Why you no like my flute? It is good, no, good size, not too big, not too small, perfect.'

Ian looked tired. 'I'm sure it is.'

Carlitos put the rag away. 'It is ready. It is easy to play, I can teach you.'

Ian replied curtly, 'No, thank you.'

With that we turned out the light and drifted off to sleep. The night air and humidity blanketed my body with a film of sticky moisture. The hum of tropical insects created an orchestral lullaby. A gecko scurried across the ceiling. I felt content for the first time in ages. I knew this holiday was going to be exactly what the doctor ordered.

It was still dark when we were woken by the beeping of Ian's alarm clock. I put a Metallica track on my MP3 player and cranked it up loud. We had to hurry, to catch the only ferry to Havelock Island. I played air guitar to the opening bars of *Enter Sandman* as everyone packed.

Suz the Nip opened the door. Seeing me in mid-performance, she dropped her bags and jumped onto Carlitos's bed with arms stretched to the ceiling, headbanging, fingers splayed in the symbol of the beast, the heavy-metal salute. She sang along with me on the chorus, before we broke into double air-guitar solos. I slid across the floor on my knees while Suz star jumped over me. Carlitos picked up his bag and shook his head. 'You are very strange, my friend. We mus' go or we miss de ferry.'

We fell out onto the still sleeping street. The day was warm but not yet hot, the air still and cool, waiting for the sun that shimmered just beyond the horizon. Hues of purple shifted to blues in the pre-dawn sky. We managed to wake a couple of rickshaw drivers . We were running late and Carlitos started to panic. We could see our ferry at the end of the jetty. He squeezed our rickshawallah's shoulder. '*Andiamos*, faster, *chello, chello* (let's go).'

The rickshaws were neck and neck as we hit the jetty ramp, becoming airborne. Dave leant over the side and screamed, 'Go, Schumacher!'

Our overweight rickshaws slammed down hard on the jetty. Dave leant further out, hanging on with one hand and pointing with the other to the boat. 'Go, James. To the batmobile.'

As they screeched to a stop we all scrambled out of the rickshaws, thrust fists full of rupees at the drivers and ran towards the boat. The ferry's engines rumbled and the crew started to remove the gangplank.

'NO!' We all screamed. The ticketseller tried to stop us from boarding, but there was no way I was going to spend another night here, no way I was eating at the nut-scratching waiter's restaurant again, so damned close to paradise I could almost taste it. Sweating, chests heaving and gasping for breath, we made it. Next stop Eden. A surge of white foam churned from the back of the boat as we pulled away. Waves smashed on the bow as we carved a path towards an island. We saw pristine beaches with turquoise water lapping gently at the shore. Luscious tropical jungle, thick and full of mystery, covered the tiny island. Apart from the little portside village the island was uninhabited. The instant my feet hit the ground everything slowed down. The moment felt eternal, like I had all the time in the world – island time.

CHAPTER 4

Paradise Lost and Found

Something about living on a remote tropical island cut off from the rest of the world put my mind at ease. None of the things that seemed important back in one's 'normal' life applied here. All of a sudden there was no hurry to do anything. In fact the more I slipped into island time the less I achieved. It got to the point where eating two or three meals, having a swim and falling asleep, nose pressed against the pages of a trashy novel, became a full day. The comforting sound of the waves synchronised with my ever-slowing heartbeat. Time came to a virtual standstill, the tightly wound coil of tension inside me began to unwind.

Woken by the roasting sun on my bamboo hut, I'd fall out of bed into yet another beautiful day and shake off the hangover caused by drinking the local island gut-rot, Smugglers Rum, into the wee hours whilst playing poker with the Dream Team. Then while doing my yoga sun salutations in the gentle sea breeze I'd savour the smorgasbord of sights, sounds and scents emanating from the jungle. Wild dogs dozed, too lazy to even chase the chickens that clucked and scratched around them. I would then head out through mangrove swamps in a fishermen's long boat to the reef and dive amongst an array of iridescent colours and movement. Totally in the 'now', this was meditation at its best.

Then after a late lunch and afternoon snooze, I'd slowly make my way up the beach, calling into the different guesthouses for cups of chai with my newfound friends from the boat, before finally meeting up with Dream Team for dinner and our nightly poker jaunt. A danger unto himself, Dave, always smiling and always losing, was the happiest loser at cards I'd ever met, always insisting we play longer and longer as he tried to win back his losses. Dave's biggest weakness was that each time he bluffed he grinned. If any of us suspected him of faking a good hand, all we had to do was ask, 'Dave, are you bluffing again?'

He'd smile from ear to ear. 'No. Definitely not, not at all, not this time.'

Ian on the other hand, always grumbled and complained. Not about the game but about everything else. This, and the fact that his delicate digestive system couldn't cope with the ravages of Indian cuisine, made him a bit of a wet blanket. Suz the Nip fast became a staunch poker player and was always the unpredictable one.

We became known as the island casino. Suz the Nip, joint clenched between her teeth, shot of straight rum next to her pile of beer-bottle-lid chips, would deftly shuffle the cards. Without looking up she would explain the rules to newcomers. 'We play No limit Texas Hold'em. Buy in is five hundred rupees. If you get cleaned out you can buy back in as many times as you like, just ask Dave. The game only finishes when the person who has lost the most wants out. So are you in or what?'

Ruthlessly we wiped out all new blood who dared play. The most notable, an English toff named James – weedy and pale with a wet fish handshake and an intense stare – had some serious Freudian mother issues. After the loosening effects of a couple of glasses of Smugglers Rum he started to express his ultimate sexual fantasy. This guy actually had a list of women who he wanted to tuck him into bed at night and nurse him when he was ill – Elizabeth Taylor and Joan Collins being at the top. An awkward silence fell over the group upon his revelation. The sound of crickets chirping filled the night air. This combined with his venomous verbal spat that all women were evil led me to believe this guy was prime psycho killer material – a real 'silence of the lambs'. We were all relieved when, after losing, he decided to leave.

* * *

One afternoon when I dropped into one of my guesthouse hangouts, I noticed a beautiful Israeli girl. I had seen her doing yoga on the beach a few times with who I presumed was her boyfriend. Maybe five foot eight, lithe, with an athletic tanned body, her long curls of sandy brown hair fell down her toned shoulders. Naturally very attractive, I couldn't help but stare at her. As I walked past her table she smiled, 'Shalom.'

'Shalom,' I beamed back at her.

'Sa Baba?' (Hebrew for lots of things, here I think it meant *cool?*)

'Sorry, I don't speak Hebrew.'

'Oh you are not Israeli?' she enquired with her thick accent.

'No, Australian.'

'Oh, like Crocodile Hunter?'

'Yep, that's me. Wrestle crocodiles and sharks and snakes and spiders and drop bears ...'

Laughing she gestured to the seat next to her. A warm smile with hard eyes, her brow was creased in a permanent furrow. 'Please sit.'

'Sure, but won't your boyfriend be jealous?'

'Ha, Nimrod, he is not my boyfriend. Little Nimrod is my cousin.'

Even when laughing her eyes looked tired. A deep sadness lay beneath the smile. Introducing herself as Merav, we shook hands, followed by an awkward silence. Was her quietness disinterest or some sexual tension? Merav broke the hush, 'I am sorry but I only speak little English.'

Relieved, I overzealously responded, almost cutting her off mid-sentence, sounding too eager, 'Yeah, that's cool, me too, I mean I don't speak Hebrew either.'

Another silence followed. Then her cousin returned. Younger, maybe early twenties, he smiled the same smile as Merav. With similar good looks but with darker features and a thick black beard, his long dreadlocks hung over the shoulders of his small, light frame. However, there was a distinct difference between him and his cousin. His smile radiated an ease and friendliness that made him appear very approachable. Also, his brown eyes were illuminated, filled with happiness and a childlike innocence. He extended his palm, 'Ah, my cousin is always attracting strange men and again this looks like no exception.'

We shook hands. 'My name is Nimrod.' He spoke excellent English. 'We must smoke to celebrate this occasion. Come, it is nearly time for sunset.'

Merav smiled with her tired eyes, 'Nimrod has a thing about sunsets.'

'Yes every sunset must be enjoyed like it is your last. After all we only have so many, no?'

We all sat on the log of a coconut tree that had fallen on the beach. Nimrod removed a leather mixing bowl that cleverly folded in half and sealed with a zip, several black label Rizzla rolling papers and a small, circular tobacco tin from his hippy-chic bum bag. It was slung diagonally across his chest like the bullet belt of a Mexican gunfighter. He opened the tin with reverence, as if it was a sarcophagus containing some priceless artefact. 'Ah, my finest collection of India's best charas. Which should we enjoy on this special occasion?'

Nimrod wiggled his fingers like an excited child. He expertly rolled a perfect looking joint. 'I need filters. I am always looking for filters.'

Merav rolled her eyes, 'Nimrod, why like this. Just use something.' She turned to me with her sad smile, 'He is always looking for filters.'

He lit the joint just as the sun started to fall to the horizon. Pushing sand between his toes, he didn't look up as he spoke, 'You must understand when we are eighteen we are made to go into the army. We have no choice. For three years. After this I promised myself I would never run when I could walk, never eat standing up and never sleep in a tent. But most importantly, to enjoy every sunset like it is my last.'

Nimrod passed me the joint as the sun sank into the sea. I paused briefly – I had abstained from smoking since Goa. I watched the smoke curl between my fingers, and then I put the joint to my lips.

***

A few days later with Ian, Dave and Suzy sunning ourselves on the beach, Dave's eyes lit up, 'In poker tonight, I have a new strategy.'

Ian smirked, 'What's that, not to lose?'

Dave's characteristic grin spread across his face, 'Yes, exactly.'

Suz interjected, 'No Dave, not tonight. It's the *Puja* festival tonight.' She turned to face me all excited, 'It's going to be awesome, all the village elders smoke heaps of bhang and chew betel nut, then everyone opens up their houses and lays on a feed. Something to do with celebrating the new season's crops and the new moon.'

Dave's smile waned, 'So, poker tomorrow then?'

Puja basically translates as prayer and is done by most Hindus twice a day. This Puja festival, *Maha Shiva Ratri*, was one of the major ones celebrated, along with Pongal and Holi. This one is dedicated to Shiva and devotees start early in the morning and it goes through the night. Brahma (god of creation) and Vishnu (god of protection), so the legend goes, were arguing over who was the more powerful. Shiva came along and transformed himself into a beam of fiery light in a celestial muscle flex to prove that he was in fact the strongest. This was now celebrated by an all night ceremony that was meant to be good fun.

Going to the puja party involved crossing the island to the western side, to Beach Number Seven. This beach was simply numbered, not named, and was reputed to be the best beach in the world. Shaped like a crescent moon, the beach spanned some two or three kilometres of a sheltered bay where half a dozen yachts took up anchor. Warm water gently washed against the white sand without rip or current. An elephant and its keeper appeared out of a tall stand of trees bordering the beach and strolled to the water's edge. I couldn't have created a more idyllic beach in my own imagination. A point in the universe – in the space-time continuum – of complete balance and harmony. We were at a loss for words. We split up to enjoy the receding day alone, each taking some contemplative time for meditation. This was some damn fine quality 'now'.

Further down the beach I came across Nimrod and Merav. Nimrod sweated as he tried to inflate a large plastic Lilo. Merav sat beside him, her arms wrapped around her legs, head resting sideways, her cheek on her knees. She seemed distant. Nimrod looked up and noticed me, eyes shimmering, '*Walla* (Hebrew for lots of things, here I think it meant *yes*), Mr Dundee, excellent, some Australian muscle, please help us blow this up, sunset is approaching and we want to be floating in the water, smoking this most amazing joint. You must join us.'

I helped and in no time at all we were floating in the bay, slowly spinning around and around as a gentle current took us out past the yachts. Smoking one of Nimrod's perfectly rolled joints we started to share our life stories. Merav, like me, had recently escaped a destructive relationship, the wounds of divorce were still tender. I felt drawn to her, not just because of her physical beauty but because I understood her pain. She gave me mixed signals. I often caught her gazing at me, but she maintained an emotional distance.

Nimrod spoke of his time in the military, of how his family had pressured him to fulfill his military service. He spoke of how the government tricked him by promising to let him serve as a cameraman and fulfill his dream of becoming a filmmaker. Instead they lied and put him in the Gaza Strip with a machine gun. Smiling, he laid on his back, blowing smoke rings into the sky. He joked, 'Why do Israeli army barracks have fences around them?'

I shrugged. 'Why?'

'To keep the logic out.'

He paused before continuing, 'You know my father still serves voluntarily, Mum too. Even my sister is a tank driver. My whole family believes this bullshit propaganda. When I told my mother that I didn't want to fight because I did not think it was right, you know what she said? She said *how can you not fight? I will be ashamed of you if you don't fight.* Can you believe my own mother said that?'

Merav interrupted Nimrod, her voice quivered on the verge of tears. 'How can you say that when my father, your uncle, was killed by those Palestine dogs?'

'Merav, we slaughter them like animals too. That's why I got out. That's why I moved to England. My own family won't talk to me anymore, no one except you Merav.'

'Because you shame your family.'

Nimrod turned to me. 'You know how I got out of that fucking hellhole? I pleaded insanity. I pretended to be crazy, fooled the doctors, the army and even my own family. They dismissed me and then I flew straight to England. Been there ever since. I want to go to film school and make amazing films. I want to move to New York. One day hopefully.'

Merav snapped at him. 'Nimrod, you are such a fool, full of dreams. And, and silly ideas.'

Nimrod continued, 'You ever wonder why there are so many Israelis in India, and no it's not just because it's cheap. They come here to kill the soldier inside themselves.'

Silence fell over us, above us the stars started to appear; we had drifted further out from the coast than we had realised. The effort to paddle back to the shore made our muscles sore. The glow of iridescent plankton glittered each time our arms struck the water. By the time I reunited with the Dream Team, it was pitch black. So dark in fact we could barely see our hands in front of our faces. A local villager carrying a torch approached us, and enquired, 'Puja?'

Like an usher at the movies he led us down the beach to a clearing under a stand of trees. We duly sat on the ground with a group of villagers. They all clapped in unison watching the central character, a village elder who, with his wispy white beard and long grey hair tied above his head in a ponytail, looked a hundred years old. Sitting cross-legged with his eyes closed, and with a toothless grin stretched across his face, he reminded me of the BBC character, Catweazle. He rocked back and forth playing a single-string instrument made out of a coconut shell. Its twanging intonation sounded like a Jew's harp. As women passed around palm leaves with sweet, sticky rice and other nibbles he sang some strange yet melodic song.

Ian got right into the swing of things, tucking into a bottle of Smugglers Rum. Chillum pipes, then betel nut were passed around in endless rotation. After a while I glanced across to Ian who chewed betel nut, red spittle drooling down his chin. Chillum in one hand, near empty bottle of rum in the other, his eyes were closed and his arms above his head. He swayed rhythmically from side to side, totally consumed by the experience. Suz smirked at me, 'Go Ian.'

After several more rounds of betel nut and chillums, Ian rose unsteadily to his feet. Looking a little pale he announced very publicly, 'I'm just popping off to the little boy's room.' Then, with a distinct purpose, he marched into the black moonless night, into the thick of the jungle, but without a torch and completely in the wrong direction – away from any path, house or any other trace of civilisation. Before any of us could ask where he was going the night had swallowed him up. When he didn't return we futilely called out his name from the jungle's edge.

Our puja usher returned and insisted we follow him back to his village. He took us from home to home, where people warmly greeted us and fed us plate after plate of food. By the time we returned to the beach we felt like stuffed pigs. Ian miraculously appeared from some nearby foliage complaining that he had a headache. The Puja usher shone his torch into Ian's face, which was covered in lumpy red splotches. We couldn't help ourselves as we all started to giggle at him. Ian didn't look impressed. 'Got bloody eaten alive by bloody mosquitoes didn't I. Yes very bloody funny. I couldn't see a thing, staggering around in the jungle, darker than, than … well really bloody dark.'

Dave patted Ian on the back. 'That's our happy camper.'

Suz had an evil grin. 'Shanti shanti Ian?'

Ian grumbled, 'Shanti bloody shanti.'

* * *

Over the ensuing days I continued to pursue Merav. I couldn't understand her – she would give me the eye then the cold shoulder. In an attempt to impress her, I tried to teach the Israeli guys cricket. An absolute nightmare – they kept changing sides, ducking off for chillum sessions mid-game and arguing over the score. One day Merav said she wanted to go somewhere nice for dinner, and then after I made a reservation at the only restaurant on the island, she stood me up. I thought she wasn't interested in me, so I backed away. Then she came looking for me and complained I had not come around to see her for a few days. After a week of this hot and cold routine I was totally confused and frustrated. I liked Merav, but I missed Amber. I liked the island but felt I should go and find Frankie. I was walking along the beach to clear my thoughts when I came across Carlitos lying in a hammock. He waved at me to join him. 'Hola amigo, wha' is wrong, you don' look happy?'

I sat down next to him and he playfully punched me in the

arm. Wearing only a lungi, his bamboo flute was stuck down the front. 'Maybe you wan' to wrestle with me?'

'No thanks mate. I'm thinking of leaving the island and heading back to India.'

Carlitos continued to punch me in the arm. 'Why you go. It is nor time for you to go.' He laid punch after punch rhythmically into my arm, making my body rock back and forth.

'Stop punching me man, or I'll hit ya back.'

Carlitos ignored my warning and continued to try and get a reaction out of me. Which he did – I turned and hit him back in his arm, hard.

'Ouch dat hurt!' Rubbing his arm Carlitos looked at me. 'You worry too much. Don' worry.'

'I dunno man, I'm meant to catch up with my buddy.'

'Hey brother, you have a sad face. I fink your problem is you have no girl, yes?'

'Well, there is this Israeli girl but she keeps giving me mixed messages. One day all friendly, looking at me like, you know, and then the next day she ignores me. Hot cold, hot cold.'

Carlitos lay back in his hammock, one hand behind his head, the other hand scratching what appeared to be a freshly trimmed beard. 'Hmm.'

'Don't know if I'm coming or going.'

'Well amigo, you nor coming.'

'Very funny mate.'

Carlitos scratched the hair on his exposed chest, which also appeared manicured. He sat up in his hammock. 'You know friend, dese girls dey sometimes do dis, but dey not look at you like a lover. No, more like a papa or big brother, someone to protect dem. Sometimes de girl that is right for you is nort de pretty one but de one that is next to you de whole time but you never see. Dis is de girl dat will be de mother of your babies. I wan' a girl like dis. I wan' to be a papa. I am getting old, my time is running out.'

'OK, Don Juan, so how is your love life going. Found anyone to play that greasy flute of yours yet?'

His scratching made me feel itchy. Rubbing my scalp I felt the small scabs from over scratching. The heat had really started to aggravate my skin – my head constantly itched. Carlitos gave me a cocky grin. 'I don' tell tales, but yes, I met a girl.'

'Good for you Casanova, is she cute?'

The smile fell away from Carlitos's face. 'No. She was nort so pretty an' she was very fat. We did it in de hammock. It was very difficult. Nort comfortable and dere was sand in everyting. I don fink it wa' such a good idea.'

Looking at Carlitos, still rubbing his chest hair, he appeared somewhat traumatised by the memory. I decided to be kind and change the subject. 'Mate, have you had a trim?'

'Ke?'

'Your body hair, it looks distinctly shorter.'

Carlitos puffed up his chest with pride. 'Yes, I cut. ALL my hair – is more sexy, no? It is for de ladies. I am being, how you say, metrosexy.'

'Metro-sexual, and yes you are Casanova.' I smiled.

Carlitos grinned as he lay back down in his hammock. He twiddled with a white shell necklace, 'No, it's simple, you are here now, stay here an' be happy amigo.'

At that moment a girl walked past us and grabbed Carlitos's attention. He jumped out of his hammock and chased her down the beach. 'Hello lady, wha' is your name, would you like a massage? Will you have my babies? I don' have much time left to be a papa. I can teach you to play my flute.'

Another week or so passed and I found myself even more irritated. I'd been avoiding the poker games and the usual hangouts. I was despondent as Merav continued her cold shoulder and I felt a little homesick. The desire to leave grew stronger, until it reached the point of no return. Getting up early one morning I packed my bag and ordered a rickshaw. The words of Carlitos rattled around my mind. 'It's nor your time to leave, you muss stay.' Already hot, my scalp itched, adding to my general restlessness and irritability. I heard a voice yell out in a fake, American accent. 'Fire in the hole.'

I turned around and saw, a few huts down from mine, a crusty old dreadlocked hippy smoking from a glass chillum. Sitting in the door of his bamboo hut wearing nothing but a dirty lungi, long ginger-red dreadlocks hung from his receding hairline. He looked forty going on sixty. He gazed up at me, smoke billowing from his nostrils like some decrepit dragon, faded tattoos, blurred beyond recognition, on his skinny freckled arms. His smile revealed rotten yellow teeth, half of which were missing, teeth of an Englishman and a face that only a mother could love, but friendly eyes anyone could love.

'Ello Guv, the name is Jimmy Bacon,' he rasped in a north English accent, which was followed by a phlegmy cough.

We shook hands. 'Aaron, pleasure mate. Unusual surname, Bacon, your father a butcher?'

'Actually my full name, as is written on me passport, is ...'

Jimmy stood up, extending both arms out wide and facing the sunrise. He proclaimed loudly like some over performing Shakespearian hack of a thespian, 'Jimmy, Ambassador of the Sunrise, Bacon.'

'You're kidding, that's your real name?'

'Depol mate, it's legal, had meself a little tax problem. Jimmy here was makin' too much bacon. But it's also coz no matter how late I go to bed I am always up at the crack of dawn to watch the sunrise. Lovely girl Dawn!'

He chuckled to himself as he continued, 'Life's too short to sleep, especially the way I live. No, plenty of time to sleep when you're dead I say. I got to get as much out of life as I can mate, here for a good time not a long time. Party hard, die young.'

He smiled as he passed me the chillum, changing the subject. 'This chillum cost me a bloody bomb. It's pure crystal. Fucking dropped it last night didn't I? See the crack. Oh well, nuthin' lasts forever.'

I squatted down holding the crystal chillum to my mouth.

Jimmy shouted in his fake American GI accent, 'Fire in the hole.'

Exhaling a plume of smoke, my rickshaw arrived. I passed the chillum back to Jimmy and picked up my bag.

'You off mate?'

'Yep, time to move on.'

Jimmy laughed, 'You'll be back mate, this place is like the fucking Hotel California, you can check out but you can never leave, it's my third tour of duty mate. I'll keep the home fires burnin' for ya.'

He winked as I jumped into the rickshaw and left my little shanti shanti neighborhood. My head was heavy from the charas but my heart was heavier. I did the *sketchy bail* (colloquial Australian expression – to leave somewhere in a hurry for uncertain reasons and without telling anyone).

The rickshaw skittled down the road, swerving around sleeping dogs and flapping chickens, past naked laughing children and along the edge of the steaming jungle. It all beckoned me to stay. I was full of doubt when I boarded the ferry back to Port Blair. I considered the past few weeks – Carlitos's advice, Nimrod's love of the sunset and Jimmy's love of the morning sunrise. I felt confused and lost again as the ferry pulled away.

Arriving back at Port Blair in the heat of the midday sun, I melted – the humidity was off the scale. My T-shirt and shorts stuck to me like oily flypaper. This backwater of civilisation felt like an overwhelming metropolis of noise, traffic and pollution after the serenity of Havelock Island. A slight panic began to rise inside me as I trudged to the ticket office for the boat back to Chennai, sweat stung my eyes. The boat was due to leave the following day, but the office was shut and the sign on the door said the boat had been cancelled. I stumbled down the street – direction unknown – into the immediately unknown and the rest of my life. I thought to myself, 'What the hell am I going to do now?'

Then from behind me I felt a punch in my arm, it was Carlitos with Dave and Ian. 'I knew you did nort leave de Island.'

Dave smiled, 'We thought you did a runner on us.'

Ian winked at me, 'Can't get rid of us that easily. Oh that reminds me some girl gave me this to give to you.' He passed me a crumpled note from his pocket. I opened it up.

Why you go. I missed you leaving
I give you my email so we can meet again yes?
I will be coming to Varanasi next month. Let us meet
Yes? I like to see you again
Merav.

The girl was a mystery. Carlitos punched me again, 'Ah the girl is hot now is? We is flying to Kolkata on a new airline, dey are offering special tickets very cheap and next week is de festival of de colours. You should come wit us Australia.'

My spirits rose again, the universe just provided the new path of my journey. After buying our tickets for Kolkata the following day, I managed to send an email to Frankie telling him of my plans. He actually responded.

```
Hi bro,
    I'm in Tiruvannamalai inland from Chennai.
I think a lot of people come here looking for
all the answers! A lot of lost people here,
probably including myself? I met a woman in a
café who wouldn't stop talking, even when I said
'I have an appointment, I have to go now', she
didn't blink an eye... she just kept talking
about how Sai Baba transported her from Germany
to America!!! I just backED away slowly and she
kept on talking... it was weird. She had earplugs
in as well. I don't think it mattered if I was
there or not.
    I got kicked out an ashram the other dAY FOR
LYING Down!!! Horizontal meditation not allowed!
All these ashrams seem just like $$ spinners for
the Indians. I should be in Kolkata before u
leave the Andamans
regards
THE KOBRA
Ps: hope the diving is going well ... find anything
in the depths?
```

We all decided to go for dinner together, a kind of impromptu farewell. We caught up with Suz who intended to wait for the next boat back to Chennai. Island time was about to come to an abrupt end. We all exchanged emails with Suz, promising to catch up one day in the future, but in our hearts we all knew we'd probably never see each other again. It's like having friendship flings or affairs. You get very close to people very quickly then move on.

The next day at the airport I got my family jewels fondled for an extended period of time by a smiling customs officer. He only stopped when I said, 'Dude, what? Do you want me to cough? And no officer that's not a gun you're holding.'

Our plane was late, and whilst watching the news on TV in the transit lounge it became evident why. The pilot had managed to crash our plane on the runway before taking off on its maiden flight. That was the moment I started to fall in love with India, everything was a risk, an adventure and a miracle. Eventually we boarded our plane and headed back to the insanity of mainland India. It kind of felt like we were soldiers returning from war, not that I'd have a clue what that felt like. Not everyone who arrived left. Except we hadn't been at war, we'd been lying on a beach for a month. No comparison really.

CHAPTER 5

Birds of a Feather
March 15 2006 – The day after the first day of the rest of my life.

I open one eye cautiously, like a tentative swimmer dipping a toe into a pool. I dip the minimum required of my senses into the pool of consciousness that is my current reality – my current 'now'. I'm not positive I want in on this day. I scan the room of my YMCA Salvation Army digs. All appears normal. The atomic peripheral shimmer of yesterday's LSD seems to have completely passed. Judging by the intensity of the heat and the brightness of the day searing through my window, I guess it's about midday.

The clatter of Kolkata can be heard and smelled outside. I close my eye and analyse the data – reality seems to be back in place. I turn my attention to my inner universe, assessing the state of my earlier spasmodically, uncontrollably convulsing sphincter and stomach muscles. No stabbing pain in my stomach – good. No overwhelming need to vomit violently or defecate – good. No fever or cold sweat – good. I feel thirsty and even a tad peckish, both definite signs of hope. The pre-dawn, post-Holi, post-party exorcist double end projectile expelling has passed. It had been one hell of a temple cleansing.

I open both eyes now and roll onto my side. Dangerous Dave's bed is vacant, and judging by the tangle of bed sheets on the floor trailing out of the open door, it appears he left in a hurry. I reach beneath the bed, feeling around till I find it. The plastic film canister containing charas, half a cigarette and I hope one more Rizzla paper. I'm in luck. I roll a joint, light it and lie back down, staring at the dirty stained ceiling. After the cathartic temple cleaning earlier this morning, I'm feeling positively post-coitus. There is nothing more overrated than a bad fuck and nothing more underrated than a good shit. Since the former is nowhere in sight, I have to settle for the pleasures of the latter.

I lie here smoking, contemplating life and the insanity of the day before, hurtling through the back streets of Kolkata in Garuda's taxi, the mesmerising stimuli of the festival of colours extenuated and exaggerated by the LSD.

My mind falls upon Frankie as I wonder at his whereabouts. I consider his last couple of emails.

```
Hey Bro,
I'm still at Tiruvannamalai, very strange place!
I have been trying to leave a number of times,
but haven't got out yet. This place has a way of
holding on to you. I will try again today... I
think I need to get out of here! Anyway will be
in Kolkata a day before Holi,
Until then,
The Kobra


Now in Puri, half way there. 10 hour train ride
to Kolkata. Will train tomorrow arrive morning of
Holi, promise ...
Government sells opiUM Here.
    K
```

An apparition of a ghost-like Dave standing in the doorway snaps me out of my daydream, his usually bushy hair, limp, dripping with water. Wrapped in a bath towel and holding his jeans with an outstretched arm, he looks sallow. The pink dye from his hair runs down across his face bleeding with the green on his skin. He has the appearance of a half-melted ice cream. The stench of shit, almost saccharine sweet, like that of a soiled baby's nappy, penetrates my nostrils. Dave, not his usual chipper persona, looks positively sorry for himself. If he had a tail, it would be between his legs right now. 'I had a little accident.'

Judging by the smell, the distance and disgust with which he holds his jeans, I guess it was more than a little accident. Dropping them on the floor, he picks up his sheet, crawls back into his partially collapsed bed and curls ups into the foetal position, groaning. 'Ouch, think I'm dying.' Whimpering to himself, he drifts out of consciousness, 'That's the last pair of jeans I had too.'

Obviously the Super Bar pizza got him too. Still feeling delicate, the scent of shit and death gives me inspiration to get up and face the rest of the day. I decide to face my karma and leave Dave to his. I sort through my clothes, selecting my cleanest dirty items using the sniff test, it's a dirty pair of white pants and a once white T-shirt.

It seemed appropriate for some reason. The spiritual epiphany during the festival, the internal cleansing of the pizza and the whitewash of the acid, a mind, body, spirit spring-clean, represented by the white robes. Going through my dye-stained pants of the day before, searching for any spare rupee, my fingers stumble across a card. I remove it. It's the ace of spades. The card I found outside of the Victoria Gardens at the peak of the trip. I slip it into my white pants. Not sure why but I sense it has some sort of significance, yet unidentified to me. Maybe a sort of tarot delivered by the universe, the ace of spades, like the tattoo on my wrist.

Making my way into the common room of the hostel I discover an equally fragile looking Ian. Slumped on a couch, the palm of his hand is supporting the side of his face, which is distorted and twisted under the pressure. He watches cricket on TV with disinterest. He has shaved off his five o'clock shadow, in the process clearing the green dye from his chin and cheeks, the only white patch on his otherwise green complexion. His eyes roll up to meet mine, forcing a smile; he doesn't look well. Next to him his roommate, Red Man is now a shade of pink. A long arduous shower, trying to scrub off the dye, has left his skin rubbed raw. Outstretched, his head is rolled back against the couch, his mouth agape, his eyes closed. With his blonde ponytail tied back too tightly he has the appearance of a corpse in rigor mortis. Smiling back at Ian I enquire, 'Shanti, shanti Munty?' (Short for munted yoga master, the name we christened him with yesterday at the height of the trip).

Not smiling, Ian can't help but sense the humour of the situation – he grumbles a reply, 'Shanti shanti.'

'Acha.' (Hindi for good or OK).

A girl sits in an armchair adjacent to Ian and Red Man, voluptuous, verging on a little dumpy, but cute, with a bob cut, maybe late twenties. She looks like a prim and proper girl, back straight, legs together, feet on tippy toes and her fingertips resting on her knees. She has a disturbing smile as she rocks her head from side to side, as if she is singing the Smurf song to herself. She has the presence of Judy Garland's Dorothy in *The Wizard of Oz*. A little kooky. The sexual deviant in me is curious to know more. I sit down on the edge of Ian and Red Man's dilapidated couch, facing Dotty the space cadet. Smiling at her and trying to muster the best 'boy next door' vibe I can, I introduce myself. She responds in a high-pitched, whining voice that I can tell won't take long to become annoying, 'Hiiiiiiii, my name is Celine. I'm from Toronto.'

'Really?'

'That's in Canada.' She speaks to me like a primary school teacher, as if I'm some retarded infant.

'I actually know that Celine. Beautiful name – Celine. It's like Celine Dion, she's from Canada too isn't she?'

'Yeeeeeesss! Hmmmmmmm, I looove Celine Dion.'

'How about that, so do I.' I smile, lying through my teeth.

Ian sighs, 'Good god.' He knows I'm selling out. I turn to him, 'What's wrong Munty, England losing at the cricket again?'

He glares at me, raising one eyebrow, 'Yes, whatever, something like that.'

Celine claps her hands, 'Wow, cricket, it's so cute. They all look so serious don't they, seems very popular. I don't really understand it though.'

I look back at Celine and wearing my best wholesome nice guy expression I steer the focus back to me. 'So, Celine what're you doing here in Kolkata.'

'Well, I'm volunteering at the Mother Teresa Centre for Homeless Children.'

Excellent, a do-gooder. 'Wow, that's amazing, what an incredible coincidence, I'm looking at doing the same thing.'

Groaning, Ian mutters under his breath, 'I don't believe this.'

Ignoring his comment I persevere, 'Have you eaten? I was going to go out for a late breakfast – I would love to hear more about Mother Teresa and the orphans.'

'Yeeeesss! That sounds wonderful, let's all go.' Celine slaps Red Man on the leg, returning him to consciousness with a startled gasp. I'm not sure he's totally aware of where he is. Grabbing Ian and my hands, she stands up and virtually skips us out of the door like we are the Lion and Tin Man. Red Man trudges after us with a sunken-eyed vacant expression and a slumped neanderthalic posture.

On the now not so surreal Sudder Street, I feel extra sensitive to the intensity of Kolkata. The brightness and heat of the sun, the orchestra of noise and the overwhelming stink of pollution are all a little too much for my constitution. Workers dig a trench across the street – jackhammers smash the bitumen away. The road is blocked and impassable; the traffic has built up. Taxis blast their horns, infuriatingly, annoyingly. Ian, clearly feeling as tender as I do, breathes in deeply as he pats his chest, 'Ah – Kolkata, Shanti shanti.'

Despite his seedy condition Ian is obviously in good spirits and apparently recovered from his déjà vu crisis of last night. The large overweight rickshawallah, also the local drug dealer, approaches us. We met him only days prior and upon minutes of our arrival into Sudder Street from the Andamans. Wearing a grimy blue lungi wrapped tautly around his expansive belly and a moth-holed, sweat-stained singlet, he had approached us with a shady grin. 'Vhat you like, hashish, opium, heroin, cocaine? All very much excellent, very best quality.'

We had purchased some hash off him and now everytime we exit or enter the hostel he follows us, raising his eyebrows with an expectant knowing expression that's a little unnerving. He saunters up to us now, wiping his sweaty palms on his dirty, once white singlet, nodding his head and winking at us. Before he can ask the inevitable Ian cuts to the chase,

'We will not be in need of your product or services today my dear contraband merchant and purveyor of everything shifty, but thank you for indicating your willingness to engage in business with your "mum's the word" all knowing omnipotent nod. Thank you, but no thank you.'

'You vant rickshaw. Me best in Kolkata.' He points to his redundant, antiquated piece of machinery in the street. The old school variety, not powered by a Bajaj motor or even a pedal bike, but only by the rickshawallah himself. This is done by holding the bars and running down the road. This is the last place in India you will find this variety of transport. Ian and I smile, we know full well his rickshaw is nothing more than a cover for his drug trafficking operation. The only function it ever serves is as a bed upon which he snoozes for the most of the day.

Sucking in his belly and puffing out his chest while flexing his flabby biceps he says, 'I big and strong. I take all four of you.'

Ian smiles graciously. 'Yes sir you are most definitely very, very big. There is no denying it, but no thank you my good man, and I think I can speak for all in our party when I say we will remain pedestrian on our little journey henceforth.'

Not fully comprehending Ian he gets the point nonetheless and returns to his sad looking rickshaw, which creaks as he places his large derriere onto its usual resting place.

We continue on our way and come across the large and still yellow goat from the night before. He looks up at Ian like someone that's been violated. There is an unspoken moment between them both. Grinning, I elbow Ian in the ribs, 'Looks like the goat fared worse than us. Wonder if your naked dancing companion got any last night?'

Ian chooses not to hear my remark. Celine kneels down

and pats the goat on the head, 'Oh, looook, he's soooooo cute!'

The goat flinches and pulls away from Celine's hand. He seems traumatised by the touch of humans. As our perverted attention is held by Celine's affection for the goat, none of us notice Carlitos approaching. Standing in front of us, hands on his hips, he slowly shakes his head in disapproval. He's tutting under his breath, 'Wha' have you been doing Australia, why de green colour?'

I glance up at Carlitos. He signals with his eyes at Celine, as if enquiring *what's with the girl, got lucky yet?*

Celine, still focused on the goat, doesn't look up. I shake my head and Carlitos rolls his eyes in disappointment. I smirk, 'You know, just getting into the festivities of things yesterday. The dye comes with the territory I guess. I can see you escaped cleanly.'

Dressed in a white kaftan, Carlitos is immaculate, not a single spot on him. 'Dis festival is for silly teenagers. You are all like children. Dis dye takes a long time to wash off, maybe one week or more.'

'Sorry Dad.'

Ian looks a little shocked, 'One week, green, well that's just fantastic. As if I wasn't conspicuous enough already.'

Carlitos remains all serious. 'I will see you later. I have to go meet a girl. Ciao.'

As Carlitos marches off, Ian calls after him, 'Flute lessons I presume?'

Further along, at the corner eatery the aromas of food emanating from the kitchen are all a little too much for me. I order a fruit salad and a plain sweet lassie. Ian requests, 'Plain toast, no butter and a black tea, thank you.'

Red Man utters the only two words I ever hear him say, in his abrasive east European accent, 'Chicken tikka.'

My stomach turns as I look at him with pleading eyes, 'For breakfast, man, how can you? I would be suss of any meat here, in fact I'm going vego from now on.'

Ian also offers advice, 'You know there is a bird flu outbreak in India as we speak, heed caution dear friend.'

Red Man looks at us both glumly, 'Chicken tikka.'

Celine reads the menu. She claps her hands, 'Hmmm, think I'll have pizza.'

Ian and I groan, clutching at our bellies haunted by memories of last night at the Super Bar. Our food arrives and while pushing pieces of fruit around my bowl, I continue to attempt to tune Celine, talking about the orphanage. She smiles with a vacant, slightly disturbing expression, 'Yeah, it's really, really, really nice. I feed the lepers and the kids with Aids that are homeless. Many have been deserted by their prostitute mothers you know. They're so cute with their big eyes looking up at me. I even get to hold their hands when they're dying. It's really very rewarding.'

At a loss for words, we fall into silence. This and Red Man tearing into his greasy, anaemic looking chicken leg becomes all too much for Ian. Pushing his plate of uneaten toast away, he stands, 'Think I will pop back and have a little lie down, feeling a bit under the weather. Namaste people.'

Celine continues talking of her charity work with the gleeful detachment of a sociopath. The girl is definitely damaged goods, but the perverted side of me, the side desperate for a shag, perseveres. I try a change of tack, 'I hear the botanical gardens are worth a look, fancy having a stroll this afternoon.'

'Yeees, that sounds lovely.'

So we leave Red Man, with his face buried in his chicken like a carrion-gorging, ponytailed hyena. Saffron infused grease is smeared all over his chin and fingers as he grunts a farewell that sounds distinctly like, 'Chicken tikka.'

We walk across the vast Victoria Park where only yesterday hundreds of Indians played cricket. Today it's deserted. The parched ground cracks as the sun sucks out any residue of moisture. The patches of surviving grass, dry and brown, crunch underfoot. It never rains in India, not until the monsoons come. Being the last couple of months of the dry season means everything is hot and dusty. The land is as thirsty as hell, the soil, the grass, the trees, all yearning for the monsoon rains, which when they come never stop.

We jump over an open sewer – the stink of human excrement slams my senses. My first impression of Celine as a ditsy bimbo appears to be slightly misguided, if not presumptuous. She knows her way around this expansive metropolis. 'We just have to pass over the train tracks, and then we can catch a ferry across the river. I think the Botanical Gardens aren't far then.'

Crossing the train tracks we make our way down a rusted carriageway to the river's edge. My first view of the mighty Ganges river steals my breath. This, the very life blood of India, from its birth in the Himalaya to here at its mouth in the delta, the Bay of Bengal, with billions and billions of litres of water billowing out into the Indian Ocean. It stretches the width of the subcontinent, the carotid artery of the country.

A river so steeped in mysticism, so revered by its people, that it's worshipped as a goddess in its own right. To understand this amazing river is to understand India. In no other culture has a feature of nature assumed so much psychological and spiritual significance. The whole river provides salvation, not in the afterlife but in the here and now. A goddess the people can see and touch. There aren't any shrines or temples built for this popular liquid deity anywhere, why bother when she's flowing right past you.

The river's mythical origin stems from a fable. It involves a sage or rishi (Hindu saint) who loved to travel across the land and sing ragas (classical Indian music). However he didn't realise he was not a good singer, until one day he came across the spirits of the ragas writhing in pain, begging him to stop. Feeling indebted to the poor souls he had inadvertently tortured, he promised to help them. The only way to do that was to ask Shiva to sing. Shiva sang whilst Brahma and Vishnu listened. The ragas were soon healed. However, the music was so sweet that the soft tones actually melted Vishnu into liquid at the feet of Brahma, who collected this liquid and fashioned it into a divinely beautiful girl, his daughter Ganga. Ganga lived in heaven and her powers made her turbulent and unpredictable. This creature of whim with the power of Vishnu was only allowed to play in the Himalaya.

There was trouble in the valley, down on earth, however. In trying to dry the seabed, so that an army of demons from the deep could be defeated another rishi had inadvertently caused a catastrophe by drinking the entire ocean's water. A king begged Brahma to allow Ganga to wash over the land and cleanse the many generations of his ancestors that were cursed by yet another rishi. Brahma finally consented to permit Ganga to descend to earth, but only if Shiva agreed to allow the divine deluge to fall upon his head and thus break up the impact of Ganga into manageable levels, otherwise the earth would have been destroyed by her immense power. Shiva agreed. Ganga had delusions of grandeur and thought she could wash Shiva away. Shiva chastened her by only letting her flow as five gentle streams from the top of his head. Ganga finally fell in love with Shiva as they were in a constant close embrace and so she became one of his wives.

The story of Ganga is an allegory about the acquisition of divine consciousness. For consciousness to flow requires great effort and if released on an unprepared mind it could destroy it. So it is first passed to a sage who can handle it, who in turn passes the knowledge down to the individual seeker in amounts they can cope with.

Standing now at the gaping mouth of the Ganges river, I watch its water, opaque, milky-green in colour, eddy in whirlpools, concealing an eternity of secrets. Its current is strong and ferries and cargo boats struggle to fight its power as they traverse back and forth. The river bullies them about like bobbing corks. Just near the ferry a gathering of Indians bathe in her filthy but sublime viscosity. Red powder and flower petals disperse into the river from a ceremony where hundreds of people rejoice, baptising themselves in the holy water. Along her banks sunken hulks lie semi-submerged, scattered in the shallows.

Celine and I board our ferry, which sits alarmingly low in the water. The water licks and laps at my toes. I remember the ace of spades in my pocket. Fishing it out I finger the card, twisting it around and around. I don't know why, but I toss it into the Ganges. It swirls in the current, and then is gone, swallowed up by her. It seems like the appropriate thing to do, a blessing at the beginning of something, at the end of the river.

I recall an experience I had a year earlier, it was the most significant spiritual moment of my life. It occurred on the Murray river, which forms the border between the states of Victoria and New South Wales – in the Barmah forest, land of the Yorta Yorta people, the indigenous, traditional landowners. After a festival of electronic music, didgeridoo, traditional 'shake a leg' dancing and a plethora of spiritual workshops, just close friends and some of the tribal elders remained. We relaxed around a roaring campfire of smouldering red gum, telling stories and sharing jokes. It was the witching hour – pre-dawn, neither night nor day. The stars had all but disappeared and it was just before the morning sun had broken the skyline. We were discussing the Aboriginal spirit world, 'dreamtime' and animal spirit guides. Perplexed I asked an elder how you find your spirit animal. He laughed and said, 'Ya don't bro, they find you.'

Needing to stretch my legs I went for a stroll to the river's edge. Watching the dark water ripple past I didn't notice someone walk up and stand by my side. 'Magical isn't it?'

I turned to see Joan, or Joan of Arc as she was otherwise known. An elderly woman, she had been an attendee of gatherings like these since the 60s. She had shells and feathers woven into her long silver hair. A knowing smile spread across her face. 'Thinking about your spirit animal still?'

'Yeah, I think I know what it is. When I was a teenager I used to keep a pet sulphur-crested cockatoo. He flew around our bush-block as he liked. I'd leave his aviary door open and he came and went as he pleased. He'd sit on my shoulder as I cruised the streets on my pushbike. I became known as the boy with the bird.'

Joan of Arc nodded, 'You certainly seem to have a strong connection with the cockatoo.'

I felt nostalgic thinking about my pet from my teenage years. I blurted on, 'Then when I turned eighteen I planned to leave home and hitchhike around Australia. Can you believe this, the week before I left, another cockatoo came and they left together. Crazy huh, it's like he knew. Even today, seventeen years later, he still occasionally goes by my parents' house, usually when I'm having problems in my life. Mum will phone saying, *That bloody cockatoo is back here again, screeching and carrying on, are you in trouble again?'*

Joan chuckled, 'Yes my dear, it couldn't be any clearer. This bird has a direct connection with your spirit.'

I continued, 'I have this recurring dream, every month round full moon. It's like a panic dream, but not quite a nightmare. I dream I've been away for the weekend. I'm rushing to his aviary coz I'm afraid he's been locked inside with no food and water. When I arrive I find the cage door is open and he's sitting in the branches of his favourite tree nearby. When I look up he looks back at me then flies off down through the valley of forest below my parents' house. It's the same dream, every month since I left home seventeen years ago.'

Joan contemplated my words. 'Now let me pass down to you a tale told to me by the elders. The cockatoo is second in the hierarchy of animals, second only to the crow. The crow's in charge round here. The cockatoo, however, is like the secretary of the forest. It's up to date with all the gossip. It chatters and carries on and wakes everyone up in the morning and tells them to go to bed at night.'

Joan placed her hand on my shoulder and steered my gaze downstream to the eastern horizon, where the black sky had started to bleach to purple tones in anticipation of the morning sun. 'The day of the cockatoo starts like this. When the sun rises in the east, when it creates a certain hue of orange on the eastern side of the tree trunk the cockatoo has slept in, he scratches an X on his branch and announces to the whole forest the beginning of a new day.'

Turning away from the river and looking towards a cluster of trees in the distance she continued, 'The whole family then flies northwest in a forty-five degree angle to a stand of trees where they catch up with relatives. Then when the day grows old and the shadows draw long the flock heads southwest at a forty-five degree angle back to the river's edge where they drink and bathe in the waters of the mighty Murray.'

Joan shifted again, facing the still dark horizon, where a couple of resilient stars twinkled in the last of the night sky. 'Then as the sun sets in the west and creates a particular hue of red on the western side of the tree the cockatoo is resting in, he announces to the whole forest that the day has passed and it's time for bed. The family then flies at a forty-five degree angle back down the river till they return to the tree where they started the day.'

Joan patted a large gum tree at the river's edge. 'He lands on the very branch he scratched the X on in the morning at sunrise.'

I looked up at the canopy of the old tree. 'Wow, that's a cool story.'

She smiled at me. 'It's your story now. Just remember the cockatoo is your grandfather, your ancestor. Whenever you see one it's a good omen for you. Always stop whatever you're doing and pay your respects to him, salute him.'

She simulated the cockatoo's crest with her hand on her head, raising it like a mohawk. 'I will tell you a ritual you can do to help deepen your bond with the spirits of the land and the cockatoo. But to understand you first have to know something of the land. Each part of the forest has a family of trees. These trees are either men or women. The women trees have a trunk that divides into two main branches, like the legs of a woman. The men trees have a trunk that branches into three main stems from its base. First thing you have to do is to look around to find the grandfather tree – he is the biggest and the oldest of all the men trees. His wife, grandmother tree, is never far from her husband. All their children will be scattered around them. The forest is made up of hundreds of these families. Even in the cities and parks you can still see the families, all you have to do is find the grandfather tree first.'

Joan, still with one hand on my shoulder whilst caressing the trunk of the large grandfather tree next to us, continued, 'Now, to be welcomed by the spirits of the land, this is what you must do. The next cockatoo feather you find, you must take it and place it at the base of the nearest grandfather tree. Then, turn and walk into the wind and once you have done this you will be welcomed by the land. Next, you must go down to the river and place your hand in the water. This will connect you with your ancestors. You see, water's timeless and it acts as a portal or a doorway for the spirit world. It's able to transcend space and time – it allows you to connect with the divine anywhere, in any lake, river or ocean anywhere on the planet.'

Later that day, after the cockatoos had announced the new day and flown off to their see their relatives, I did just as Joan said. Found a cockatoo feather and placed it at the base of a grandfather tree, walked into the wind and placed my hand into the Murray river.

A couple of weeks after I had conducted the ritual with the feather and the tree I had my full-moon monthly dream. However, this time it was different. This time it was a lucid dream. A dream where I knew it was a dream, so there was no sense of panic – I knew the cockatoo was sitting safely in a nearby tree. I also knew that he was my spirit guide. I looked up at him and smiled. Then as he flew away, I flapped my arms and took off up into the air, right up next to him. I flew down through the valley where I'd spent my childhood. My arms were wings, covered in white feathers. I looked across to my friend and felt overwhelmed with happiness. He turned and smiled as he spoke to me, 'Hey bro, I've been waiting a long time for you. Why do you think I kept coming back? We just wanted to take you for a fly.'

That was the last time I had the cockatoo dream; he's never returned to my sleeping world since. It was like it was his final parting gift to me. All these memories flood back now as I kneel down and place my hands into the waters of the holy Ganges. It laps just below the open deck of the ferry – it licks across my fingers inviting me in to cleanse my lifetime of sins.

* * *

Crossing the river, Celine and I taxi our way to the Botanical Gardens. We stroll through the expansive parklands and ramshackle gardens that, despite their state of neglect, provide tranquility from the frenetic bustle of the city. Without pausing, Celine talks of her experiences at the orphanage like it's a school camp, and with the same gleeful detachment I found so disturbing earlier. She also reveals that she has volunteered in China and I get a born again Christian vibe from her. I tire of the game of seduction that, frankly, I feel incapable of performing. So I decide to mix it up with a bit of shock treatment when she asks what I did during the festival of colours. 'I took a dose of LSD, you know, acid, and tripped like a trooper.'

Expecting her to scream in horror and run for her life, she smiles at me instead. 'Acid hey, yeah I used to take a lot of that in college, as well as ecstasy and coke and smoke like lots and lots of weed, not to mention have lots of orgies and kinky sex. But then I realised it was all just so self-indulgent and typically middle class and that I really wanted to do something, like,

105

positive for the world. We all have to grow up eventually.'

Celine smiles sympathetically at me again, like I'm a simple child – maybe she's right. We stop at a banyan tree, the highlight of the gardens and reputed to be the largest in the world, some two hundred years old. These trees are of particular spiritual significance, considered sacred by Hindus, and Buddhists alike. The tree represents eternal life because it supports its expanding canopy by growing special roots from its branches. These roots hang down and act as props that form an ever widening circle that reflects the Sanskrit name *bahupada*, one with many feet. This tree looks more like an entire forest than a single tree.

The banyan tree is considered as a place of rest and meditation, its leafy canopy providing a cool respite from the heat of the day. It's also believed, however, that many spirits or ghosts are harboured there. The local people don't sleep under the banyan tree at night. Well, that's what the sign under the tree says. Standing there next to Celine, I start to feel slightly guilty for my presumption that she is a bimbo I can easily seduce for the sake of feeding my desperately deficient ego. She's obviously a lot sharper than I thought. I can almost hear the tree spirits laughing at my misguided, foolish soul – not a cockatoo feather in sight to save me here. Celine takes my hand with the same empathy I imagine she has for the dying orphans. 'Come on silly, let's go home.'

CHAPTER 6

One's Company, Two's a Crowd

I wake suddenly, clammy from a nightmare. I was under the banyan tree at night being hounded by the tree spirits. The tree was an asylum or some sort of spiritual rehab clinic and I was in a twelve-step program for ascension. Very bizarre, we all wore hospital robes like in *One Flew over the Cuckoo's Nest*. Ian, still green, painted in sad clown make-up, clutched at his stomach. In pain he walked in little circles mumbling, 'Shanti shanti.'

Dave was screaming, chased by gremlin-like playing cards with stumpy arms and legs. Frankie, a half serpent, half bearded man, coiled on a pile of writhing, skimpily-clad Israeli girls. Celine, dressed in a sexy nurse's outfit, skipped around and dished out flowers, whilst the giant yellow goat followed eating them. My feet were stuck in mud as I desperately tried to reach the open door of Garuda's taxi. I knew it was my path to enlightenment. Garuda smiled at me, cigarette clenched in his crooked rotten teeth, beckoning me to come. I woke just before I reached the Ambassador's door.

It's late morning and my room is empty. There's a note on Dave's bed. Rubbing my eyes to focus, I read it.

Didn't want to wake you, I have decided to leave this morning.
Heading for the hills, needed to get out of the city and get some fresh air.

Send me an email and maybe we can catch up later for a friendly game of poker.

Take care.

D.D.

Dave's done the sketchy bail. He's taken everything except for his soiled jeans that are pushed into the corner of the room. Quite frankly I totally sympathise with him and feel like doing the same, I'm sick of waiting for Frankie and listening to Ian complain about his stomach upsets. I feel claustrophobic from too much time with fellow travellers – a change of scenery is definitely on the cards. I get up and head to the alleyway chai stand. While sipping tea and contemplating my options, Carlitos slumps next to me. He weakly punches my arm. Still wearing his white kaftan from yesterday, he looks tired.

'So how was your date yesterday?'

'It was nor a date friend, we were jus' talking about yoga.'

'Yeah right, whatever – get any?'

'I don tell tales, but yes I did. But she is not so pretty, we did it in de hostel, in de dorm room. I got nor much sleep.'

'Classy mate, geez you're a real charmer Carlitos.'

'We did it three times, but I did nor come. I don like. It takes away my prana, I jus' fuck, but nor how you say, ejaculate.'

'Fuck man, do you mind, I am trying to enjoy my tea here. Please, spare me the gory details, Christ. And by the way, if you wanna be a dad you're going to have to come sometime.'

Carlitos changes the subject. 'I *chello* Kolkata today, fink I will go to Darjeeling, then Sikkim to hike in de mountains, it is too hort here and de air is nor clean. Wha' you do Australia?'

My head itches again – scratching my dirty fingernails across my scalp I scrape off scabs and draw blood. 'Dunno, but getting away from this heat sounds good, it's making my skin crawl.'

'Well if you wanna go to de mountains with me here is my email.' He whips a card out of his pocket – it has a symbol of an OM on it with his name and email.

'Very fancy mate, don't tell me, it's for the girls right?'

Standing up, he winks at me, patting my back as he walks out of the alleyway disappearing back into Sudder Street. Change is in the air. I check my emails, no word from Frankie but one from Merav saying she will be in Varanasi in a week. I head back to my room with plans of leaving – the social unit is starting to collapse. I bump into Ian outside our hostel – he stares blankly at the road where yesterday workers were digging. A large hump of dirt now covers the trench. Ian looks at me. 'Amazing workmanship, you wouldn't even notice they had been here at all.'

'Hi Ian.' I'm tiring of his sarcasm in regards to India.

He continues, 'My stomach just goes from bad to worse, had the runs all night, what I wouldn't do for a good English breakfast and a real cup of tea. Seen Dave today?'

'He's split, so has Carlitos, thinking of doing the same, head up to the north somewhere to escape this heat for a bit.'

'Yes, you're right, let's go. My ponytailed roommate, the red one, left last night unannounced. Either that or the chicken tikka got him.' Ian has just invited himself to tag along with me. He is starting to feel like a girlfriend, but a fat bald one whom I don't have sex with. We go to the train station to buy a ticket to somewhere, anywhere, originally agreeing on Varanasi, the holiest city in India and where I know Merav will be next week, but at the last minute deciding on Darjeeling instead, the old British tea station in the eastern foothills of the Himalaya. We book two sleepers on the Darjeeling Mail Express, due to leave that night.

* * *

Back in my room I'm shoving handfuls of clothes into my bag, when all of a sudden I hear a voice singing, 'It's a long way to Tipperary, it a long way to go …'

It's Frankie. It's an 'in' joke between us. One time eighteen years ago, when we hitchhiked around Australia, we had been stranded for hours in the Simpson Desert waiting for a lift to take us to Uluru. Frankie needed a respite from the heat and flies, so he went to get us a cold drink. In the five minutes he was gone the first car for hours pulled up and offered me a lift. A sexy older woman in a short skirt and driving an air-conditioned four-wheel drive – I laughed as I climbed in. She drove me the whole five hundred kilometres to the turn-off for the National Park, where I set up my tent and started cooking dinner over a campfire. It was sunset, some ten hours after I had last seen Frankie. Then on the horizon I saw a bedraggled, sunburnt and exhausted Frankie limply dragging his bag down the middle of the road towards my camp, singing the song he's singing now. The irony is beautiful. He surges through the door. 'Hey Baba Ji.'

He looks pale, thin and pasty with dark rings under his eyes. His beard is all crooked and his hair is mangy, I think he cut it himself without a mirror. He slaps me on the back. 'You look good man, all brown and healthy, island life obviously agreed with you.'

'Thanks man – you look like shit. Where the hell you been bro? Been waiting all week for you.'

'I know, I know, sorry. There was this cute Israeli girl in Tiru, which made leaving hard but then she left and now she is waiting for me in Varanasi. What can I say – it's Kobra power. Then I got stuck in Puri. Man they sell opium there in these government controlled shops, got caught in a rut, time got away from me.'

I tell him about my adventures on the Andamans, about my poker wins and meeting Merav. I tell him about Holi and the acid trip and my epiphany in the back of Garuda's Ambassador.

'Cool man, it's only been a month since I last saw you but you seem like a new person. You seem to be getting into the whole India experience now. Go dragon power. You're getting your mojo back dude.' Teasing me, he pats my back – he's referring to the Chinese dragons tattooed on my shoulders.

Frankie then shows me photos of Tiruvannamalai, his entourage of young Israeli nubiles and the current love or infatuation of his life, who is waiting for him in Varanasi. He shows me pictures of the highlight of this city, Arunachala Hill, a Mecca for devotees and lost hippies alike. He excitedly explains how legend has it that Shiva once appeared here as an infinite beacon of light so bright that no one could look at him, so Brahma and Vishnu asked Shiva to appear in a form more accessible to the people. So he did, by transforming himself into this hill. Frankie with fire in his eyes utters the words of Shiva, 'As the moon derives light from the sun, all holy places can derive illumination from here.'

Apparently Shiva went on to say that the hill was OM itself and he would appear once a year as a fiery beacon on its summit, sometime in November and align with the Pleiades constellation, Frankie's 'home galaxy'. Devotees would flock here for every full moon to worship Shiva's flaming apparition and march solemnly the eight miles around its base in bare feet. Frankie, like a man possessed, elucidates, 'I looked at the mountain everyday for weeks. It was like it was calling me, until one day I was drawn there. It was really fucking hot and I had no shoes. I climbed the hill – man the ground was so scorching I burnt the soles of my feet. I had no water. When I reached the summit it had a really intense energy and there was an eagle circling overhead. I don't know, but it was like I went up a couple of notches on the ascension to the divine, man. Then coming back down was full on, almost hallucinating from thirst and sunstroke, staggering around, nearly died, tripping on loose stones. No shit dude it was full on. It was like when Jesus went into the desert and saw the burning bush. Then, check this out, when I got to the bottom of the hill there was this really old rickshawallah, he looked about ninety. Nobody else around except this old guy, like he was waiting for me. Bizarre. Really fucking weird.'

'Sounds like my Ambassador taxi.'

'Exactly, real twilight zone material. He said he had been expecting me, and when I told him I didn't have any money, he didn't care. He reckoned I was a sadhu. Said I was a very wise and holy man and it was his honour to take me wherever I wished. He rode me back into town past a pile of rubble he said was the remains of his house that the government had bulldozed to the ground. Said he had lived there for years but now he was homeless and slept in his rickshaw. Don't know if it was bullshit or not. I thought it may have been a scam to get money out of me, but I'd already told him I was broke.'

'Strange.'

'Gets weirder man, check this out. He takes me back to my guesthouse and I was feeling sorry for the old dude. So I invited him to come in to sleep on the floor, coz it was getting late. He comes up and is sitting there telling me how I'm a great and very holy man. Then he reaches over and tries to undo my fly.'

'What the … ?'

'No shit. I'm like saying exactly that. What the fuck you doin' dude?' He reckoned he wanted to pay me for my generosity. I was like, man I really ain't into this, just go to sleep on the floor. He kept trying to open my pants. He wouldn't give up. I had to push him out of my room eventually. He wanted to blow me coz I was a holy man. Fuck, it totally creeped me out, I split the next day. The whole place was giving me bad vibes after that, apparently it happens if you stay there for too long.'

'What, old guys start offering you blow jobs?'

'No, the weird vibe, it's like the energy is just too powerful there. So I headed north to Puri to chill out and ended up smoking way too much opium.' Frankie notices the half-packed bag on my bed. 'Why you packing, you're not going are ya?'

'Well, yeah I am actually. I've already paid for my ticket to Darjeeling. Man I've been waiting for you all week.'

'Shit, yeah fair enough. I'm sorry dude. Look I gotta get out of the country in a few days, my visa is about to expire. I was thinking of Nepal to do a visa run, that's not far from Darjeeling. Wanna come to Nepal?'

In Frankie's haste and eagerness to leave Australia for India, he had purchased his six-month visa three months prior our departure and therefore it was now about to expire. I consider his offer, 'Sounds cool, could be fun. Then we could bus it down to Varanasi together, chase up our Issie chicks.'

Frankie looks at me with a serious expression, 'I don't know if you heard but things are pretty hairy in Varanasi right now. Last week some terrorists let off a couple of bombs in a temple. So it wouldn't hurt to take our time to get there. Things are also a bit shaky in the north of India too, along the border with Nepal. There are Maoist communists running amuck and Nepal looks like it could go off in big way. Man the whole area is a potential firecracker dude, could end up being something epic.'

The bombings in Varanasi were suspected to be the work of Muslim extremists, possibly from Pakistan, although nobody was claiming responsibility. Varanasi is a holy temple town and is to the Hindus what Mecca is to the Muslims or the Vatican to the Catholics. The first bomb exploded in a popular temple at its busiest time. Another bomb detonated at the main train station, next to the tourist information centre. A further two more bombs were discovered and diffused at a market and beside the Ganges river. Fifteen people were killed and another sixty injured. The attack was designed to create the maximum amount of havoc, aimed at both Hindus and tourists.

The problem in the North West of India and Nepal is a different story. Nepal has been caught in a civil war between communist Maoist rebels and the monarchist government for the last decade, killing thousands, displacing many more and disrupting development. Tension was heightened in 2001, after the Nepalese royal family was massacred. Some people in Nepal, which is ninety percent Hindu, believed that the king was the reincarnation of the god Vishnu and the massacre threw much of the country into disarray and further unrest.

The royal family was revered amongst the general population and the King was very popular and well liked. Supposedly, it was one of the King's disgruntled sons who open-fired on his whole family before turning the sub-machine gun on himself. The King's younger brother, who became the successor to the throne, was conveniently absent from the palace the night the massacre occurred and there has been a lot of speculation that this prince organised the assassination in an ambitious political move to gain power. The suspicion and mistrust the Nepalese people now have of the monarchy they once worshipped is further destabilising the country. The Maoists now control the rural areas and move back and forth across the Indian border at will.

I smile at Frankie, 'Nothing to fear but fear itself, Frankie.'

'Yeah that's true, we could get killed crossing the road.'

'Yeah, but crossing the road in India is probably more dangerous than the revolution. Anyway, I go to Darjeeling tonight, I can wait for you a couple of days then we can head to Nepal by bus. But don't take forever getting there, OK?'

'I promise, Scout's honour. I'll come tomorrow.' Frankie has never been in the Scouts so this doesn't fill me with confidence.

Ian then appears at the door and I introduce him to Frankie. I'm concerned they won't get on. They are poles apart in personality and beliefs. There is a bit of an awkward moment between them, especially when Ian starts to talk about his theories of Gandhi, theories he always entertains in the presence of new company. I think it's his way of being radical. 'You know Gandhi, really, when you look at the facts, was just a troublemaker. I mean he made out like he was an everyday Indian but really he was a rich kid, educated in Britain, who moved to India, carrying on about freeing "his country". In actual fact the British were about to give India back when Gandhi started stirring things up. Then there was the whole bloody mess with Pakistan. The whole damn thing could have been avoided. Actually, I think he was just a political opportunist taking advantage of the situation for his own gain.'

I flinch, expecting a torrent of abuse from Frankie, but he remains surprisingly restrained and even gracious. I give Frankie a big brotherly hug. 'It was great to see ya bro, however briefly, it's like a tag team across India. Get your ass to Darjeeling tomorrow.'

Frankie grins, *'Sab kuch milega.'* (Everything is possible)

* * *

At the frenetic and madly crowded Howrah train station, we appear to be the only tourists and judging by the constant stares we're obviously an entertaining spectacle. I don't know why, maybe because we're both still green. We spend a tediously long five hours waiting to board our train. One of the few benefits from the days of the British, trains are one of the things that operate with reliability here – apparently even more so than British Rail. It isn't until we're well underway and start chatting with our travelling companions in our six-berth compartment that we discover the reason for the delay. A Bangladeshi family heading home after a Kolkata shopping spree explain how Maoist terrorists had planted a number of bombs in the carriages. The officials had to sweep the whole train from end to end in search of explosives. It sends a cold chill down my spine. Ian and I look at each other. Ian jests, 'Don't worry old chap, we're on holidays, nothing ever happens to you when you're on holidays.'

The air of tension also explains the high police presence on board. They are armed with machineguns instead of their usual bamboo sticks. As the train rythmically shunts along the track, the family tells us that the Maoists control all the roads in and out of Nepal and are using rocket launchers to blow up any traffic trying to enter or exit the country. Apparently, they are being quite pleasant about it – telling border officials when they can and can't use the roads. They are even issuing tourists with receipts when they demand a 'tax' payment, a receipt, that when presented to other Maoists, allows free passage.

The deranged, deformed and destitute constantly pass our berth, trying to sell, beg, bribe or steal. It's an endless stream of chaiwallahs, kids with masala nibbles, families of performing acrobats, dancing transvestites, snake charmers and children sweeping the floors. Conversation with the Bangladeshi family reaches a natural lull and we all enjoy the silence and consider setting up our beds. Then out of nowhere a very drunk, fat Indian Sikh, wearing a purple turban and lots of gold necklaces and rings approaches us. He looks like an Indian Liberace with a Salvador Dali moustache. He staggers up to Ian, eyeing the spot of vacant bench next to him. I wouldn't say it's an empty seat, more like enough space for one butt cheek. He leans heavily on Ian's shoulder, supporting his mammoth weight. His other bear-like hand, shiny with sweat, stretches out to Ian, 'Hello my good friend.'

A tentative Ian, reluctant to accept the perspiring man's paw, finally submits, being the polite Englishman, 'Um, hi.'

Ian's newfound friend violently shakes not only Ian's hand, but his arm and upper body as well. 'Yes, it is most very, very good to meet you sir. Is this seat being taken?'

Ian glances at me desperately, trying to rope me into his predicament. I want no part of it. Pulling my cap down hard over my eyes I think to myself, *you're on your own buddy.* The Sikh still shakes Ian's arm as he stammers, 'Um, no, no I guess it's not.'

'Excellent.'

Our newest companion then squeezes his robust and ample posterior into the impossibly small space. At no point does he stop shaking Ian's hand, while placing his other hand on Ian's upper thigh, gripping firmly. He continues to tell Ian what a pleasure it is to meet him and Ian continues to attempt a gracious smile to cover his discomfort. This goes on for some twenty minutes, until he has a terrified Ian in a bear hug. Ian isn't having any luck with the ladies, but is certainly a natural with the inebriated and insane.

The Sikh then diverts his attention to me, pressing Ian's face into his armpit for safekeeping. His friendly macho, verging on homo-erotic bear hug has transformed itself into a wrestler's headlock. Ian's bald head goes purple under the Sikh's arm, as his muffled voice pleads for help. Looking at me, the Sikh tries making eye contact, reaching out his hand to me. 'Hello my good friend.'

I wave at him, avoiding his offer of a handshake,

Our Bangladeshi family is laughing as they film it all on their video camera, no doubt to appear on Bangladesh's *Funniest Home Videos*. The purple-turbaned Sikh then announces he will fetch some more liquor to drink with us. The moment he vacates the seat we all promptly set up our beds, turn off the lights and retire, faking sleep when he returns. I'm sure Ian is relieved to be on the top bunk and safely out of harm's way.

* * *

It's late morning by the time we arrive in Jalpaiguri, a poor, small, dusty city at the base of the mountains, with little interest for us other than being a necessary transit point to Darjeeling. From here we manage to negotiate a Land Rover to take us the remaining seventy-five kilometres up some two and a half thousand metres of altitude, a spine-shaking four hours of hairpin bends winding through small villages and into the clouds. Our driver hoodwinked us saying that only four would be riding in the back – there are ten of us crammed in. On one side I have an old lady's ample breast pressing against my arm; she smiles at me each time I look at her. On the other side an old man with no teeth and bad breath rests his hand on my leg and winks at me. In my arms is someone's sleeping infant. The whole way Ian complains: a) It just isn't fair we have to share with 'these people'. b) That his tummy hurts and he needs to go to the toilet, and, c) That it's too cold (after weeks of complaining of the heat). He is becoming more annoying every day.

Reaching Darjeeling, the air is thin, cold and every little exertion makes me short of breath. Checking into a hotel we are delighted to discover it has hot water and cable TV. After a scalding hot shower and an episode of *Friends*, I'm rejuvenated. Walking around the town, the cold air makes my cheeks rosy. It feels distinctly different to the rest of India – the people are more petite and look Tibetan. They are more relaxed with no hard sell tactics, maybe something to do with the predominantly Buddhist influence of the region.

The buildings adhere to impossibly steep terrain and are interspersed between tea plantations. People harvest the leaves, placing them into wicker baskets strapped to their waists. Low-lying clouds conceal the giants behind – the mighty Himalaya. The clouds fall as light damp mist in the afternoon, shadowing everything with an enchanting mystery. Periodically the deep tone of the nearby Buddhist monastery's bell can be heard. There is a definite Swiss cottage vibe going on, complete with cake shops and hot chocolate.

After a cup of this sweet inspiration I feel brave enough to venture into another great Indian institution, the barbershop, for a shave. The Indian beauty industry is almost exclusively tailored to the needs of men. These guys are nothing short of amazing. Old school. Cut-throat razors, sharpened on wide leather belts. The position of barber is so revered that these guys have to be able to lather up a balloon and shave it without popping it to qualify for this prestigious title. To nick the skin of a customer is a death sentence for the Indian barber.

My painfully polite barber seats me in the traditional barber's chair, straps on the gown, lathers up my face, shaves, lathers up again and shaves a second time. Then aftershave, three different skin lotions and moisturisers, finishing with a scalp and face massage. All cheaper than the price of a disposable razor, the result is a face smoother than a baby's bum. By far the best shave I've ever had.

* * *

After a few days of hot chocolate, hot showers, cable TV and barber visits I feel like a new man. We even managed to find somewhere that served bacon and eggs, Ian's proverbial English cooked breakfast. Not that it stopped his complaining though. My patience wears thin as we become the odd couple, spending our days on dates – the zoo, the tea plantations, the cake shop and then evenings in front of the TV. Again there's no word from Frankie who's proving to be a most unreliable best friend. Also there is no sign of Carlitos, so hiking looks like a no go. On the fourth day, on our way back from visiting a Buddhist monastery, we bump into a surprised and sickly-looking Dave. A shadow of his former self, the Kolkata runs obviously took its toll and he has shed a few pounds that he couldn't really afford to lose. Self-conscious he stammers, 'Hey, fancy meeting you guys here. I was going to send an email.'

Dave can't help himself – he is his own worst enemy, despite his obvious desire to travel solo. 'So, how about one last game of poker tonight boys?'

Dave rocks up to our hotel that night with two bottles

of red wine, a block of real cheddar cheese and non-masala flavoured crackers. He managed to source the goodies from one of the many shops catering exclusively for tourists. However it doesn't feel like India anymore and I'm now, for the first time, really ready to tackle the full depth of this country alone. Also, for the first time, Dave wins at poker – definitely a sign. The following morning over our breakfast of bacon, eggs and hot cocoa I announce to them, 'As the great Confucius once said, *Change is the only constant in the universe.*'

Ian interrupts, 'Actually it was Heraclitus, a Greek philosopher and what he really said was …'

I cut him off, 'Whatever, anyway I've decided it's time for me to move on and begin my spiritual quest alone. I plan to return to the river bank of the holy Ganges in Varanasi, the city of the dead and experience the burning ghats.'

Ian, holding a fork full of bacon to his lips, 'What are the burning ghats?'

Dave, eyes me suspiciously over his mug of steaming cocoa, 'It's where they cremate their dead Munty.'

Ian drops his fork and pushes away his plate. 'Oh god, count me out, I am staying here in my little Britain till I am on the mend.'

Dave flits his gaze back to me. 'So what you're really saying is that you're going to try and shag that Israeli girl you met in the Andamans and you don't want us cramping your style.'

'Exactly.'

And that was the end of the poker Dream Team. I left Darjeeling after emailing Frankie to warn him of the polite rocket launching Maoists and to make sure he caught a bus to Nepal on a day they approved.

CHAPTER 7

Big Wheel Keeps On Turning

Back in Jalpaiguri after descending from the mountains, I sit in the open doorway of the carriage of my still stationary train. For the first time, I'm comfortably alone and no longer feeling desperately lonely. Frankie's right, I'm finding my mojo again. Mother India has seduced me, the smells, the delays, the crowds, and the persistent hustle and bustle of the streets now all feel harmonious and not nearly as aggravating as it had seemed in the beginning.

It will take some fourteen hours to complete the first leg of my journey to Varanasi, to the city of Patna in the state of Bihar, the poorest and most politically corrupt in all of India. Usually avoided by travellers, in some ways it feels like a personal pilgrimage into the very essence of India. Watching the landscape change as the train descends to lower terrain, it becomes flatter and drier. Afternoon transforms to dusk, the train rockets past rice paddies where exhausted but smiling workers walk home beside the tracks, waving as we pass. Through the open window a warm breeze, thick with the aromas I've come to savour, washes over me.

My fellow passengers are the everyday Indians, thin, lean, brown, in worn clothes, years of hard work showing on their bodies. Tired but not complaining, resigned to their fates in this incarnation. Old ladies carry large baskets of vegetables into the bigger towns, to sell at the markets. Young families migrate with all their possessions contained in a cardboard box, to start a new life somewhere – eyes full of hope.

This isn't like the Darjeeling Express, full of affluent Indians heading to the hills for vacation, no – this train hauls the less fortunate. As night falls across the land, the train is completely full, even the floor is covered with the poorest of the poor. Bodies wrapped in sarongs and baskets of cargo take up every last square inch of space. These are the untouchables, or the lowest of the seven castes. Under the adjacent bench a young woman curls up cradling her baby. Leaning against my seat is a sleeping elderly lady with silver nose rings connected by chains to her earrings, long white hair spills out of her sarong hood. Thin, wiry, skin and bones, but she looks resilient. Her head rocks from side to side with the clickity clack of the train's momentum. The same rhythm drifts me off into a light sleep.

We reach Patna early in the morning. It's still dark but the level of poverty is very much visible. All the buildings lining the tracks are either makeshift slums or rundown to the point of no return. People look hungry, the homeless sleep on the platforms, under their lungis. I feel like the rich and spoilt cousin. Most of the world lives like this, struggling from hand to mouth, from day to day. How frivolous and conceited of me to come here from my more affluent, but morally effluent culture, on my little spiritual safari. I wince at an image of myself in the future. At some fancy restaurant, telling people of my decadent adventure to find myself, while these people starve and struggle.

Waves of people scramble on and off the trains – everyone here has a sense of quiet desperation about them. Nobody speaks any English, and trying to fathom the ticket stalls is utter chaos, with miles of queues and people pushing and shoving each other. Giving up on the idea of buying a ticket I figure I will just jump on the train for Varanasi and work it out with the conductor.

Waiting for the train on the platform, I watch commuters step over a sleeping beggar as if he isn't there at all. Walking closer I realise with horror that he isn't asleep but is in fact dead. Rigor mortis has already set in as flies crawl in and out of his open mouth and around his closed eyes. He's wrapped in his lungi in a foetal position. Obviously an old man, he must have passed away in the middle of the night. But now in the light of day nobody looks twice at him; it's like he doesn't exist.

I know Indians don't see death as final but merely as another point in the wheel of life and that the body is nothing more than a vessel in which to carry the soul, but I still find this disturbing. It's sad that there is nobody to bury him, burn him or mourn him. We enter this world alone and we leave the same way.

According to Hinduism the soul is immortal, while the body is subject to birth and death. The spirit goes on repeatedly dying and being reborn, changing bodies as if it were no more than clothes, discarded at the end of each life. The reason a soul reincarnates is because of karma, which is the sum total of a person's actions during their life. This determines how we are reincarnated into the next one. A soul desires to be born into a body because it desires worldly pleasures. These pleasures of the flesh aren't seen as sinful, but they will never bring a lasting inner peace, so after many births and deaths a soul becomes dissatisfied and seeks fulfillment through spiritual experience. Then, after much practice, a person finally realises his/her own divine nature, that the true self is the immortal soul, rather than just the body or the ego.

Only then, when all desire has vanished, will a person not be reborn again and will have reached their salvation, freed from the cycle of rebirth. You keep coming back till you get it right, almost like a test we need to pass before we can reach the next level. Like a cosmic PlayStation.

As my train departs, I contemplate this big old wheel, wondering how many more rounds I'll need till I finally work it out. The poor dead beggar has gone on to whatever awaits us all, but here and now in the land of the living I'm surrounded by many smiling faces and big bright eyes. Once again I have become a spectacle of entertainment for my fellow passengers. Smiling back, I smile to myself. All is well in the greater picture. As tragic as the image of the beggar's corpse is, it's somehow balanced by these smiling faces. As chaotic, frenetic and overwhelming as this country can be, it starts to make some sort of divine sense in a way that I can't explain, only feel. The sun begins to heat up the land, another hot, dry day. Staring over rambling fields of yellow grass and dry rice paddies, the rhythmical rocking of the train again gently seduces me into sleep.

A jovial, rotund-bellied conductor wakes me and I'm not sure how long I've slept. 'Ticket please, sir.'

I tell how I don't have a ticket, of the confusion at Patna station. Looking gravely at me he explains I'll receive a hefty fine. I hand him my passport. He flicks it open. 'Sir, you are Australian?'

'Yes mate.'

'Very best cricketers Australia. I very much admire Ricky Ponting.'

'Thank you.' As if I personally appointed him to his captaincy.

'Most excellent indeed ...'

The conductor pauses, he gently pats my shoulder. 'Vhere are you going today sir?'

'Varanasi.'

'Oh yes, a most holy place indeed, it is most very, very good.'

He looks at me as if he's considering something. 'Very good, very good – Australia is a very good team.'

Standing up, the conductor puts away his notebook, appearing to have a change of heart. He passes back my passport and raises a finger in the air. 'You must take blessings at the mother Ganga. Varanasi is the next stop, be sure not to fall asleep or you will vake up tomorrow in New Delhi.' With that he goes.

Looking out the window I occasionally see fleeting glimpses of the Ganges, shimmering silver like a giant serpent. Then we suddenly pass over a large bridge, spanning the river, giving me my first view of Varanasi, the holiest Hindu city situated on the banks of the Ganges. Considered both the cultural capital of India and abode of Lord Shiva, at 3000 years old it's the oldest living city in the world, famous as the city of temples.

As well as the belief that bathing in the Ganges washes away all sins, Hindus also believe that dying in Varanasi circumvents the cycle of rebirth and provides a permanent place in heaven. Whatever is sacrificed, chanted or given in charity here reaps its fruits a thousand fold more than those good deeds performed elsewhere. Some say that three nights of fasting in Varanasi city is the same as many thousands of lifetimes of ascension. Because of this Hindus from all denominations have made pilgrimages here for longer than history can recall. Even Buddha performed his first sermon not far from here.

Stopping at Varanasi, I catch a pedal rickshaw to the ancient city centre. Having been in transit for some twenty odd hours, it's always the last leg that's the hardest. Hungry, tired, sweaty and desperately in need of a shower, this bone-shaking rickshaw over cobbled streets into the old city takes an eternity. The streets become increasingly narrow, as my rickshawallah weaves deeper and deeper into the old city. In places the path is barely wide enough to squeeze our vehicle through – catacombs of ancient laneways. It reeks of history, literally.

We pass a cow languishing in the gutter. A flick of her tail splatters my face with filthy muddy water, a small amount enters my mouth, it tastes of sewage. Spitting, I consider whether it's an omen or a blessing. After all the cow is considered sacred by Hindus and the symbol of abundance and sanctity of all life – she gives without asking for anything in return. Although Hindus do not worship the cow, it's respected by some sects as a mother figure and has an honoured place in Indian society. Killing a cow is taboo and most Hindus do not eat beef. So, cows are able to come and go anywhere in India, at their own whim. They often block traffic and eat the market vendor's precious produce or flick dirty water into unsuspecting tourists' mouths.

As my rickshawallah turns into the main bazaar at the epicentre of old Varanasi, he's exhausted and barely able to pedal my weight of ninety-four kilos plus backpack. I'm afraid the little grey-haired man will keel over at any point with a coronary and expire at my feet under a blazing sun. The bazaar is packed with merchants, lepers, beggars, pickpockets, scam artists and other shady characters. For a place steeped in spiritual kudos there is a dark side to Varanasi – tourists apparently go missing here on a regular basis. Maybe they fall victim to foul play at the hands of the con artists who don the orange robes, imitating sadhus. There's an ominous vibe in the air. A gaunt looking Indian in dirty clothes with a pinched face and shifty eyes starts jogging next to my rickshaw, his hand on my arm. He has a hunger in his face and the demeanour of a rat. 'You vant opium, hashish, vhat you vant?'

I do my best to ignore him. However, sensing my discomfort, he's like a hyena that can smell blood. He knows I'm new and have no idea which way is up. He persists till I snap at him, 'No, *chello, chello.*'

He snarls back at me, '*Chello* Pakistan'

I tell him the same, '*Chello* Pakistan yourself buddy.'

This incites a deep fury in him. To say *chello* Pakistan, meaning 'go to Pakistan' to an Indian, is like saying go to Hell. Gripping my arm he looks at me with daggers in his eyes. '*Chello* Pakistan.'

With that he leaves – another omen? The now wheezing rickshawallah stops, sweat drips off him. The alley is now too narrow even for a solitary vehicle to pass. Continuing on foot, I weave deeper and deeper into the heart. Lanes so thin that people hardly have enough room to pass each other. Lanes cast in perpetual shadow from overhead buildings and cloaked in a mist of kerosene smoke rising from street stalls and their boiling vats of oil.

Beggars, stoned hippies, scores of Israelis, sadhus and cart pushing vendors all try to go in the opposite direction to each other. Blindly following my intuition, turning down narrower and tighter paths, I squeeze past a large white buffalo munching on garbage and find myself at a dead-end outside a '*Shiva Hotel*'. Checking into a room, relieved to finally close my door to the world, I enjoy some precious solitude. Well as close as I can get to it in India, large monkeys with fangs, beady eyes and pink asses stare at me through my barred window, noses pressed against the mosquito mesh.

* * *

After settling in, I decide to take a walk to get my bearings. I get lost within five minutes. The paths meander left and right like spider webs. Countless old people, sleeping on small beds, are scattered in the shadows, no doubt waiting to die, as funeral processions pass by. Families gaily march their deceased on stretchers, the bodies covered in ornate robes dripping with flowers. Singing, dancing, burning incense and playing instruments, they make their way down to the river, to cremate their lost loved ones. It sounds more like weddings than funerals.

Following a procession to discover the path to the river, I emerge from the warren of lanes onto the bank of Ganga and at one of the many ghats. The ghats are basically temples that have steps down to the river's edge, where people wash and bath. A small girl, maybe six years old approaches me to sell her wares, small paper boats containing a tiny candle and a flower, 'Sir, sir, you vant? To make puja, for luck.'

I happily pay her too much and she assists me to light the candle as I place it in the river. She has both the playful abandon of a child and the world-weariness of an adult. We watch as it floats away, the one solitary candle flickering in the gentle afternoon breeze. Taking my hand, she smiles at me. 'A blessing for your family. You vant another one?'

Laughing, I grin. 'No, maybe tomorrow.'

'Karma promise?'

Not sure what a karma promise is, 'OK, karma promise.'

She skips off in search of new prey. In the near distance

over a ridge of steps I see spiralling clouds of smoke. With my heart in my mouth, I realise I'm approaching the burning ghats where the dead are cremated on the riverbank. From the top of the stairs I gaze down on a hive of activity. Maybe four or five bonfires are ablaze, tended to by young boys. They dutifully maintain the flames. Thick white smoke billows up into the sky. One of the fires has just been lit while another is nothing more than a smouldering pile of ashes. I see the funeral procession I just followed setting up, the body already placed on a large stack of wood as a priest pours hot oil over it while another applies a flame. Stray dogs mill about the periphery of the area. I shudder to think what they're waiting for.

One of the fire tenders approaches me, a bandana tied over his face to keep out the ash. He explains how they burn up to five hundred bodies a day, each using some two to four hundred kilos of timber. It must be imported from many miles as the surrounding area has long since been deforested.

I thought the imagery would be disturbing, at least macabre, but it isn't. Not even when the bodies start to disintegrate and smouldering limbs begin falling off. They are picked up by one of the boys and nonchalantly tossed back into the flames. No, it's surprisingly serene. There is no crying, or sobbing from the mourning family, just a quiet reverence. People are happy. It feels real. In India, death is not shunned, hidden behind euphemisms, kept behind closed doors and under hushed tones, no, it's brought out into the open, literally.

By fate or miracle I manage to find my way back to my hotel in time for sunset on my rooftop. Doing my sun salutations taught me by Dr Mohanti in Pondicherry, everything feels as it ought to be. Trying to hold onto the space of nothingness between my thoughts, between the relentless cyclic banter of my mind, I focus on the flow of the twelve asanas. Connecting to breath, I inhale, stretch, release – exhale. Vertebrae unlock, muscle fibres unravel, as my mind empties like sand from a closed fist. I imagine energy coming up through my feet from the ground like Dr Mohanti told me to until every cell tingles from my toes to the hair follicles in the top of my head. A nearby mosque starts singing hauntingly beautiful prayers as a shimmering red sun sinks into the horizon, silhouetting the skyline of the ancient city. It's like nothing has really changed here for thousands of years.

Families of monkeys screech and scramble across the rooftops – people may dominate the laneways below, but up here it is the city of the monkeys. Kids fly kites from balconies, filling the sky with movement and colour while young men play cricket on rooftop courtyards, balls tied to pieces of string to prevent them from being lost over the side. Twilight fades into night as the stars emerge, the river sparkling from the light of hundreds of floating candles lit by devotees performing puja. Sitting, meditating, soaking up the 'now' and being grateful for my solitude, I learn to like myself again. Eventually I hear from Frankie.

Hey Dragon power, howz things? I made it to Kathmandu after a hell bus ride. 15 hours on a bus to go 250 kms!!! The bus stopped at blockade because of the Maoists' curfew and we waited for 6 hours. We didn't arrive in Kathmandu until the next day!!! I was pissed off.

Nepal has been mostly annoying from the start with the visa application, it's one giant tourist trap!!! Not really into it. Apparently there're

protests starting in two weeks so I was going to
split by then. What are your plans, besides having
no plans? You are planning to stay in VArranisi for
a long time? I'm THINKING ITS PROBABALY getting
hot there now? Anyway we'll keep in touch. I'm
smoking too much, need to kick it 'again'. The
mountains will help, take care bro.
The Kobra

After four days of yoga and solitude, I hear from Merav.
Kidding myself that I came here for a spiritual workout, it's
really an erogenous one I hope for. Having been celibate for
four months, not for lack of trying, I'm keen to break the
drought. I haven't been laid since my pizza delivery sessions
with Amber back in Australia. I shower, even shaving my balls
and puffing talcum powder into all my crevices, just in case.
Wanting to look my best I wear my cleanest dirty clothes and
change the sorry looking condom that's degraded past the
point of no return in my wallet. With my most Zen spiritually
enlightened face, a steeled expression similar to what Frankie
the Kobra uses, I head out of the door. In the rickshaw I pass
a bewildered, lost and clammy looking Ian. He's standing in
the middle of the bazaar being hounded by the hash hyenas.
Noticing me he calls out, I yell back as we scuttle past, 'Hey
Munty, I'm just in a hotel down the lane way back there, turn
left then two rights, can't miss it, I'll meet you a bit later.'

'Um, righto, will do …'

Knowing full well he didn't have a hope in hell of finding
me, I tap my rickshawallah on the shoulder telling him to
chello and not stop for anything. I'm determined not to fall
into Ian's grasp, now I have a real girl to pursue, one with all
the good bits.

Meeting Merav, we walk along the river and watch the burning ghats. Kind of feels inappropriate for a date, if that's what we're having, so we continue walking. There's a sexual tension in the air, but also an awkwardness. There is chemistry and now is the moment to kiss, but something stops us. For some reason it just doesn't feel right. She looks so beautiful, long flowing curly locks of her hair catching a light breeze against the backdrop of the river with bathing pilgrims and majestic eroding temples. Perfect romantic setting but something isn't clicking. It occurs to me she slightly resembles my ex-wife Stella. I start to question my motives. Looking at the river Merav speaks. 'Yesterday I was walking here and I saw a pack of wild dogs. They were eating something. It was the body of a baby floating in the river. It was blue and rotten.'

Well, that certainly kills the mood. After that we struggle to make conversation. Without her cousin Nimrod we seem to have nothing to say to each other. Attempting to keep the conversation alive, I persevere. 'So, where is Nimrod?'

'He went to Rishikesh to study yoga.'

Another pregnant pause, until Merav speaks again. 'You know there is a solar eclipse today. People are going to watch on my guesthouse rooftop, we can go.'

A solar eclipse due to occur this afternoon completely passed my mind in anticipation of a possible sexual encounter. Agreeing to the idea, I hope it takes the pressure off our stifled conversation. On her rooftop, there's a crowd of Israelis, a new crowd I don't know, but as I'm with Merav they reluctantly include me in their tight-knit social circle. The guys frequently cast me suspicious glances, as if insinuating *what you doing with one of our women?*

As the moon begins it trajectory in front of the sun, one of the guys cuts lengths from a roll of film and passes it to everyone – Merav turns to me smiling, 'Hold it front of your eyes to watch the eclipse.'

The Israeli guy passing out the pieces jokes, 'You can use this to watch a nuclear explosion too.'

Contemplating if they're taught that in the military as well, I hear a slight tone of animosity in his voice. Smiling at him I accept his offering. I turn to Merav. 'Well that's a shanti shanti thought.'

After the solar light show and as the sun sinks away once again, an impromptu party starts. Not a Goa style party but a shanti shanti sitting in a circle playing bongo drums and acoustic guitar party. Passing joints, drinking chai and singing songs by Bob Dylan, Cat Stevens and half an hour renditions of John Lennon's *Give Peace a Chance*.

As insipid and outdated as these little gatherings are and as aggravating to my punk rock sensibilities as this is, I can't help but get a warm fuzzy feeling inside. The same kind I get from sentimental chick flick movies starring Tom Hanks and Melanie Griffiths. Films, incidentally, I normally have nothing but contempt for. Films that are vacuous, free of any kind of true substance or significance – films that however, when I watch them alone, make me cry like a baby.

Merav now leans against me and it's nice to be in such close proximity. Suddenly Carlitos appears on the rooftop with another friend from the Andamans, Dylan, from the States – late twenties, tall, a good-looking surfie hippy and a bit of a lady-killer. He's wearing a 'Fuck Bush' T-shirt and does acappella rap of his own poetry. Wearing a tailored short lungi made in Goa, he's very hippy chic.

Dylan came to India for a friend's wedding in Mumbai and was only meant to stay a week, but he keeps extending his flight home. He's also being increasingly seduced by India.

'Ya know man, it's like, just come to India for my buddy's wedding then go back to the States. But then I discovered Goa, then Gokarna and the Andamans. Wow, like full power, 24 hour. So much universal love, good vibrations, ya know what I'm saying man. Keep getting emails asking, hey Dylan, like when are you coming back. I'm thinking hey, I ain't ready, and if the guys could see me now – like, wearing a dress, like wow man.'

Carlitos, quiet, looks at me. I sense a tinge of envy from him. The tight circle of Israelis keep Carlitos and Dylan confined to the periphery. Eventually, realising they aren't welcome, they leave. Carlitos gives me a not so subtle nod as he exits.

Eventually one by one the group dissipates as midnight approaches, when guesthouses, including my own, lock their doors for the nightly curfew. The streets are not safe here at night. They're dominated by packs of rabid dogs that have a predilection for human meat, as well as by homeless and murderous gangs that will stab you for your few rupee without a moment's thought. Merav gazes up at me. 'It's late. I think you will be too late to get into your guesthouse. If you like you can stay in my room.'

Perfect. Even though there had been an inability for either of us to consummate the physical side of our relationship, despite all the build up of sexual tension, sharing a bed together is nothing short of a sure thing. I'm glad I shaved my balls now. Show time. The Israeli guy who earlier gave me evil stares now approaches Merav and starts having a heated but hush-toned discussion with her in Hebrew. I may not understand the lingo but the message is loud and clear. He doesn't approve of our little arrangement and lays a massive guilt trip on Merav.

After several minutes of his dictatorial tone she returns to me. Her head hangs low in shame and without eye contact she mumbles, 'If you like you can share a bed with one of the guys. Amit (as she points to the now gloating prick behind her) doesn't feel comfortable with them because he does not know them. So, he will share with me. Sorry.'

Fuck that for a joke. I've just been cock-blocked as we say in Australia, where one prevents another from getting laid just because of spite and jealousy. No, I'd rather take my chances in the streets with the rabid dogs and murderers than the humiliation of staying here. Picking up my dignity I stride proudly out the door into the darkness. Actually pitch bloody blackness, another power failure has extinguished all street lights. I literally feel my way along the lanes with my fingers touching the wall, blind, stepping tentatively, hoping not to tread in something indescribably disgusting.

Trying to remember whether it's right, left, right or left, right, left to get back to the bazaar. Somehow I work it out and rickshaw round the corner to my locked guesthouse. Luckily the hotel next door is open, so I sneak in and up onto the roof, climbing the dividing wall to eventually reach the safety of my room. Falling asleep I swear to myself to become celibate for the rest of my journey in India. I'm finished chasing girls. It's time to really focus on all the spiritual stuff.

Happily alone again, I tell myself I'm relieved at my decision to give up playing 'the game', even if I am masturbating so much I expect to start growing hairs on my palms. I practise my yoga and meditate obsessively, struggling to clear my mind. Remembering Janardan, the chuckling meditation guru from the gardens of Auroville, I try to just focus on my environment, the sounds, the smells and the vista of the Ganges from my rooftop. The past jumps into my mind, memories to irk me. I breathe, inhale, exhale and I tell myself, *no, I am here in the present, in the now.* Then anxieties of the future bounce in. Diaphragm inflates, deflates – I let go of thoughts and I'm back in the moment for the moment, back in the now for now, breath by breath – it takes work. All the little insecurities, niggling negativities, grudges and regrets – each a little pebble carried, small weights together heavy on my heart, one by one drop away. I email Frankie.

```
Hey Kobra,
I have had an epiphany. I've taken a vow of
celibacy. I'm over all the bullshit, now I have
clarity. It rocks - you should try it too. You
got your visa yet? When you comin?
Later,
the Dragon
```

* * *

Feeling strong and even slightly self-righteous I stride through the bazaar. I see Carlitos marching past with a determined gait and carrying his pack. I stop him with my hand. 'Hey bro, why the hurry?'

'I am going to dat guesthouse where de party was.' He breathes heavily, panting, trying to catch his breath as he leans on my shoulder. 'Der is only one room left. I want it. So many pretty girls der. Maybe I can find one who will have my babies. I mus' go.'

Gathering his strength and wiping the sweat off his brow, he continues down through the market. I call out, 'Good luck mate.' God knows he'll need it.

Back at my guesthouse rooftop I watch the afternoon fade

away while doing my yoga regime. From the opposite roof, I hear a familiar voice. 'Fire in the hole.'

Scaling the dividing wall I see Jimmy the Ambassador of the Sunrise Bacon with Dylan, sparking up his trademark, cracked but still surviving, crystal chillum. Hearing my ruckus Jimmy turns to me. 'Hey Australia, so we meet again.'

Joining them, my earlier self-righteous, self-conceited, spiritually superior sanctimonious attitude evaporates in a moment, along with the hopes of my sunset yoga session. My eggshell thin willpower collapses as I accept Jimmy's chillum. In the red glow of the afternoon we watch the monkeys cause havoc on the rooftops. They fight, squabble and raid houses for food or anything else they can get their hands on. Jimmy tells us how today one had made its way into a woman's room and stolen her clothes. Then right on cue a monkey wearing a woman's underwear, its skinny arms through the leg holes as if it were a cape, dashes across the dividing wall, baring his teeth at us. We all laugh.

I take a backwards step hanging with Jimmy and Dylan over ensuing days. Slipping into smoking again and avoiding my yoga, procrastinating, café hopping, futilely trying to chat up girls once more and drinking the marijuana-laced *bhang lassies* (Indian milkshakes) or special *lassies* as they often appear on menus. Glutinously thick, sickly sweet and an unappetising green colour, these things will knock your socks off.

Unlike smoking dope, the *bhang lassie* will just keep on coming on. When you reach the point of 'OK, thanks very much I have had enough now' it persists, further enveloping your senses, drowning your consciousness past the point of the 'OK this isn't funny anymore' stage, and the 'I'm totally fucked' stage – until your brain hits the cognitive 'flat line' stage. Not a good look, dishevelled bed hair from the fifteen hours a day you sleep, crusty chocolate on the corner of your lips from endless munchies and eyes so bloodshot that there are no whites left.

Stumbling along the ghats, Jimmy, Dylan and I stop for a chai. It's hot – the hottest day yet, pushing the low forties Celsius. The place has been getting ridiculously warmer every day for the last week. My scalp is itchy again, worse than ever. The air, warm, still and stifled. Every movement is an effort; combined with the *bhang lassies* and the smoking my limbs feel heavy. Despite this, the heat of the chai tea refreshes. Sitting in the shade, the slightest of breezes, scented lightly with the smoke of the burning ghats, is the only respite from the weather. Sipping our tea and staring at the river, I wonder why only the western bank is populated and the eastern bank completely barren. Jimmy, third time veteran of Varanasi, sheds some light. 'Well guv, it's where the Aghori sadhus live.'

I stop sipping chai. 'The what?'

'The Aghori babas, these guys are spooky. They live in graveyards, talk to ghosts and eat human flesh, something to do with proving their devotion to Shiva. Any floaters that pop up they consider fair game, so that side of the river is feared by the locals. You've also got the packs of dogs there too that will tear you to shreds.'

Shuddering I remember Merav's story of the dead baby. Dylan looks perplexed. 'Wow. Man, that's like really intense. Eat people. Man. But I thought they burn all the bodies and just throw the ashes in the river?'

Jimmy smiles revealing his few remaining crooked teeth and coughing his phlegm-rich laugh. 'No, mate, there's five types of people that don't get burnt. Children, pregnant women, lepers, sadhus and people that die from cobra bite. They get chucked straight in the drink. There's so many bodies in there it's like soup, and to think they wash in it and even drink the bloody stuff.'

Dylan stares at the bottom of his now empty chai glass. 'Nasty man, that's totally crazy.'

Jimmy knocks back the last of his tea as well. 'Very Nasty mate. Varanasi can be vari nasty.'

I also finish my drink. 'Man that was one good cup of chai, who's up for another round?' Both nodding in agreement, I signal to the chaiwallah – who smiles. 'Most certainly sir, I must be getting more vater first.'

He picks up a bucket and lightly springs down the ghat steps. He cheerfully hums to himself as he scoops up a bucketful of river water, skips back up the stairs and pours it into the teapot on the fire. The three of us look at each other with the same worried expression.

We're realising it's not the chaiwallah's secret herbs and spices that gives his brew its extra tangy flavor, but actually mother Ganga, and all her children. Suddenly losing the taste for tea we cancel our order. Dylan turns pale. 'Guys, I think I will go and, like, drink a bottle of iodine or something, maybe have some antibiotics. Man, wow. Think I need to seriously meditate.'

Jimmy grins nervously. 'What won't kill ya only makes you stronger.' He slaps his stomach and winks. Dylan meekly smiles back before shuffling off. Watching him leave, Jimmy elbows me. 'Kids today huh, got no bloody grit.'

'Yeah, you can say that again.'

Not feeling as confident as Jimmy, we make our way home to our rooftop for our daily ritual of sunset chillums. Jimmy looks up at me with a devious smile as he passes me the pipe. He winks. 'It's got a little something extra in it today… opium.'

Holding the chillum to my lips I pause. It has been ten years since I gave up heroin, the drug that nearly destroyed me. The drug that took the lives of some good friends and ruined the lives of others, the drug I struggled to quit and when I did, cold turkey, vowed never again to succumb to its temptations. And now I look down the barrel of the same substance in its rawest form. Face to face with my own devil. In a moment of ultimate weakness I let myself go. 'Fire it up Jimmy boy.'

Filling my lungs it tastes familiar, bitter in the back of my throat, rasping and cutting the soft tissue of the capillaries in my lungs to shreds. Exhaling, I sense a wave of aesthetic wash over me. Feeling dirty inside, polluted, the opiates finger their way into my blood and surround my brain. I'm detached, desensitised and comfortably numb. The molecules lock into my synaptic receptors, saying, *hi remember me.* Yes I remember. Staggering down the stairs, I blunder my way into the night like Mr. Hyde.

Filled with a sense of unease, I make my way through the lanes, somehow ending up in the bazaar. In the market there is panic and mayhem everywhere. People rush towards me with terror in their eyes. Everything is in slow motion, my vision blurry. As I approach the centre the tension intensifies. It soon becomes clear why. Two huge bulls, one black the other white, are sparring, charging, slamming their immense weight against each other and locking horns. They knock over stalls, smashing everything in their path. Oblivious to their destruction, the beasts trample silk and fruit into the dust.

The cow, symbolic for giving, is now taking away. Yet another omen? Shopper and merchant alike scramble out of the path of the animals – they climb up lampposts and over each other. The crowd surges, like waves of fear. People are crushed and fall under foot. It's a disturbing and surreal vision. Ducking into a side alley I snake my way back through the labyrinth of paths, eventually reaching the confines of my guesthouse and fall into bed. Drifting off to sleep I watch the fan spin while drowning in perspiration.

Awakening, my room is devoid of light. I can't see anything. Another blackout. My mattress, soaked wet from sweat. It must be the middle of the night – everything is silent. A sharp stabbing pain in my stomach makes me grimace in agony. Blindly stumbling out the door into the corridor, I reach the toilet. This is not like Kolkata, no much worse. As soon as I shit, I violently vomit. My stomach muscles convulse in spasms. I spend the rest of the night wrapped around the toilet bowl, throwing up and shitting till there's nothing left. By morning I'm weak, drained and barely able to crawl back to my room, the pain is relentless but I'm empty inside. Pale and greasy with sweat and fever, I curl up in a ball on my bed. Maybe it was the tea, maybe the opium, maybe just India.

Slipping in and out of nightmares, my fever makes it impossible to distinguish between waking and sleep. I have visions, visitors from my past life. Stella dressed in a sequined dress dancing seductively, laughing at me, morphs into Amber. Tossing and turning, the bed sheets damp and knotted. The monkeys at my window laugh at me, saying, 'Fire in the hole, fire in the hole.'

My next conscious thought – I'm aware it's morning. Shadows stretch along the floor and race up the wall like phantoms, the heat of the sun's rays through my window sears my flesh as it passes over my body, but I'm too weak to move. In moments dawn transforms to dusk and the angry blood red sun falls from the sky. Dreaming of lost loves, family and friends, oceans of faces rush past me, a river of writhing snakes and worms while black and white bulls fight, horns locked in an eternal battle. It all swirls around like a kaleidoscopic Dante's hell. Vertigo. The chanting of the mosque, the smell of burning flesh, I fall into an abyss. The monkeys scratch, it sounds like they are in the room now and running around my bed, prodding, poking and teasing me. 'Mother India is bottomless, down, down, down you go.'

I wake up again. It's pitch black, power failure. Intense pain still in my stomach. Was it a dream? My head throbs and I shiver in a cold sweat, I'm dehydrated.

Opening my eyes again – it's bright and hot outside. It must be midday. Staring at me, the monkeys grin, exposing their teeth. I don't remember what is nightmare and what is real. Feeling weak and sweaty, mouth dry and tongue swollen, I see a bucket next to the bed –did I put it there? I roll over and try and throw up. A small dribble of bile falls into the bottom of the bucket. It exhausts me. Falling back down on the damp bed, I stare at the stationary fan above. I desperately need water. I slip from consciousness again.

I'm standing in a forest. It's Yorta Yorta land. Behind me the trees are thick, strange and foreboding. It's dark and no light permeates the canopy. I can hear the monkeys inside, inviting me to come in. They mock me. At my feet I notice a white feather. Looking up I see a cockatoo flying overhead. Turning, I watch him fly towards a beautiful sunrise. I follow him, leaving the forest behind me until I reach the Murray river. Kneeling down, I drink. The sweet water soothes, cool and refreshing. It quenches my thirst.

I awaken suddenly, outside it is pre-dawn. Chronically dehydrated – my dream makes me yearn for water. On death's door, I force myself out of bed. My room reeks of sickness. How many days have I been tossing and turning in bed, slipping in and out of sleep? The cockatoo dream was a warning – I need to drink water. Climbing to my rooftop I wait for sunrise, swatting mosquitoes as I linger for the shops to open. Did smoking opium trigger a visit from my old devils, the monkeys in my head trying to draw me back into their jungle of addiction? The bullfight in the market, the struggle of darkness and light, the flick of the cow's tail the day I arrived, were these all premonitions? I decide it's wise to heed caution, and take note of the signs the universe has provided. I decide to change my ways.

My fever lasted three days. Three days without food or water. It's said that three days of fasting in Varanasi is equivalent to a thousand lifetimes of ascension. Let's hope so. After replenishing my fluids and resting, I ascend to the rooftop to visit Jimmy. Climbing the wall, there is no sign of him in his usual afternoon position. Trying to descend the stairwell to his room, a big male monkey blocks my path – he looks mean and hisses at me revealing long yellow canines. Backing away, I climb back to my hotel and down the stairs into the lane. There, a large white bull stands in my path. Each time I try and pass him he blocks me with his horns.

Eventually squeezing past him I climb the stairs to Jimmy's room. His door is ajar – he's sitting on his bed and looks a mess. Stoned to the gills, his eyes roll back in their sockets, as he nods in and out of sleep, almost falling off his bed, waking just in time to sit upright again, only to repeat the cycle again and again. Caught in a loop – it's sad and a little pathetic. He barely recognises me. Scratching his nose he holds an unlit bent cigarette. 'Hey man, how you going?'

'I've been sick as a dog mate.'

Jimmy, continuing to roll forward and sit up with a jerk, smiles at me with his eyes closed. 'Yeah me too brother, they had to change my bed, shat myself in my sleep didn't I. I tell 'em downstairs, *excuse me Guv, but someone has shat in my bed, it's simply not good enough.* They gave me a new one.' Laughing to himself he puts the cigarette to his lips and lights his Zippo, holding it a foot from the end of the fag and inhales. Not realising it's not lit, he exhales an imaginary plume of smoke. Continuing to roll forward, falling asleep and sitting up in an awkward motion, he slowly scratches his nose again. 'Got some brown sugar mate, strictly medicinal of course, want some?'

He passes me a piece of aluminum foil, black with soot underneath, with residues of the brown heroin on the top. Jimmy had obviously been chasing the dragon.

'Think I'll pass buddy, thanks anyway.'

I notice Jimmy has small cuts on top of his head that are bleeding. 'Man, what happened to your head?'

Jimmy has the expression of a baby with colic as he rubs his wounds. 'Last night I fell asleep sitting up. I bloody fell head first into me bag. Woke up with my head in there (points to his bag on the floor) and me ass in the air. When I pull my head out, I got a couple of dreadlocks caught in the zipper, ripped them clean off. Fuckin' hurt too.'

With that, Jimmy drifts off to sleep, mumbling to himself, scratching his nose and smoking his unlit cigarette. Monkeys hanging from the bars of his window reach into his room, trying to steal anything their little fingers can touch. They grin at me as they torment Jimmy. Leaving him in his homemade hell, I know I need to move on, away from the heat, away from this city of death and away from Jimmy and his monkeys. I want to chase Ganga up to the mountains into heaven, not dragons into the abyss. I decide to head to the cooler climate of Rishikesh, home of India's best yoga schools, and hopefully find Frankie escaped from the revolution. A few days of working my way back onto food and building up my strength, I email Frankie telling him I'm leaving. He responds,

```
Dragon,
Still in Kathmandu waiting for visa. A lot of
hassles, there's a strike here so I can't see
me leaving for a few days. I want to go now, I
was sick myself last night, vomiting, diarrhoea,
don't feel too good. Varanasi sounds bad, what
did you get food poisoning from? Rishi sounds
better! Anyway, I think I'm going to go back to
bed. I will try to get to Rishi within a week
if nothing else happens! I can't see me going to
Vari-nasti sounds very nasty!!! TAke care man,
Kobra
```

Walking through the bazaar one last time I feel lighter in my stride. Passing an old man with a set of bathroom scales I pay him a rupee and jump on. Weighing in at seventy-two kilos, I've lost some twenty-two kilos in a bit over a week. That explains why my jeans keep sliding off and I've run out of holes in my belt. Now that's a form of weight loss you don't see on late night TV. As I board the slow train to Rishikesh I feel I have left something of myself here – twenty-two kilos to be exact.

CHAPTER 8

Spiritual Supermarket

Without doubt this is the hardest train ride yet. The heat is so intense it's unbearable. Outside it's forty-eight degrees Celsius, in the shade. Inside, stuck inside a metal box, the train feels twice as hot. Roasting like living legs of lamb, the walls are torrid to the touch. Even the resin of my sunglasses scorches my skin. Stopping every hour or so, at small towns, we let the express trains pass. When motionless the heat overwhelms us, but when the train moves it's no better. The breeze through the window is like opening an oven door. Sweat pours into my eyes, stinging and blurring my vision. My water bottle, nearly boiling, gives no relief as I drink or decant it over my head. I'm literally cooking from the inside out.

Outside people move slowly about under the blazing intensity of the midday sun. They endure this cruel hardship to survive by either tilling the soil or carrying impossible loads on their backs. Villages consist of small huts made of mud with grass thatch roofs. Malnourished dogs languish in what little shade there is while sari-clad old ladies symmetrically arrange cow patties to dry in the sun, the fuel for their kitchen fires. This expanse of backwaters has no Taj Mahals, just countless poor folk trying to scratch subsistence out of the heat and dust. The skin on my scalp crawls. Scratching, my fingernails draw blood as I reopen angry wounds. My stomach is still not right, I feel weak. Outside vultures ominously circle up above. Even the usual parade of train performers struggle, the dancing transvestites look wilted while the acrobats and snake charmers have just plain given up.

I befriend my carriage travelling companions, three generations of an Indian family from Hampi. Grandpa and grandma who smile and nod a lot, their son, his wife and their two young children. Only the son speaks English. Exchanging pleasantries, we share our food. I trade my stale masala-flavoured chips for their homemade sweets and crispy nibbles. For dessert Grandpa hands out serves of paan (betel nut, chewing tobacco and other spices). Being gracious I accept it even though I'm not overly keen on its bitter taste or mildly narcotic effect. Sitting there, chewing and slurping red spittle, the son explains how they've been saving up for years to make this trip. They're heading for Haridwar, another holy town just south of Rishikesh, and also on the Ganges. For them this is a once in a lifetime experience; ecstatic, he rocks his head from side to side,

'We vanted to be going all the vay up into the mountains. Up to Gangotri and make the most sacred walk to Gaumukh, the very source of Mother Ganga. It is where Ganga comes out of the head of Lord Shiva himself. But my parents are too old and we cannot afford the expense. It is unfortunate indeed but ve cannot complain. Actually, it is very much a blessing to be making this vonderful journey and ve are very, very happy.'

A distinct pang of guilt fills my heart, as I decided only on a whim to travel to Rishikesh, nothing more than a moment's thought given and no more than a handful of loose change spent, whereas these people have planned and saved for a lifetime. Contemplating how I'm certainly privileged to be able to make a journey many consider to be sacred, I'm determined not to belittle the experience.

＊ ＊ ＊

After a week of constant diarrhoea, unbelievably, I'm now constipated. Pains in my digestive tract come and go in waves. It's nowhere near as debilitating as in Varanasi, but enough to make me continually trek back and forth to the squat loo, assume the position and stare down the hole to the tracks rumbling past below – all for another false alarm.

On one of my futile return trips from the toilet a long thin but muscular arm, as black as the ace of spades, stops me. Reaching from a top bunk, a gangly Rastafarian with dreadlocks speckled with grey and a long dreadlocked beard gazes down at me. Sitting with ease, cross-legged, in the full lotus yoga pose, he must be in his late forties. His eyes burn bright. 'Hey mon, do ya have di time?' He drawls slowly, in a thick, deep Jamaican accent.

'Sorry mate, don't carry a watch, hate the bloody things, life goes fast enough as it is.'

'True enough mon. Do you know how long de train will take to arrive in Rishikesh?'

I smile. 'I reckon it will take exactly as long as it takes. One thing India has taught me is if you have no expectations you will never be disappointed.'

His serious expression crumbles into a slight smile. He chuckles lightly in a deep, resonating tone. 'Hmm, good answer.'

Releasing his giant hand from my shoulder he extends out his palm. 'My name is Victor.' Victor uncoils his legs and with the grace of a jaguar slides down from his bunk, standing tall and towering over my six foot two stature. His dreadlocks, as thick as rope, fall down below his waist. A big friendly grin spreads over his face extending smile lines to his ears and revealing his pearly white, crooked teeth. 'So den, are you making de holy pil-grim-age, to bathe in de sweet waters of Mother Gan-ga? Maybe you want to wash away de burden of your sins?'

'Yeah something like that.'

As the stranglehold of the day's heat releases its grip, and slips into the twilight of the late afternoon, Victor and I start to chat, sharing stories. He tells me how he's been an Astanga yoga teacher for the past fifteen years, giving exclusive private classes to high flyers in Manhattan. I drop hints as to how he should teach me a yoga class. Victor eyes the dog-eared *Lonely Planet* I hold with a certain disdain and changes the subject. 'Why do you carry dis book? You do not know where you are? You are much better to just trust your instincts. Dese books are only for de faint hearted and de fearful. Dey are for de tourist, not de traveller, throw de damn ting away mon.'

I consider what Victor says in his rich accent. 'Yeah, you're dead right, it's like my security blanket.'

With that I toss the book out of the window. Victor looks surprised. He waits a moment before speaking dryly. 'Shit mon. I was only speaking metaphorically, I wanted to have a look at dat.' Maybe I was a bit rash. Now I'm not sure where to go or how to get there. Maybe I'm just a tourist and not a traveller after all. With this thought spinning around in my mind I retire for the evening.

Morning rolls in with the clang of the chaiwallah tapping against his pot of hot tea to advertise his arrival. Outside the landscape has changed. No longer flat plains of red dust and dry yellow grass, now smatterings of green foliage and undulations in the land start to appear. The distinctly cooler temperature indicates the three hundred metres in elevation and the few hundred kilometres north we have travelled, allowing us to temporarily elude the finale of the dry season. Disorientated, I disembark from our train to be submerged in a throng of taxiwallahs all bidding for trade – we're in Haridwar, Rishikesh is another half an hour away by bus. Victor, already on the platform, notices my mildly perplexed state. 'Good morning mon, de bus is just outside de train station.'

The short bus ride up to Rishikesh sees us nearly hit an overturned truck. It lies on its side like a beached whale. On a blind corner, it's surrounded by a group of Indian men all staring blankly and scratching their heads. Our path blocked, the driver has to swerve to the wrong side of the road to avoid a collision. In the process an unfortunate motorcycle rider is bullied off the causeway and disappears into the bushes at the kerb's edge. I wonder if that counts as another strike against our driver's 'five and you are out rule'.

Not what I expect – Rishikesh is just another dirty, busy Indian town. Victor senses my disappointment. 'We must go to Laxman Jhula – dis is where it is shanti shanti on de river.'

Sharing a rickshaw, Victor and I head up a steep winding road shouldered by pine trees into the hills. Its overworked motor groans all the way as our driver grinds through the gears. At the top of the hill we continue on foot, down stairways tucked between countless gem stores, the path scattered with old sadhus begging for food. Finally we arrive at a suspension bridge spanning the Ganges to the small community of Laxman Jhula. Steep forested hills fall to the river's edge – the jade-coloured water looks clean and inviting.

An orange-robed sadhu chants and blesses us with a sprinkle of water. He then ties some red cotton thread around our right wrists and places a flower in each of our hands. Crossing the narrow bridge, dodging cows, motorbikes,

Indian sightseers, sadhus and the usual stoners, I look down to the swirling currents of the river below. There are hundreds of giant catfish, some more than a metre long swimming in a perfect spiral formation, eating bread thrown to them by the captivated audience above.

Scores of monkeys balance on the wire handrail of the bridge, robbing unsuspecting people of fruit from their bags and even an ice cream from the hand of a screaming child. I decide to do a little puja of my own and toss over my flower, watching it disintegrate into petals as it falls down to the water. For the first time since the Andaman Islands I have a sense of sanctuary.

Breathing in deeply, the air is clean, cool and fresh. Crossing the bridge and reaching Laxman Jhula, an Indian dressed from head to toe as the monkey god Hanuman again blesses me. He places a red dot in the centre of my forehead, between my eyebrows. Apparently it's the location of the sixth chakra, the seat of concealed wisdom or the third eye and the exit point for Kundaline energy. This dot or 'bindi' is said to retain the energy and strengthen concentration. It's meant to protect me against demons as well as bad luck. My entrepreneurial Hanuman then waves a fifty rupee note in front of me. I give him ten.

An orange temple some five stories high stands next to the bridge; it looks like a giant witch's hat. A path winds around its exterior all the way to the top and along it there are rows of bells and an endless stream of people ringing them. It creates an atmospheric orchestra of continual chiming akin to that of a small village church on Sunday morning. At a small fruit market in front of us I order a sugar cane juice. The juicewallah winds a big handle turning cogs as he feeds sticks of cane into it, spurting out my green drink at the bottom. From behind I hear a familiar voice. 'Hey Australia, is dat you?'

Turning, I feel a punch on my shoulder from Carlitos. Dressed in an orange sarong and yellow Hindu prayer shirt he holds a stick of burning incense. He squeezes my arm. 'Wha' happened to you big man? You are not so big now, where is de rest of you brother?'

'Left it in Varanasi, but as a friend there said, what don't kill ya only makes ya stronger.'

Carlitos grins then punches me again. 'But you are not so strong now.' Carlitos then generously sorts out accommodation for both Victor and me. He gives me the Laxman Jhula lowdown. 'Dere is many people from de Andamans here, everyone goes just up de road to de Freedom Café.'

Just then, a roar of mechanical thunder interrupts us – from down the road we see a convoy of Royal Enfields roll into town. The crowded market divides like the red sea for Moses as a dozen bikes rumble past. The Shiva Riders have made their entrance like a scene out of the Wild West. Long hair, bandanas, dreadlocks, tassels and leather waistcoats flap in the breeze as they pass. Behind them they are ghosted by a mist of red dust from a thousand miles of road. Sexy tattooed Israeli girls in knee high boots ride pillion on the back.

They have come up from Goa, which means the season has officially finished and they too are escaping the heat. On the back of one of the bikes I see an old bearded Indian wearing a distinctive rainbow coloured top hat. It's Rainbow Baba, the charas donating sadhu from New Year's Eve. He must be hitching a ride back to his village in the mountains. I wave as he passes and he gives me a knowing wink. They will wait for the north to thaw before heading up to Dharamsala, home of the Dalai Lama, then continuing on to the dope plantations of Manali and the Parvati valley. There they will party till the end of the monsoon and head back down to Goa to start all over again.

Pausing, we watch the spectacle pass. Carlitos turns to face me with an urgency in his eyes. 'I will see you later, I mus' go, I have a meeting.'

'Don't tell me man, a girl?'

'You tink too much about sex brother, no dis is about a yoga class I wan' to do.'

'Is she pretty this time?'

'Dis is a very holy place, nort some playground for teenagers, sometimes you are like a child Australia.'

With that Carlitos again scurries off on what I suspect is nothing more than another hare-brained scheme to plant his seed and realise his dream of fatherhood. He deserves to be a dad – he certainly works hard enough at it.

Totally run down, I'm exhausted. India has taken its toll on me – I'm anaemic, underweight, constipated, itchy and I have the beginning of a head cold coming on. Then combing my hair after a shower, I notice small things crawling and squirming in the comb's teeth. I've been suffering with head lice for two months without realising it. With my runny nose, sickly cough, itchy head and gurgling stomach, I venture out in search of a doctor. It turns out Laxman Jhula is a spiritual supermarket, with ayurvedic medicine, reiki, yoga, iridology, crystal healings and spiritual satsangs (lectures) from various gurus advertised on every second door. I don't have to wander far before I find an ayurvedic doctor, a grey-haired Indian man with a friendly smile. 'How can I be being of assistance today sir?'

Breathing in a lungful of air I announce, 'Well. I've lost twenty-two kilos, got stomach pains, have trouble going to the toilet, also have a nasty cold and to top it all off, today I discover I've got head lice.'

If I was a dog, I'd be put down due to being terminally mangy. The doctor checks my tongue, squeezes my lymph nodes, looks under my eyelids and in my ears and grunts, 'Hmmm.'

Pulling out a set of scales he starts weighing up portions of mysterious powders, seeds and herbs, grinding them all together with a small mortar and pestle. Pouring this onto a piece of paper and deftly folding it up into a little triangular parcel, he passes it to me along with a small dark-coloured jar. 'Mix a spoon of this powder with some of this honey and take three times a day.'

He then grabs another two dark-coloured glass bottles from a shelf behind him and passes them to me one at a time. 'This is a vitamin supplement, take one spoonful every morning, and rub this ointment into your hair, it will kill the lice. Just continue with all the medicines until they are finished and you will be making a full recovery.'

With no idea what's contained in these undefined dark little jars and in the paper package, I follow his instructions. It works, and after a couple of days I have colour in my cheeks, no more pains in my gut, snot in my sinuses and not a louse to be found anywhere on my now itch-free head. I feel rested, light in mood and after a shave at my local barber I have a spring in my stride and even graduate to solid foods.

* * *

Hopping from yoga school to yoga school, I search for the perfect teacher. The first is a bit sleazy with the girls, always focusing on correcting the posture of their asses with gentle caresses, while completely ignoring the men. The next has an ego issue, spending more time showing off his headstands and flexible dexterity than instilling anything helpful into his students. None of them really measure up to Dr Mohanti in Pondicherry. I finally manage to convince Victor to give me an evening yoga class on my rooftop. He pushes me to the limit of my comfort zone, edging the boundaries of my ability further and further out. Muscles burn, tendons stretch taut, and sweat darkens my T-shirt in the small of my back as I hold the warrior pose till I shake. Knee bent at ninety degrees, the other leg straight back behind at forty five degrees, front foot forward, back foot perpendicular, hips to the side, both arms out making a T shape with my torso, head forward eyes staring in front. In his laconic drawl Victor encourages, 'Dat is good mon – now hold de pose, imagine you are in between two sheets of glass, keeping every ting in a-lign-ment.' Then when he knows I can't hold it much longer he slowly counts down from ten, lingering for ages on, 'three, two, one … and rest.'

Meditating together at the end of the session we sit cross-legged lotus-posed on my hotel rooftop. The Ganges swirls past cutting through the gullies of the Himalayan foothills, lined with forest and boulders polished smooth from high water marks. Shadows grow fast in crimson light as the sun dips behind the peaks. The air cools. Listening to the chiming of temple bells and smelling the Nag Champa incense Victor has just lit, I follow his instructions to close my eyes. He lightly taps a Buddhist prayer bowl that reverberates and intones, 'De con-scious-nass is like de ocean and all your thoughts create a stormy sea. Focus on slowly calming de waves so dat de water does move wit even a ripple. Den you will be in de supreme bliss of *Ananda-ma-ya.*'

Every day at dusk Victor coaches me and word soon

spreads among travellers – the class swells till every square foot of the rooftop is covered with yoga mats. Under the guidance of my new mentor I improve in leaps and bounds. Who would have thought I would come to India and study yoga from a Jamaican Rastafarian? Still no sign of Frankie and after sending a couple of emails he finally responds,

```
Hey Dragon,
Can you believe it, I'm stuck in Kathmandu. I've
had my Indian visa for a week now. There is
a general strike here and no-one's allowed to
cross the border. There's a curfew and lots of
beatings, killings, riots and protests, it's all
a bit hairy! I've been sick twice and want to
leave, hopefully the border will open soon, then
I'll go straight to Rishikesh or where ever u are
… maybe MAnali?
    I got off the pot, vomited a lot ... diahhrea
(however u spell it!), but feeling purified now,
I even shaved my head. I look like a freak. I fit
right in on 'freak street', Kathmandu! Nepalese
women are beautiful!
The Kobra
```

Hiring a lime-coloured motorbike I spend days exploring the surrounding area – the gravel road hugs the contours of the hills and follows the meander of the Ganges. Barely one lane wide, scores of taxi jeeps speed past, careening around blind corners. The road's edge is not protected by a barrier and falls steeply away to jagged rocks on the banks of the river some fifty metres below. I fantasise about signing up with the Shiva Riders. Discovering a series of waterfalls one day and an amazing vista of the region on another, I wind through forests and remote farms. The flicker of dappled light through the trees mesmerises as the sound of cooing peacocks emanates from the shadows, the occasional bird dashing across the road in a flash of colour and feathers.

I spend afternoons relaxing at the Freedom Café, an outdoor open-air establishment with lots of carpets and cushions to lie on. It's situated with premium views of the river. A tall dope plant grows out of the gutter next to the entrance where the sign hangs at a forty-five degree angle and a cud-chewing cow with sleepy eyes is tethered. Dylan arrives from Varanasi with a striking looking Icelandic girl named Frida, buxom, late twenties with long blonde hair and blue eyes. She speaks in a thick Welsh accent, as she has been working in Wales as a professional photographer. Intelligent with a razor sharp wit she keeps Dylan on his toes. Soon after Nimrod appears with a pretty Israeli girl, petite and dark, a feminine version of himself. He met her at a yoga ashram, another Indian affair. I ask what happened to Merav.

'Hah Mr Dundee good to see you. My cousin Merav met some Israeli guy in Varanasi and ran away to Goa, she wanted beach, party and sex.'

* * *

One morning I meet Carlitos at the fruit market. 'Hey Australia, wha' you do now? I am going to swim in de river, maybe you will come?'

A chance to finally wash away all those sins, start with a clean slate seems all too tempting. We walk just outside the township to a small sandy clearing. I would call it a beach, but it feels kind of inappropriate to say that. Stripping off to our boxer shorts, Carlitos boldly dives in, surfacing he lets out a scream of delight. A little more tentative, I take my time. Stepping into the water up to my ankles stops my breath. It's icy cold, coming straight down from the heights of the Himalaya.

The jade-coloured water flickers silver like the scales of a snake. Small particles of metallic sand capture and reflect the sun, making the water shimmer. The current is strong, pulling at me, beckoning me to venture deeper. Cautiously, I step up to my waist. The sharpness of the cold makes my balls contract with fear and my torso shiver. Letting go I completely surrender to the tempestuous goddess and dive in. The powerful current carries me downstream. Swimming back to the safety of the shallows, I'm not sure if my karma is cleansed, but I certainly feel invigorated. I turn to Carlitos. 'Just what the doctor ordered, a karmic fresh start, what a way to begin the day.'

Carlitos looks at me seriously in his dripping wet underwear. 'Dis is no joke, if you do nort really want to repent from your sins, dis will nort work. De sins jump out of you and hide in de trees before you enter de river, and when you come out, if you are not serious, dey will jump back into you again when you leave.'

'Sorry.' Feeling foolish of my flippancy, I duck in the river, quickly submerging myself one more time for good measure. Later I read how one of Shiva's wives, Parvati, jealous of Ganga, complained she made salvation too easy. Shiva scoffed at her claim and set out to illustrate by example. He pretended to be a dead body at the river's edge and instructed Parvati to play the role of the grieving wife. She was to tell anybody that tried to console her that an apparition of Shiva said that her husband would be re-animated if somebody, who had been cleansed of their own sins by dipping in the river, touched his corpse. However, if the bath had not cleaned all sins, that person would also die. Not surprisingly, nobody offered to take the risk. Enter stage left, the village's notoriously murderous criminal thug, blind drunk and announcing to all his lewd activities of the previous night at a brothel. He became so filled with remorse upon hearing the wailing widow's story (a.k.a. Parvati) that he volunteered for the job, saying, 'I am the village's biggest sinner but I will repent and wash away my sins in the Ganga, then I will surely be able to help you.'

Realising he was about to commit the first good deed of his life, he dipped into the river with genuine repentance and approached the corpse with a great reverence. As soon as he touched the body it transformed back into Shiva, who jumped up and proclaimed to everyone watching, 'Of all that have bathed here, only this man has true faith and repentance. Only he has gained salvation by dipping in the Ganga. The rest of you only got wet.' Pondering this, I wonder if I too only got wet.

* * *

Our afternoons at the Freedom Café are interspersed with visitors and a waxing and waning of friendly faces. Joints and chillums are rife and I try my best to abstain, only smoking with the Baba. Mid to late forties, partially-dreadlocked, flecked silver hair falling over lean, leathery, scarred brown shoulders, the Baba is always barefoot and robed in a dirty orange sarong. He is always wearing a yellow scarf around his neck and stroking his greying beard. Traditional sandalwood and rudra beads adorn his neck. With his light build and short stature, Baba Krishna is a sadhu of somewhat dubious origin but none-the-less, one of good intent. He always enters the café holding his iron Shiva trident in one hand and a bunch of flowers in the other. He always greets us smiling, with arms extended. 'Hello my children. Everybody meeting. This is the season.'

Today he passes out a flower to everybody at the table before he sits. 'This is the good life. Good vibrations.' He then places his trident on the table and lights some dhoop on it, a black paste incense that sadhus use, made from ghee, herbs and dhoop wood chips. It smoulders – aromatic smoke lingers in the air. 'For puja.' Surreptitiously he places his chillum pipe on the table. 'Good for making meditation. For relaxing and enjoyment.'

He is vying for a smoke. Nimrod smiles, picks up his circular tobacco tin. 'Hey babas, if I make a smoke can we use your chillum?'

'As you like my child.'

This is how he survives, from the gifts and charity of others – not a greedy soul, he only takes what he needs and gives everything else he receives away. Dylan takes his cue from Nimrod. 'Baba, my man, would you like something to eat?'

'I will take some chai for the drinking, Baba Krishna will eat this.'

He picks up a piece of chapatti bread, long since discarded from one of our plates. He has a pride about him in his humility. Dylan calls out to the caféwallah, 'Hey Ji can we have a chai, and can I have some extra love in that? *Dhanyavad* (thanks).'

This is Dylan's new buzzword, 'extra love', everything he orders he asks them to put some 'extra love' in it. Finishing the mix, Nimrod passes the bowl to the baba, who packs the chillum and hands it to Dylan. He always smokes last, after everyone else. Chanting the prayer to Shiva, he lights up the clay pipe for Dylan.

'Alakh, alakh boom
Alakh, alakh boom, boom
Alakh Shiva Shambo'

Once the chillum has circled everybody, the baba taps out the ash on his hand and blesses us all with a dot of the grey powder on our foreheads. He often gives us gifts – yesterday Nimrod got a pendant, the day before Dylan and Frida, shell necklaces. Today apparently it's my turn. He places a shell in my hand the size of my thumbnail, it has been cut in half and polished and has a spiral in the cut edge, these are commonly called *Shiva eyes*. Cupping my hands with his, the baba looks at me. 'Better for seeing the world and helping the meditation.' Rubbing the little finger on my right hand, 'Be making it into a ring and putting this finger, making sure it is touching the skin. It will help you in the life.'

* * *

The days merge into weeks and start exclusively at the Freedom Café, with chai and shakshuka, (Israeli scrambled eggs), blessings and chillums with the baba and then meeting later for sunset rooftop yoga with Victor. I become prolific in my quest for self-improvement, studying yoga, attending various satsangs on spirituality, eating healthily, receiving ayurvedic massages and contemplating life on the banks of the river. When I find a course to study reiki I decide to give it go.

Originally from Japan, reiki is a technique for stress release, relaxation and healing. By the 'laying of hands', one is able to transmit a life-force energy, from the universe and into the receiver. Previously I've only been on the receiving end of reiki and I'm never sure if it's placebo or if something more significant occurs. Frida, Dylan and Victor also come along for the ride.

I could say that we study reiki, but that would be a lie. We are actually initiated through a series of rituals. Now, I try my hardest not to be skeptical of the process. We're initiated by 'Reiki Masters', an old German lady and her elderly Indian lady-friend. The process entails sitting down with our eyes closed as they motion secret invisible symbols in the air with their hands. Sounds flaky? Well it kind of is, but there's a nice atmosphere, and it only costs a tenth of what they charge in Australia. We receive the reiki then practice on each other, it's all very shanti shanti, and a bit touchy feely. I don't really feel anything, but after each day I am energised, positive and happy, so it can't be all bad. I also sleep the best I have since I can remember, my insomnia and nightmares of Stella finally begin to wane.

Our master explains how practising on ourselves will assist meditation and help clear and align all our seven chakras. Chakra is sanskrit for wheel or circle, sometimes referred to as part of the 'wheel of life'. In Hinduism these are considered to be the metaphysical and energising bionexus of the human body. Located at different points on the body, from our clackers to the crown of our heads, each chakra has an organ associated with it as well as a metaphysical function, elemental force and even a colour and sound. Part of me wants to really believe all this and part of me, the inner cynic, wants to laugh heartily out loud and chorus, *What a load of bullshit.*

However, I don't want to be a party pooper, as everybody else seems to be lapping it up and who am I to judge? I have enough humility to realise that I'm an ignoramus in the greater scheme of things. I consider a personal philosophical proverb – *a wise man once said nothing.*

Even when our master further extrapolates that using Buddhist singing bowls will assist our reiki by focusing our meditation and the energy pathways of Ki flow – creating a harmonic convergence and chakra alignment with the universe, I think to myself, *give me a break.*

A few days after our chakra tune ups, Victor enters the Freedom Café. He's quiet and somewhat reticent. Nimrod asks what he's been doing. 'Well I just had my fortune told be de ayurvedic astrologer. It was very interesting to say de least. He knew many tings about my past dat makes me wonder about his predictions of de future.'

Curiosity too much, one by one all of the clan go to see this enigmatic character. The story and excitement of each person inspires the following visitor. At first I'm a little dubious, but when nobody comes back saying they were Cleopatra in a previous life I consider it warrants personal investigation (I've met too many girls that reckon they were the Egyptian Queen in a previous life. Not all of us can be Egyptian royalty). So I decide to give it a go. When I enter his establishment, it's so dark I can barely see, blinking to adjust my eyesight to the dim conditions. The man's smile radiates a warmth and geniality that feels reassuring. He simultaneously stares into my eyes with an omnipotent intensity that is a little disarming. Placing his palms together in a silent greeting of Namaste he says, 'Velcome my friend, you vould be liking to know your future?'

'Yeah, I guess so.'

He asks for my exact time and place of birth to work out my star chart. I feign an imperturbable equanimity, but really consternation fills my heart. What will be revealed? He reputedly can tell you the day you will die. A strong aroma of incense is in the air. He holds a piece of paper with a series of monograms and hieroglyphics scribbled on it. 'A most interesting chart indeed.' The suspense is nearly killing me – hopefully not literally. I wonder if there is a code of conduct amongst these guys. If they see that you will die unavoidably really soon – like next week, do they just say 'you will have a long a prosperous life.' Looking up at me the astrologer grins. 'You will have a long and prosperous life.'

He wobbles his head. 'Would you like me to tell you the day you vill die?' Enquiring casually like a sales clerk at Mickey Dees asking what extras I'd like on my burger. 'Do you want cheese with that?'

'No, no, no I don't want to know. It's not next week though is it? Tell me it's not next week.'

'No it is not next veek. You vill live to be an old man.'

That's a relief.

'As long as you stop smoking. Hmm, I sense some heat from your throat chakra. You used to have problems with breathing as a child.'

OK, that's a lucky guess. I had asthma as a kid.

'I can see you used to have some problems vith the law. But those days are behind you now and drugs, you have taken much. It is time for this way to end now. This is not your path for the future. If you continue it will have bad karma for you in the future.'

Deduction – a man walks into your shop covered with tattoos, safe bet he has a shady past.

'You have been sick, I see heat coming from your solar plexus chakra, from the stomach. You are OK now, but there is still something there, you must drink much vater and it vill pass.'

Come on every second traveller has a case of the Delhi belly.

'Your heart chakra is blocked. I can see you vere married, but that has finished. It was not good, there vas much fighting.

165

This has finished now. This is best. Leave the past in the past.'

I feel my heart in my mouth as the old wound tears open.

'I see another love, she is much younger than you, hmm, strange, have you been to Africa?'

Shielding my surprise. 'No, why?'

'This girl, she vas from Africa vasn't she? But there was a problem you had to leave her in a hurry. '

Now it's getting spooky.

'I see an artist, yes you are an artist. I see you tried many different things in this life. I see the stage, are you an actor?'

'Yeah, in the past.'

You also have a healing energy, you should study some energy vork, like reiki – you have the hands of a healer.'

'I actually just did a reiki course.'

'Excellent, and yoga, this is good for you.'

'Already do it.'

He then proceeds to advise me which yoga poses are good for me and which are not. Pausing, he has a serious expression on his face. 'Do you ride motor bikes?'

'Yeah, sometimes.'

'No, no, this is not good, you must stay away from motorbikes, especially green ones, these are very bad for you.'

I think of my green bike parked outside my guesthouse, uncanny.

'And your left knee, you have a problem vith your left knee.'

'No I don't.'

'Vell you vill and very soon.'

He continues, 'I see a romance in the very near future.'

God I hope so.

'I see many places, you are on a long journey around the vorld – this trip is blessed. I also see you living in a hot place, somewhere tropical, maybe South America. Also you vill meet your next wife in September this year. This vill be a good marriage, a happy one. She is younger than you. This is better for you, girls that are younger in age.'

The filthy old man in me couldn't agree more.

'It is good for you to stay away from Australian girls. They are not good for you.'

Touché.

'You need to meditate much, it is important for your busy mind. You have a strange and dangerous adventure in front of you. Take care on this quest.'

My head swims with all this new information. Have I overdosed on good vibrations, chakras, reiki, yoga, shanti fucking shanti harmonic alignments, karma cleansing sanctimonious swims in the Ganges, satsangs with disturbingly happy, vacant-eyed society dropouts, ayurvedic everything, chillums and chai? Have I gone too far, lost myself on the quest to find myself? Whoever the fuck that is anyway. I was an ex-punk rocker, ex-drug addict, failed actor, divorced truck driver from Australia. Shitty as it was, at least it was still a clearly defined label. But now, what am I now? Just another anorexic, spiritually spit-polished and rewired Indian travelling space cadet cliché that's about to slip through the cracks of this esoteric maze and into the abyss of this apparently bottomless subcontinent? It happens every day here.

I walk out of the astrologer's establishment with the same stunned expression Victor had days earlier. His words, 'take care on your quest', rattling around in my brain. How could he know my future, he certainly guessed my past. Surely he just uses the power of suggestion, appealing to my subconscious and my desires. Bet he's one hell of a poker player. What I wouldn't do right now to be beamed like captain Kirk from

Star Trek, to my local, a smoky working-class bar in the outer suburbs of Melbourne. I'd sit with the old alcoholics and down a few quiet beers. But they'd no doubt view me suspiciously, with my now long hair and orange 'dress' and dot of make-up on my forehead.

Needing to clear my head, I take my green, bad luck, motorbike out for a spin. I wind the bike out, up the road, around hairpin bends into the hills, going faster and further than ever before. It's a beautiful, blue-sky day, perfect riding conditions. I stop to admire the view from atop a crest in the road.

From nowhere, imposing black clouds roll across the horizon and in moments the sky goes dark. The temperature cools and the smell of negatively charged ions saturate the atmosphere. The birds stop singing. A cold breeze descends from the mountains, as thunder and lightning crack and rumble over the rise. Turning around, I retreat down the hill. Lightning and thunder chase me – wind and rain bite at my heels. By the time I reach the outskirts of Laxman Jhula the storm has fully enveloped me. Soaked to the core I ride tentatively on the wet road. Around a corner a taxi jeep comes careering towards me at an alarming speed. The back wheels spin out, swinging the car across the road, approaching me like a wall of steel. The Indian driver smiles nervously at me, as if to say *we are both screwed, sorry.*

I've nowhere to go, I ease on the brakes to slow down but the road is slick with oil, I start to slide towards my apparent destiny. I'd like to say my entire life flashes before my eyes, but it doesn't, just the word *FUCK* passes. Everything is in slow motion like some ghastly waltz. Just before the moment of impact the jeep manages to gain traction, swinging the back end away and creating the smallest window of opportunity.

Miraculously my bike also grips rubber to bitumen and I throttle through the gap to safety. Not wanting to tempt fate again, I return the bike. Then the next day I hurt my left knee doing a yoga pose my astrologer advised me not to do. Time to go buy a Buddhist singing bowl and be on the look out for romance, who am I to argue with such celestial forces?

* * *

The next day I don't go to the Freedom Café till the late afternoon. Only Baba Krishna is there, he looks up at me smiling. 'Yes friend, sit. I have been waiting.' He threads a large, textured brown seed with a piece of cotton twine. The size of an olive it looks like a small walnut. He ties it in a loop and auspiciously places it around my neck, while singing a chant.

'*Om Namah Shivaya*
Om Namah Shivaya
Om Namah Shivaya.'

Gently he pats me on my shoulder. 'This is for you my child, now you are my student.'

'What is it Baba?'

'Rudra, for making protection and for health. I made vith my blessings, it is for your long journey.'

Rudra seeds are also called The Divine Bead or The Tears of Lord Shiva. They are the original Vedic beads of power worn by yogis of India and the Himalaya for thousands of years. Believed to maintain health, they create self-empowerment and a fearless sense of life on the path to liberation. When worn, they're reputed to rid the soul of sin and help attain the supreme goal of enlightenment. The seed goes through a process of blessings – washed in a mixture of cow's dung, urine, milk, ghee and curd, this explains its pungent aroma. Baba Krishna places the bead under my T-shirt. 'You must be wearing it like this, it is to be touching the skin. Come child, it is time to be making puja.'

We stroll along a narrow path by the river stopping at a tree covered in red flowers. The baba picks some and passes them to me to carry. 'This is my place of sleeping, many sadhus here.' Continuing, we meander through a small settlement, emerging on a main road. A few moments later we pass a temple, long since neglected, buried beneath weeds and overgrown vines. 'This vas the ashram of the Beatles, but ve are not having the time to be seeing it today.'

It's true, there was an old temple built in the 70s here by the Beatles during their acid phase, I'm surprised it's so lack lustre, I thought it would be exploited as a tourist highlight. Continuing we enter the next village on the river, Ram Jhula. The baba picks flowers. Ram Jhula is a hive of activity, devotees everywhere, sadhus smoking chillums while people are converging at the river. Baba leads me to a large temple. Entering, we remove our shoes and descend down a carpeted stairway to a polished white-marble ghat. At its base sits a twenty-foot statue of Shiva meditating in the full lotus position. The ghat quickly fills with disciples. The baba sits me down. 'Vait here child I vill be returning soon.'

Passing me his iron trident he leaves me holding the bouquet of flowers as he disappears into the crowd. On the stage in front of the statue, boy monks in immaculate orange robes prepare wood and oil for a ceremonial fire. They then dutifully sit in formation and await their mentor.

As the sun starts to set the swami enters, he has long, rich black hair and a thick beard that flows in the breeze. He has fire in his eyes and the presence of a rock star. A band starts up, and with a swish of his hand he indicates for the choir of young monks to start singing. Their sweet melodies resonate as the swami sways to its rhythm. After an hour the music crescendos and the swami spectacularly ignites the centre piece fire – the monks light oil lanterns from it and pass them around the audience, all of whom join in the singing. It is like the ultimate cigarette lighters in the air routine during the ballad at a rock concert. Dark by the time the music stops, the congregation starts to dissipate, passing the river and tossing in flowers and lighting floating candles for puja.

As I start to wonder of the whereabouts of the Baba, he appears smiling. 'Yes, you like the singing? Come, it is time for our puja and blessings.' Under the statue of Shiva the baba leads me into the water. Breaking the bouquet in half, he passes a portion to me. 'Be putting it in Ganga, but be using only your right hand.' He then dabs water on my forehead and sprinkles some over the crown of my head.

Walking with Baba back towards the Freedom Café, he stops at the path to his tree where he sleeps. 'My path is going this way. You must be going that way my child.' Pointing up the road to Laxman Jhula, 'Follow your path with eyes open child, it is important in the life.' Smiling, he walks off, calling over his shoulder, 'Namaste child.'

Back at the Freedom Café there is a party, Victor leaves in the morning for Delhi. It's a happy vibe, much laughter and merriment but it's the end of another phase, the end of an era – but can one month be considered an era? One by one the group goes to bed until I sit alone. Rolling the rudra bead the baba gave me between my fingers, I consider the last month – the predictions of the future, wondering who the girl will be that is supposed to appear, and about meeting my next wife later in the year. I think about green motorbikes, chakras and my karma, wondering if it's all just a load of old bollocks or something amazing and mysterious.

At my side is a sleeping puppy. All skin and bone, he's on death's door. Listless and panting heavily, he's been here for days and his condition is deteriorating. He hasn't the strength to move now. Thinking *what the hell*, and with nobody about, I apply my hands to the dog and give reiki. I do it without cynicism and with good intent. Astonishingly the dog responds straight away, moving his little body under my hands to receive the energy to where he needs it. After about five minutes he's on his feet, wagging his tail and running around like little puppies should. Smiling, I feel content and enjoy the moment, the proverbial 'now'. Under the full moon, its light dancing on the rippling surface of the river, I open my diary and start writing a personal proverb, *We are called human beings, not human doings, so just be, for that's all I am doing.*

CHAPTER 9

Smoke and Mirrors

'Dey beat me with sticks and said dey would kill me and throw my body in de river.' Carlitos bruised black and blue, slumps down at our table at the Freedom Café. Today it's hot as an unsettling wind blows up the river from the delta plains below. The heat has finally caught up with us. Appeased for a month, a luscious remission, but the temperature has been edging up the scales a degree or two every day for the past week. It's creating a tension and feeling of unease in the village. Carlitos rubs his arm, which is covered in red welts. A small cut weeps blood above his eye and his left hand is swollen pink. Rushing to his aid, Frida dabs his cuts with a tissue like an Icelandic Florence Nightingale, cooing to him in a syrupy Welsh accent. 'My goodness, are you OK, you poor baby. Who did this to you?'

'It was the taxi drivers near de bridge.'

Judging by his shaken demeanour and the marks on his face and arms he has received a substantial beating. I pat his shoulder. 'Shit bro, they really gave it to you, what the fuck happened?'

'I was just trying to get a taxi to Rishikesh. He told me it would cost fifty rupees but I know it is only five for de locals. I said he was a thief to charge so much. He got angry and pushed me away. So I pushed him back and he fell over. Den some of de other taxi drivers came over. Dere was much shouting and pushing. I tell dem to "chello Pakistan" and dey all go crazy. Many more of de taxi drivers come with bamboo sticks and start hitting me. I fight back but dere are too many. Dey chase me up de street until I fall over and dey all are hitting me with dare sticks. I was screaming for help but nobody came. They were all around me saying they were going to kill me and throw my body in de river.'

Everyone at the Freedom Café is stunned into a silence. I break it. 'Fuck man, that's not very shanti shanti.'

Dylan slides over to Carlitos's side rubbing his hands together. 'You need some full reiki power man and some comfort food.'

He turns to the cáfewallah. 'Hey Baba Ji my man, can I please have an iced chocolate with double ice cream and double serves of extra love down here. Remember I want two serves of extra love in that for my buddy here Ji. *Dhanyavad.*'

Dylan applies reiki and Frida tends to his wounds. For the first time the sanctuary of Laxman Jhula feels undermined. We all stopped doing yoga when Victor left and have since slipped into a hash hole, smoking way too much. Also the heat is becoming annoying; we are constantly feeling heavy, lethargic and clammy with sweat. There's been a murmur of discontent among the group and disintegration seems imminent. Nimrod is pensive. 'I thought this was a place without violence.'

Frida glances over to him. 'This is not the first case of violence I've heard of. Apparently there's a rapist in the area, only last week a girl went missing and her body was later found in the river. She had like a dozen different men's semen found inside her.'

Nimrod and I look at each other in shock. 'Fuck, that's terrible,' Nimrod contributes. 'It is sad that this is happening here.'

Frida continues, 'At least the body of the last poor girl was found – often the girls just go missing without a trace. Nobody seems to care though, and whoever's doing it is getting away scot-free. They're probably local and everybody's protecting them or they're too afraid to do anything. I wouldn't trust those taxi drivers. Look what they can do to a grown man in broad daylight – imagine a girl by herself at night.'

* * *

It's sweltering the next morning. I can't rest, thinking about my astrological reading, wondering when the supposed romance will happen, thinking about Frankie stuck in Nepal in the middle of a revolution and thinking about Carlitos's un-shanti shanti beating. The urge to do the sketchy bail grows strong inside me, but the path has not yet emerged. I go to check my emails and hear from Frankie. It's been nearly a month since he received his visa.

```
Hey Dragon,
    I'm still in Kathmandu. This town has gone
to the pack! The border is still closed. Fucking
revolutionaries. Can't remember if I told you in
last email but I've been sick 3 times since I've
been here. Last time temp reached 40 degrees, in bed
for 34 hours, maybe another case of food poisoning,
maybe amoebas. Either way, I'm just feeling better
now. I have a couple of things to do then I come to
you, wherever you are. The border should be open in a
week or so. Are you staying in Rishi? Keep in touch!
K
P.S. howz the reiki?
```

On the street I walk towards the Freedom Café. The dry, uncomfortably warm breeze blows dust and debris up into people's faces. Out the front of the café the Shiva Riders have kitted up their Royal Enfields and are warming up their engines in preparation to make the journey north, indicating that the snow has receded enough for the way to be open. Again, another sign it's time to move on. Rumbling like an orchestra of fire and brimstone, the last drags of joints are smoked, ends of cups of chai swilled back and sunglasses adjusted as one by one they ride out of town. In slow succession they weave through the markets heading for the open road, where they disappear over the horizon in a blaze of psychedelic glory.

Inside the Freedom Café, Dylan, Frida and Nimrod are sitting in their usual spots, but this morning something is different, there's a certain trepidation in the air. They seem excited, all smiling conspiratorially at me. 'OK, what? What is it, why are ya all looking at me like that?'

Nimrod radiating his signature grin produces what looks like a small eyedrop dispenser from the leather pouch strapped across his chest. Giving it a little shake, he winks at me. 'Care to come for a journey into the unknown my friend, to fly through the inner universe?'

'What?'

Dylan smiles too, passing me a joint as I sit down. I pause before accepting; I wasn't going to smoke today and now I am toking before breakfast. The day starts to look like it may be a washout. Dylan nudges me. 'My man, we're going to meet Alice in Wonderland, wanna come down the rabbit hole.'

Frida quips, 'Yes and we're short one mad hatter and you can't have a mad hatter's tea party without a mad hatter now can you?'

'Getting the message,' I reply, 'So you're all tripping today?'

Nimrod nods. 'Liquid LSD 25 my friend, natures finest.'

After my near death, cathartic purging in Varanasi, I had decided to try and turn over a new leaf. The prophetic dream where my spirit guide the cockatoo led me away from the jungle of opium monkeys to the sanctuary of the river's edge and away from temptation continues to resonate. However a non-addictive psychoactive substance, taken in such an auspicious spiritual place as this, could be a real third eye opener. But still, an unsettling feeling makes me uncertain. Leaning closely to me, Nimrod takes the joint from my fingers and whispers, 'This is liquid lightning friend, straight from the chemist's brother – he is one of the Shiva Riders.' Returning to his inclined position, he adjusts his plastic gold-rimmed Elvis glasses (circa *Viva Los Vegas*) acquired from one of his recent love conquests. Smoking the joint like a Marx Brother cigar, he proclaims loudly, exaggerating his Israeli accent, 'Anyway, he is Israeli, so it must be good.'

Frida scratches the stubble under my chin. 'Come on you old dog, come and play with us.' Dylan slaps me on the back. 'So you on the team dude or what?' He squeezes the back of my neck with his hand, giving me a little massage. 'Yeah, he's on the team guys.'

Nimrod sits bolt upright, and everybody leans inward as he slowly unscrews the lid. Lick. Sip. Suck. Lick the drop of volatile liquid Nimrod carefully dispenses to the the back of my hand. Tentatively sip in a lungful of air as the acid's metallic flavour trickles down the back of my throat. Suck in the day, as I know it will be a big one, sensory overload and reality distortion expected in approximately forty-five minutes.

We decide to head up the river and find a quiet location to let it in or let it all go. Parched, I buy a bottle of water on the way. I unscrew the lid. I'm just about to put the receptacle to my lips when a passing cow casually swishes her shit-encrusted tail across the top of the bottle. Nice. Suddenly I'm not thirsty. Feels like another sign. 'A fuck you and your karma buddy' or a 'I flick shit in your general direction' sign. Pondering the words of warning from the astrologer about me dallying with such things, the school counsellor from the cartoon series *South Park* comes to mind. *Drugs are bad, OK.*

We cross the bridge. My attention is drawn to the river. The water level seems low, the lowest it's been since I've been here. The flick of the cow's tail, the warning from the astrologer and for some reason the river having dropped a couple of metres overnight fills me with a sense of foreboding. We stumble over rocks, trying to find the perfect spot – vertigo sensations of giddiness already begin to pervade the fabric of my reality, as we slip from one consciousness into another. Finally we all agree on a location.

The unsettling feeling that rode in on the morning breeze seems to intensify as the acid grinds through the cerebral gears of my subconscious. I just can't shake it. This all just feels wrong. I feel a tad conceited, even sacrilegious. Coming on strong now, senses heightened, everything starts to shimmer.

I like to consider this shimmering effect in the context of quantum physics. Objects such as the rock I'm sitting on, the river and the air blowing around in the breeze, are all made up of atoms. Atoms in turn are made up of smaller stuff that's ultimately made up of energy. Now energy is not something that's tangible, like matter, like the rock upon which I sit. But, energy is ultimately the smallest building block of matter, an interesting and slightly perplexing paradox. Everything is nothing and nothing is everything.

Now all these atoms are in close association with each other, their proximity to one another determines whether they form a solid, liquid or a gas. These atoms aren't static, but always moving, or vibrating, as they're made up of intangible energy. Everything vibrates, the rock, the river and the breeze – everything therefore has a vibrational point. Tripping is kind of like the Magic Dot pictures that were all the rage a few years ago, but in reverse. First you see the 'picture' or sober reality, then as the acid kicks in you see the dots behind the picture. Then, once you see the dots, or the vibrational point of everything, then you can see anything.

Fast approaching the magic dot stage of the trip, I still can't shake the niggling feeling that something about the vibe of the place (vibe being short for vibration) isn't right. Frida approaches me smiling. She's as bug-eyed as me even though her eyes are concealed behind Nimrod's five-buck Elvis glasses. 'Why don't we all do some yoga?'

Anything to help shake this sensation, jumping up I organise the posse into an impromptu class. We start moving through the twelve positions of the sun salutations, but it feels inappropriate, like we're belittling everything we've learnt over the last month rather than celebrating it. Totally disrespectful, it reduces the experience to nothing more than a psychedelic joyride. I abruptly stop. 'Think I need a swim guys.'

Wading into the river, the water provides no respite – in fact the sensation intensifies when I dip my head under. Staying submerged as long as my breath allows, I hope the icy chill washes away the sense of foreboding, but it doesn't. Then floating on my back I listen to the others talking as they too enter the water, voices tinged with trepidation. Dylan is first. 'Wow, that's fresh, full reiki power. Man this is amazing, really feel cleansed.' Something in his voice seems to suggest an apprehension too.

Nimrod is next in. 'Yes, full power, 24 hour, no shave, no

shower.' Quoting the famous party phrase from Goa. Frida shrieks, 'Oh, it's so invigorating.'

Still edgy I get out and squat on my close association of atoms that's still choosing to appear as my rock. Dylan sets up his MP3 player and portable speakers, playing The Doors, while he and Frida spin poi (coloured balls on the end of string twirled from each hand, very popular in the trance music scene). Nimrod rolls a joint – it's all so trite.

A boat passes by full of Chinese tourists with a mad grinning Indian at the helm. I had watched it for half an hour upstream, as it bobbed back and forth from bank to bank down the river through swirling rapids and currents. The captain appears to have little or no control over the vessel as he careers past us and into a huge dead-end boulder that protrudes from the riverbank adjacent to our position. They're all so busy looking at us and taking photos that not even the captain notices the impasse until it's too late. The boat becomes wedged, and to compensate the captain revs the vessel's motor till thick plumes of smoke billow from the engine. Eventually he clunks the engine into reverse and manages to limp the boat backwards with what's left of the motor. Grinning they all drift backwards around the rock downstream and out of sight. Painted across the canopy of the boat's roof in large letters are the words *Enjoy Boating*.

Contemplating this as a possible mantra or at least a T-shirt slogan, I stare at the giant rock that blocked the boat's path. It morphs into a stampede of Ganesh elephants, galloping and falling over each other in perpetual motion without actually moving, trapped within the confines of the atomic context of the rock. The acid is in top gear now. Dylan comes up to my side looking acutely disturbed. 'Err dude, um, can I speak to you for a sec?'

He looks really freaked out, but I'm tripping so hard it takes me a moment to focus. He continues, nodding his head behind him. 'Man, like um, over there.'

Struggling to comprehend, I look in the direction that he's tilting his head. Across the river, there are some people lying on the river bank, basking in the sun, all appears normal, but I'm not sure if I can trust anything I see right now. Dylan continues to nod with increased urgency and I again look across the river. For some reason I think he's suggesting that the people are having sex. Looking harder now, it looks like they are. Dylan's nodding starts to look like a nervous twitch. Does he want to start an orgy? Man that's kind of fucked up. I consider the logistical aspects of having group sex on the banks of the river Ganges, wondering whether it would be shanti shanti or not. Does he want me to start or something, should I take off all my clothes to kick it all off?

Looking at Dylan again, he looks desperate for me to understand him. I look at the other side of the river again. No, they're definitely not having sex on the beach, OK just visual and perceptual distortion – an X-rated magic dot picture from the gutter that is my mind. Dylan grabs my shoulder, whispering in my ear, 'Not over there man, just there.'

He points to some small boulders at the water's edge just a couple of metres from where we are. The unsettling feeling that has been bugging me all day comes back in a flash, like a bolt of lightning through me. Maybe it's a momentary telepathic link with Dylan or just my intuition, but my mind is burned with an image of something ghastly. Looking at him sternly, 'OK, dude, before you burst my bubble, just go and double check on whatever it is that's freaking you out, OK?' Nodding, he tentatively walks to the small pile of boulders and returns swiftly. 'Bubble bursting time dude.'

With my heart in my throat, I get off my rock and slowly walk to the water's edge. Reaching the destination, the image rolls into view in slow motion. The small boulders reveal what has been disturbing Dylan so much. Feeling a little giddy as adrenaline rushes through me, I squat down to the ground beside the stones. Thinking to myself, *Wow, this cow carcass looks remarkably like human remains.*

But it's no cow. Glistening in all its ghastly glory, sparkling in the reflected light of the river in which it lies, is a very decomposed human body. Spellbound for a moment my eyes are transfixed by the macabre image. The ribs, the vertebra, scapula and pelvis are all clearly defined – there is no mistaking what this is. Milky-coloured flesh hangs from the bones. Missing the head, the body lies face down, half buried by stones in a shallow grave, semi-submerged in the water. Hit by a hardcore reality rush, now I know why the place felt so wrong, we've been dancing on somebody's grave. Maybe I had subconciously seen it the whole time but was unable to focus on it. I didn't expect to see a dead body here so I didn't see one. I always was lousy at those magic dot pictures. Sighing I mutter, 'Stop the world I want to get off.'

We've been swimming in the water with this rotting corpse, I suddenly feel unclean, the complete antithesis of what the river is meant to provide. At first I think we've just stumbled on some family tomb, but then it occurs to me – Indians burn their dead or throw the bodies directly in the river. They never bury them. This body has been buried quickly in a makeshift grave, face down and without the head, hardly a respectful funeral. It's only been revealed today because the river dropped so low overnight. Somebody didn't want this body to be found or identified. A feeling of dread grows to a sense of panic. Sensing foul play, have we inadvertently discovered a possible murder scene? Remembering the stories of the missing backpackers Frida mentioned over breakfast, I shudder as I stand and return to Dylan. Smiling at him through gritted teeth, 'Mum's the word mate. We keep this to ourselves, OK?'

Dylan is on the verge of losing it – his eyes are as wide as saucers as he nods in agreement. This place doesn't feel so fucking shanti shanti now. The stories of missing girls, rapes, murders and the merciless beating of Carlitos by the taxi drivers all flood my mind. We've wandered from the main drag. I scan the hills behind us – maybe the killer is up there watching us right now, like a wolf salivating at a flock of sheep strayed from the path. My spine tingles with fear, I feel exposed and vulnerable. Painting the best casual smile on my face, I try to appear languorous in my approach to Nimrod and Frida. Dylan is ready to flip and two more would be a real problem. 'OK guys, I reckon we should head back to the Freedom Café or to one of our rooms or maybe even just over there, away from here anyway.'

Nimrod and Frida both complain in chorus, 'No, we like it here.' I look back at Dylan who's sitting on my rock holding his legs in a foetal position. He's staring at the body and rocking back and forth. 'No, come on guys, we need some water.'

Nimrod is just about to say something, but he looks in my eyes and decides against it. 'Yeah OK, maybe it is time to go.'

Picking up the poi, Frida begins to walk towards Dylan and the location of the body. 'I'll just get the music then.'

Dylan and I both dramatically yell, 'NO!' Dylan, scrambles to his feet and grabs the MP3 player. 'It's OK babe, I, I've got it.'

My heart beats hard as we clamber over the rocks along

the river back to the village. I have time to mull over the consequences and implications of our morbid little discovery. What do we do? Should we report it to the police? What Pandora's box will that open for us? Should Dylan and I even tell the others? What about moral obligations? My head swims with these thoughts by the time we reach Dylan's room. He is a mess as he paces back and forth on the little balcony of his room – I can almost see the thoughts bouncing around inside his skull.

We spend the rest of the afternoon on the balcony. As the sun begins to set and the sky bleeds into twilight, Dylan gives me a knowing look. The trip has subsided and he indicates that maybe it's time to inform the others of what happened. I nod in silent agreement and turn to them. 'You may have noticed that there was a bit of a change in the vibe at the river, that me and Dylan started to act a little strange? Well it's because we found something.'

We then both explained in detail, mentioning my suspicion that it may have been a murder. A quiet falls over the group. Nimrod is the first to speak. 'I picked up on something from you when you said to leave. It's funny, well not funny, but strange. I think I saw it too but just didn't really see if that makes sense.'

It made sense alright, and I think I may have also seen it without seeing it, before I allowed myself to actually see it. Frida speaks, 'Well I'm grateful you didn't show me whilst I was in that state, thank you guys. But I think we have to go back there tomorrow to investigate. If it is a murder we must do something about it, what if it's some poor tourist who's been killed. Maybe it's one of the missing girls? Imagine the pain and suffering the parents are going through not knowing what happened to their child.'

There is a consensus. Tomorrow we will take action. Night falls. The bellowing of a cow emanates from beneath the balcony and we all peer over the edge. A sick and old white cow breathes heavily, bawling again before falling to its forequarters, it appears to be dying. Looking up at us her eyes roll back in her head. We all watch in silence as life slips away from her, the merciless wheel of life grinding on. Dylan, resolute, picks up a small bag from the floor of his room. 'Guys, I'm going to the river, I need to make puja.'

Following him to the riverbank, Dylan removes a water bottle filled with kerosene and another set of poi from his bag. This is fire poi. Pouring kerosene over each ball, he ignites them and starts swinging them around. It's an impressive sight. They're going so fast it looks like he's in the centre of two rings of fire, like fiery comets orbiting him. The flaming poi make a roaring sound as they whiz past. They mesmerise. It feels respectful and it feels appropriate. The flippancy and casualness of our foray this morning has certainly been met with a resounding slap in the face.

It's long and solemn faces that greet each other the next morning at the Freedom Café. Nobody has really slept. After a light breakfast that none of us eat, triple chais and several joints for Dutch courage we decide to return to where Dylan and I saw the body. Not wanting to bring unnecessary attention to ourselves, we approach with stealth. Sure enough in the light of the new day there's no denying what we saw yesterday at the peak of the trip. A headless corpse buried face down in a shallow grave. It appears to have been underwater for some time, weighed down by the stones. It is definitely very suspicious and most likely murder. It's like living in a Sidney Sheldon novel. Frida is adamant. 'We have to do something, this is simply terrible, we have to go to the police and report it immediately.'

Dylan agrees. 'Yeah man, it's like we were drawn there guys. We all agreed that was the spot to hang yesterday. Maybe it's the universe wanting us to help this person.' Nimrod strokes his beard considering the situation. 'I agree something must be done, but I am not sure we should go to the police.'

Frida is almost indignant. 'Why ever not, we cannot shy away from this, it's up to us to make a stand.'

I butt in. 'I agree with both of you, we must report it. But, I do think it's wise not to go to the police in person. Man, you hear some horror stories about Indian police – they could try and pin the thing on us for all we know. We may be stuck here for months.'

We all agree to make an anonymous phone call to the local police. Frida volunteers for the job. Paranoia high, we take a vow of silence agreeing not to tell anybody, after all it's a small town and word can spread fast. The last thing we want is to inform the killer that we've uncovered his grizzly crime. It takes Frida several attempts, calling until she finds someone that speaks English. We spend the following couple of days hanging in vantage points from the other side of the river waiting to see when the police arrive, but they never come. Meeting again we discuss the situation in hushed undertones and whispers, agreeing the police obviously don't care. Then Frida has an idea. 'I'll go back and take photos of the body and the area. We can send them to the newspapers, if they print a story about it the police will have to get involved.'

Nimrod looks bewildered. 'Are you crazy? We cannot go back there. We have been there twice already. To go again would draw attention to us – people will start to recognise us. It is too dangerous.' We all agree it's too risky to return, although Frida is not happy about it. The next morning over breakfast, Frida has a mischievous look on her face as she places her camera on the table. 'I did it.'

Nimrod looks up from his shakshuka, fork laden with scrambled eggs suspended in the air. 'What?'

'I went down to the river this morning and took the photos, set up a false email address and sent them to two major newspapers.'

Dylan looks the most surprised. 'Wow, I didn't even realise you left this morning.' Frida pats Dylan on the head and says, 'Yes babe, when a job needs doing, get a woman to do it, I came back and you were still asleep my dear. Honestly, you lot are a bunch of old men.'

Nimrod, a little indignant at the remark, continues shovelling shakshuka into his mouth. 'Well it was very foolish to do that without telling anyone.'

Again we wait and watch, and again nothing happens. At a loss we decide to take counsel with Baba Krishna. Explaining to him the situation we ask him what he thinks we should do. Baba looks at us smiling with arms extended. 'This is the way of India my children. You let this be, there are many bodies in mother Ganga. It is not being your place to be looking at this.'

Frida interrupts, 'But Baba, this is a murder, something bad has happened.'

'Point is point child. My word's practical. It is important in the life. The season is finishing now, time to go. Better for you to go to Gangotri, and the source of Ganga, where she comes from the head of Shiva. It is a shanti shanti place. Making it for meditation. Many powerful sadhus live in the caves. They make magic there, healing the bodies and the mind. I am hoping there you be feeling better. Now let's be making puja, and making chillum for blessings.'

* * *

The next morning is overcast – a cool refreshing breeze blows from the north, from the mountains. A charge energises the air, it smells like rain. A new character sits at our adopted table at the Freedom Café. He has a wiry build, without an ounce of fat on him, frizzy brown hair, a pointy goatee beard and long waxed moustache. His fashion sense is straight out of the 70's, a flamboyant dresser. A yellow string sleeveless vest, flared jeans embroidered with Chinese dragons and Oms and white leather disco loafers. He looks like a flower power Peter Pan that never grew up. A road map of wrinkles, his face looks like leather. Appearing to be mid-forties he is actually in his mid-fifties. There is a small tattoo of a swallow on his hand, it's faded and blurred and may well be a prison tatt. He has a sparkle and a glint in his azure blue eyes. Already befriending Nimrod, who introduces me, he speaks in a thick Scottish accent. 'A pleasure to meet you, the name is Alexander, Alexander Templar.'

I raise an eyebrow as we shake hands. 'As in the Knights Templar?'

'Yes indeed the Knights Templar, a direct descendant no less.' Winking at me, he puffs out a smoke ring of charas from one of Nimrod's trademark joints of perfection. Momentarily hovering in a perfect circular formation above his head it dissipates only when Alexander snaps his fingers. 'Smoke and mirrors my friend, smoke and mirrors. Life is nothing more than an illusion.' Chuckling, he glances out over the river. 'Ah, a new day, a new one out of the box. A beautiful day to be alive.'

His charismatic way makes conversation flow with ease. We talk about religion, philosophy, quantum physics and about being present in the beautiful 'now'. And we talk about ourselves. A Scottish expat that moved to Amsterdam in the 70's he has a PhD in Biochemistry, practises Kundaline yoga and has studied shamanism around the world. A long-time veteran of the Indian circuit, on his ninth tour of duty, he calls India one of the great loves of his life. He speaks Hindi, sings mantras and quotes the Vedic scriptures to us. He's been travelling the world continually for the past decade. Only days earlier, he escaped Nepal's revolution and now waits for his young female travelling companion. Interested I enquire, 'So the border's open now?'

'Yes, has been for a bit over a week actually. I was just waiting for flights to begin again, decided to spoil myself and avoid the overland journey.'

Smoking chillums and Marlboro Reds like a trooper, Alexander tells us how he loves his psychedelics and refers to himself as a psychonaut, an astronaut of the inner universe. But he's a staunch non-drinker and ex-heroin addict. 'Terrible thing addiction and heroin is the mother of them all. It brings out the worst in everybody. It got me into real trouble, in more ways than one. Had a great little smuggling operation in Amsterdam I did. Hash from India inside transistor radios, cocaine from South America inside whiskey bottles. It was quite ingenious. That really was a golden age for smugglers back then. But those heydays have long gone now, much harder to pull it off now – especially with all this fuss about terrorists and the like. But it was the heroin that got me caught out, made me lazy and sloppy.'

Loving a good smuggling story, I can't resist. 'What happened?'

'Well, on a return trip from Thailand, I got busted at a Swiss airport with just ten grams of china white in the sole of my shoe. The dogs picked it up straight away. I was too stoned to stash it properly, thought it would be OK, but it most definitely was not. Pulled me three years in a Swiss jail that did.'

Smiling to himself Alexander lights another cigarette. 'Can't complain really though. It was very comfortable, more like a hotel than a jail. Kicked the junk, got healthy and read a lot. I even did my degree in there. A walk in the park really.'

Tapping the ash from the tip of his fag over the balcony rail, Alexander seems wistful as he gazes over the river. He holds the pause for a moment as he rolls the cigarette back and forth in his fingers. He has silver rings on all of them, inset with turquoise, emeralds and a Shiva's eye. 'The worst part was not getting busted, that was inevitable really. No the worst was how it happened. It was definitely my lowest ebb. I tried to use my stepdaughter as cover, trying to appear like a good middle-class family man. It was the shame of that, of dragging my loved ones through the mud that really hurt. After that, I vowed never to take heroin again, that was over ten years ago now and I have been as clean as a whistle ever since.' Turning back to us he smiles again. 'Yes, a beautiful day today indeed, a new one out of the box. *Sab kuch milega* (everything is possible).'

Nimrod leans over to me and whispers in my ear. 'Let's tell this guy, about you know what, I trust him. What do you think?'

I nod in agreement. We need another opinion, and he's been in India many times before. So we tell Alexander our story. He contemplates the information while tweaking the ends of his moustache. 'Yes, something needs to be said indeed, attention needs to be brought to this unfortunate soul's fate. Listen, I speak some Hindi, leave it with me, I'll go and speak to the police in person. I know how to deal with these people.'

While Nimrod and I wait for Alexander to return, Dylan and Frida arrive at the café. Both are carrying their backpacks. Dylan has to catch a bus in the afternoon down to Delhi to make his flight back to the US the following morning. 'Hey guys, its *chello* time. I've extended my flight so many times the airline is saying fly tomorrow or lose the ticket, so I gotta go.'

Frida, a little crestfallen, holds back the tears. 'Yeah and I've decided to head to Dharamsala, it will be much cooler there and I think I need a change of scenery, mountains, Buddhist temples, you know.'

Nimrod and I tell them we have informed Alexander and that he is at the police station right now. When he comes back, half an hour later, he's only half smiling as he sits cross-legged. 'Not good news I'm afraid people. You won't believe the officer's response when I told him that there was a headless corpse buried in a shallow grave. I even pointed to its location out of the station window.'

We're hanging off his every word. 'The bastard just leans back in his chair grinning without even looking out the bloody window, put his hands behind his head and says, *That side of the river is not our jurisdiction, so it is not our problem.*'

Frida responds, 'Well that does not surprise me, I'll write to the newspapers again in Dharamsala.' Alexander looks at her smiling. 'Chai, chillum, masala, *chello* Dharamsala!'

We all giggle as Alexander lightens the mood. Frida looks at Nimrod and me. 'What will you two do now?'

Nimrod answers, 'I am thinking of going to the Parvati Valley, there are many Israelis there and many parties and of course the best charas in all of India.'

Alexander again quips, 'Ah, Chai, chillum, chapatti, *chello* to Parvati'

191

Making us all laugh again, I smile and answer Frida. 'Dunno yet, but I'm considering taking the Baba's advice and heading to Gangotri and the source of the Ganges. I've followed the river from its mouth in the Bay of Bengal to here, so it'd be good to go all the way to its beginning.'

The sky blackens into ominous rain clouds. The earlier light breeze from the mountains picks up into a strong wind. It blows napkins and tablecloths about. The barometer drops rapidly as the temperature plummets. It gets dark. Thunder begins to rumble from the mountains up the river. Moments later there is a crack of lighting near the suspension bridge and large droplets of rain splat heavily into the dust. Alexander looks up at the sky. 'Lord Shiva is flexing his muscles. Be warned.'

By the time Dylan and Frida have to go the rain has set in – another ending, another goodbye. The rain continues steadily for the rest of the day, gutters overflow as water cascades from rooftops into rivulets down the road, washing away the dust and debris. It continues throughout the night until the early hours. By the time I rise and go to the Freedom Café it's cleared, pools of water steam in the hot morning sun. Yet the river has risen significantly overnight. The case of the headless body is again hidden under several metres of water, swallowed up by Ganga – her secret concealed once again.

When I enter the Freedom Café I see Nimrod and Alexander. They're both talking to two girls. Nimrod looks like he's turning on the charm chatting up a leggy, green-eyed, honey-coloured blonde. She couldn't be more than eighteen. The other girl, a bit older, maybe late twenties makes me start. She's petite, with long blonde dreadlocks snaking down her back, blue eyes and a perfect brown complexion. A tanned, fine-featured china doll. Wearing pink hot pants and a matching crop top, she's a hippy Barbie doll. I'm instantly infatuated. Despite her classic good looks there's a hardness in her face that reminds me of Merav and my ex-wife Stella. I ignore the flashing warning lights inside my brain as I sit down. Smiling at her as I chat to Alexander, I wonder if this is the girl he's been waiting for. Is this his girlfriend? Alexander notices I ogle in awe. 'Ah, Aaron, this is Dahlia, my dear this is Aaron.'

His tone is not as warm as yesterday, he seems a little reserved. Dahlia turns to me, forcing an unimpressed smile from the corner of her mouth – her eyes are half-closed as she gives me a little, uninterested wave. Declining my offer of a handshake, she leaves my hand awkwardly hanging in the breeze. In a flat voice she utters, 'Right, hi there.'

I endeavour to strike up a conversation with her, but she only gives short monotone answers without looking at me.

'So, where are you from?'

'Sweden.'

'Wow, Sweden, I bet it's cold there, good skiing yeah, do you ski?'

'No.'

'Really? Why not?'

'Hate the cold.'

'So that's why you're in India I guess?

'Maybe.'

I struggle. 'So is this your first time in India?'

'No.'

'Really, how many times before?'

'Once.'

'Cool, and you have just come from Nepal?'

'Yes.'

'Did you have to escape the revolution?'

'Yes.'

Nimrod introduces me to the other girl. Her name is Rianne from Holland. She has a spaced-out air about her that makes her come across as a bit ditsy, even stupid. She's a little knock-kneed and almost cross-eyed, but after chatting for a while I realise she is intelligent, just a little fucked up like the rest of us. She was also trapped in Nepal for the past month. All three of them were doing a visa run, like Frankie. Unusually, she speaks with a thick Israeli accent. Apparently she has a thing for them, adopting their phrases and intonation. Smiling at me, she enquires, '*Shalom, shalom. Sa baba?*'

I smile back. '*Wallah. Acha* (Hindi for good).'

She laughs. *'Acha.'* She talks about her travels. 'I was travelling with my Israeli boyfriend but he had to go back to Israel, so now I'm all alone.' She squeezes Nimrod's arm, he grins like a Cheshire cat. I steal him a knowing glance.

Alexander decides to go shopping, Rianne decides to join him, so consequently, Nimrod follows. This leaves me and Dahlia alone. I try and strike up another conversation, 'Your boyfriend Alexander is a fascinating guy, we talked for hours yesterday.'

Dahlia smirks. 'Alexander is not my boyfriend, we're just friends. We met in Gokarna six months ago and have been travelling together ever since. I don't have a boyfriend.'

'Oh.' Trying to contain my excitement, I'm positive this is the romance the astrologer predicted. Tying her dreadlocks in a plait she tosses it over her shoulder and appears a little more relaxed as she pulls a tobacco pouch from her bag. We spend the afternoon chatting. She tells me how she escaped from Nepal with five others, including Rianne. They hitched rides with some Israeli guys on Enfields, through back roads to the border. It sounded pretty hairy, escaping from terrorists, lifting the bikes over roadblocks and dodging rocket launcher craters in the road. Ironically the day after they crossed the border the revolution ended and the roads were open again. Dahlia gazes across the river. 'It's good to be back in India again, the smells, the sounds, everything. Feels like home.'

She seems a little melancholy, even sad when she explains how she went from dead-end job to dead-end job, like me, searching for something with meaning. Forcing a smile she turns to me again with closed eyes. 'That's why I came to India. To run away and join the circus.'

She starts singing a tune that sounds like a circus song or that of a merry-go-round at a fair, while moving her arms and upper body stiffly like a mannequin. We both laugh; it's kind of both tragic and amusing. Her self-deprecating humour seems an attempt to simultaneously deflect my scrutiny while being an admission of how lost she feels. Curious I enquire, 'What is it you really want from life, what do really you want to do?'

Turning away to the mountains, she considers my question. 'You know, it's strange, but nothing. I want to do nothing. I don't really feel like there is anything for me to do in this crazy fucking planet.'

I nod. 'Same, I'm still trying to work out what I am going to do when I grow up.'

'Yeah right.' She answers almost sarcastically, making out she is tough when really I suspect she is actually masking some deep underlying vulnerability.

I persevere. 'I don't know why I asked that, what do you want to do? Doing is overrated. I made up a proverb the other day about this very topic. We are called human beings not human doings, so just be, for that is all I am doing.'

She looks at me flatly. 'OK, that's nice, and how's that

working for you?'

She has just shot me down in flames. Dusting myself off, I try again. 'The road to Gangotri has just been opened; thinking of heading up there, to go to the very source of the Ganges. You guys should come. It's getting so hot here and everybody is leaving.'

'I don't think it's too hot, I like the heat and if everybody goes it's better. More quiet.' Shot down again, this time I stay down. We fall into silence.

The others return from their shopping spree. Alexander wears a belt made of silver, and has a rainbow coloured bag slung over his shoulder. He looks a little camp as he does a cat walk parade for us, walking up and back, fag hanging from his limply cast wrist. 'So what do you think? I think it's dashing.' Sitting down he presents the bag to us. 'Now this is amazing, this is a baba bag, it has nineteen secret compartments. It took the baba three months to make it.'

He starts rummaging through the bag trying to show us all the secret pockets, but he has forgotten where about six of them are. Dahlia shows disinterest. She gets up, brushing herself off. 'Think I will go for a swim or maybe a sleep, bye.' With that she leaves, before anybody has a chance to answer her.

Alexander looks at me, smiling. 'I see you have taken a bit of a shine to Dahlia, you would not be the first young man.' Laughing, he removes a chillum from one of the bag's secret compartments. 'Ah, there it is.' He passes it to Nimrod who is already making a mix; these two make a dangerous team.

Alexander looks at me and continues, 'She has a reputation of being a wee bit cold, she has been given the nickname of "Ice Queen" by many of her friends. But she has had a bit of a rough trot of late. She broke up with her boyfriend in

Gokarna some time back and I think she is still getting over it. She likes to keep to herself a lot. Quite a private person.'

I get the impression Alexander is actually in love with Dahlia and maybe feeling a little threatened by my intentions. He smiles at me but there is a prickly air about him. I try to quell his fears. 'I suggested both of you come up to Gangotri and hike to the source of the Ganges, but she didn't seem too keen. It's getting so hot here it's uncomfortable now, season's over, everybody's moving on.'

Alexander nods in agreement. 'It's true it is very unpleasant in this heat. Gangotri hey, sounds fascinating. I've never been up – I'd like to go. But here's the thing about Dahlia, if you want her to do anything you have to make her think it's her idea. She will never accept it otherwise, very stubborn. However if you let her suggest it as her idea, then she will do it happily and without complaint.'

Over the ensuing days I subtly try and coax Dahlia to suggest going up to Gangotri. But she defiantly struts about lapping up the heat while the rest of us melt.

* * *

Nimrod and Rianne hook up and leave together to go to the Parvati Valley, the Israeli stoner mecca. Again the group splinters into smaller units. Getting increasingly agitated, I really want to leave Rishikesh. Having been here for over six weeks I feel the need to move again but I'm hypnotised by Dahlia and I don't want to leave without her. Later that afternoon Nimrod and Rianne unexpectedly return to the Freedom Café. I'm surprised to see them again. 'Guys, what's going on? What happened to the Parvati Valley?'

Perspiring heavily, Nimrod's beard glistens with sweat.

'The bus to Parvati is cancelled. But there is one to Gangotri at 4:30am tomorrow morning, let's do it, let's all go as a group, keep the family together.'

At that moment, right on cue, Dahlia swans into the Freedom Café. Looking fantastic as usual, airing herself with a Chinese fan she wears a different skimpy pink outfit, sunglasses and a plastic tennis sun visor. She looks like she has just stepped off Venice Beach L.A., rather than from bathing in the Ganges. She only seems to wear pink. 'I've been thinking, it's getting too hot here, why don't we all go to Gangotri, what do you think?'

Nimrod, Rianne, Alexander and I all exchanges glances and chorus, 'Yes.'

'OK right then.' Spinning on her heels she exits the café. Breathing a sigh of relief, we all spend the rest of the day relaxing, as tomorrow will be nothing short of gruelling. Fifteen hours on a bone shaking public bus. I email Frankie.

Frankie,
Where's Wally!!! What are you doin' still in
Nepal? I know the border opened about a week ago,
coz I met some people here who got out. It's too
hot in Rishi now dude, I'm heading north soon.
The season's over here, everyone's chello...
A.

Frankie actually replies.

Dragon,
Sorry dude. I lied to you, I met a Russian girl
and she's been playing nurse for me, what can I
say, Kobra strikes again. But she will leave in

a day or so now, so I'll be coming soon,
Kobra

I meet Baba Krishna as I walk to the Freedom Café. 'Ah my child, it is time you are leaving.' Smiling softly, he removes a shell necklace from around his neck and places it over my head while chanting.

'Om Namah Shivaya
Om Namah Shivaya
Om Namah Shivaya.'

Holding both of my hands he looks me in the eye. 'For making blessings on your journey. Be respectful of Shiva on your path child.' He pats my shoulder as he shuffles off into the night.

At the café there is much laughter and talking over dinner. At one point Alexander calls for everyone's attention. 'Sorry to interrupt the mirth and merriment of our little gathering, but I feel obligated to inform you all of something serious. Since we are all travelling together, you should all know that I'm HIV positive, just in case anything should happen. I'm not sick, far from it. I actually cured myself with a wonderful shamanic substance in a sacred ritual in South America, but that's another story for a different day. So, how about a chillum blessing beautiful rainbow people? *Sab kuch milega.'*

But what could possibly happen? Like Ian used to say, *we're on vacation, nothing bad happens on vacation.*

CHAPTER 10

Stairway to Heaven

Still dark when we creep out of the sleeping streets of Laxman Jhula, there's no sign of the approaching dawn. Crossing the suspension bridge in single file, the air is cool and still. Dahlia leads the party – after all it was 'her' idea to go. Stopping halfway across she squats down and picks something up. Turning to me with a puzzled look she holds a card in her fingers; it's the ace of spades.

'Lucky me.' She tilts her head, smiling cheekily, and is being slightly sarcastic. Wrapped in a pink poncho, her blonde dreadlocks tied back in a rough ponytail, I consider kissing her right there on the bridge over the Ganges, but I know she'd never let me. I remember the ace of spades I found during the festival of colours in Kolkata and tossed into the river. As Dahlia examines the card, I step closer to her. 'Maybe you should throw it in the river, like a sacrificial offering to Mother Ganga, kinda like a blessing for our journey?'

Glancing up at me, she half smiles. 'Yeah, or maybe I could keep it.'

She slips the card into the back pocket of her jeans. 'Now you aren't the only one with an ace up your sleeve.'

Behind me Rianne complains in her adopted Israeli accent, 'Why like this? Lets *chello*.'

Nimrod joins in, 'We will miss the bus.'

Crossing the river we wind up the narrow stairs between the gem dealers, where six weeks earlier Victor and I had arrived. Waiting for us at the top of the hill is our Ambassador taxi. Nimrod enquires, 'Black Cobra?'

The tiny driver nods, his skin so dark he could almost be African. Yesterday the taxiwallah told us with great reverence that we would be driven to the bus by the Black Cobra. Only India can make the simplest and most mundane of tasks feel mysterious and auspicious. All squeezing into the car, our bags are lashed onto the roof. Then deftly driving through the backstreets of Rishikesh like a formula one driver, the Black Cobra gets us to the bus terminal in good time.

Buying our tickets as dawn's first light breaks the horizon – we have enough time for a little contemplation and for a cup of hot chai. Smiling, Alexander lights another cigarette. Breathing out white smoke and looking up into the sky, he adjusts the silver rings on his fingers. He speaks in his Scottish accent, thick as treacle, 'Ah. Another one out of the box.'

Nimrod sips on tea from behind his gold-rimmed Elvis glasses. 'Sab kuch milega.'

Rianne looks at us all, her hands squeezed into her tight, dirty blue jean pockets, raising her shoulders. 'Sa baba?'

Smiling to myself I think what a funny thing it is to travel, the people you end up making your family. Grinning to Rianne, I tip my truckers cap. 'Acha.'

I sit down on my backpack, take off my shoe and carefully remove my sock. A small cut on the heel of my foot is sore and inflamed. Stupidly, I caught it on the corner of the screen door of my room a few days earlier. It's just a graze but it isn't healing. Applying a fresh cast, I gingerly put my sock and shoe back on. As the night's shadows recede we board our bus and are pretty much the only tourists. Crunching through gears, the bus lurches off. Creeping upwards, we wind around hairpin bends on a road that clings to the sides of steep hills. Below us Rishikesh falls away. The shimmer and haze of the new day floods the valley with colour and warms up the bus.

By morning tea we've clawed our way to the top of the Himalayan foothills and begin to ramble along the ridge-top. Ganga snakes along beside us in the valley far below, shimmering emerald in the morning sun. Having only been on the bus a few hours, my body already aches. The wooden plank seat has no padding and each bump in the road jars my tailbone and spine. At least I have a seat as many of our Indian travelling companions stand without complaint. It's going to be a long day. Dahlia grimaces, holding her stomach. I enquire the obvious, 'Are you OK?'

'Yeah, just been having a stomach problem, do you have any Imodium?'

I turn round to Nimrod and Rianne. 'You guys got anything for Delhi Belly?'

They both shrug and shake their heads. From the seat behind them a girl, early twenties with a sandy-blonde bob cut, leans forward holding a small foil blister pack. Smiling a big toothy grin, she interjects in a Canadian accent, 'Hey there, I have some Imodium.'

Our eyes meet for a moment. 'Thanks.'

We stop for lunch in Uttarkashi, a small but sprawling city of tumbledown buildings and dirt roads. After a simple meal of thali, I'm standing at the front of the bus picking out pieces of meat from my teeth with a toothpick. The Canadian girl comes up and introduces herself. Mary is dressed in a dowdy green pullover and brown cotton slacks – sensible travelling clothes. Plain lass with a nice smile, she's an outdoorsy, clean-cut, girl next door type. My first impression of her is that she is a bit of a 'goodie two shoes' and wet behind the ears. Making polite conversation, I enquire, 'So why ya come to India?'

'Oh you know, thought I'd try and find myself.'

A wry smile spreads across her face – she's being ironic. I chuckle. 'Ah, that old chestnut, if you do manage to find yourself, let me know, maybe I'll find me there too.'

Continuing to chat until it's time to leave, it turns out my original evaluation is wrong. At twenty-two she's already a veteran traveller, having started at fifteen on a foreign exchange scholarship to France. She's travelled for five years throughout Australia, Europe, Latin America and now Asia. She has also managed to squeeze in an Arts degree in that time. As the bus pulls out of town it's me that feels wet behind the ears.

Continuing to follow the sparkling Ganges in the valley below, we pass through small derelict villages, fields of wild hemp and throngs of laughing, waving children. In the distance the ominous, magnificent and mighty Himalaya begin to grow out of the horizon. By afternoon the air has a chill as our elevation rises, inching ever closer to the sky. The terrain either side of the road becomes steep, rocky and rugged. The vegetation is sparse and alpine, with small groves of beech trees interspersed with the occasional patch of snow. Creeks and brooks cascade crystal-clear water over rocks down into the Ganges. Ganga is different here, tumbling downstream in froth and foam, swirling and spinning in rapids over water-polished boulders. We all dig warmer clothing out of our packs as the day's sun sinks behind the mountains. The shadows elongate, sucking all warmth from the air. As the last of the afternoon's light disappears, the banquet of colours turn to tones of blue, then purple and finally black.

By the time we reach Gangotri our breath is short and strained due to the thin, high altitude air. A remote village,

Gangotri's only function is to serve pilgrims that come here every year to pay homage to the Bhagirathi river, the Ganges' principal tributary that is considered its source. It has the appearance of a chocolate box painting of Swiss villas. Legend has it that Shiva sat here and let Ganga spring forth from his head to the valley below.

Clambering off the bus, stiff and aching, we're inundated by hotelwallahs each desperate to convince us their accommodation is better than the next. Mary approaches me and appears a little apprehensive. 'So, hi again. Do you guys know of a good place to stay around here?'

'Haven't a clue, but if you want you can hang with us.'

'Hmm. That would be cool, maybe I will. If you guys don't mind?'

Alexander raising both hands, radiates a warm smile. 'Of course my dear, the more the merrier. We are growing into quite an interesting entourage it seems.'

We all huff and puff up into the village and check into a guesthouse, sharing a large room with enough beds for all of us. As night falls the temperature drops away quickly; it's freezing cold. I unpack my sleeping bag for the first time since leaving Australia. It smells a bit stale, but I'll be grateful I brought it tonight. As we prepare for bed Alexander hangs a large brass Om above the door, lights some incense and sings a mantra.

* * *

Sleeping in late, I'm the last to rise. Outside the sun shines, but it's still cold in the shadows. Nimrod, Rianne and Alexander have gone for breakfast. Dahlia and Mary sit quietly on a large balcony area. Mary wears a sensible denim sun hat and reads a Himalayan hiking guidebook. Dahlia, wrapped in her pink poncho, smokes a cigarette and gazes wistfully up into the mountains. The view from our balcony, previously shielded by the cover of darkness, now reveals a spectacular vista. Huge white boulders shoulder the rumbling Bhagirathi river that tumbles past us. When I look to the rocky escarpment below I notice something unusual. There are indentations in the boulders that form small rock pools. However they're filled not with water but with a mysterious red liquid. From where I stand they appear as pools of blood. It sends a chill down my spine. I choose not mention it as rubbing my hands together I ask, 'You girls had any brekkie? I'm starving, must be all this fresh mountain air.'

We hop from café to café, as Dahlia picks over the menu. She wants yoghurt and muesli with a fresh fruit salad. I start to realise that as well as having a delicate stomach she's also a fussy eater, like some pedigree Siamese cat. Eventually we find an establishment worthy of her approval. When the caféwallah is asked if he does fruit salad, he grins and replies, *'Milega'* (Possible).

'What about muesli?'

'Milega.'

'Yoghurt?'

'Milega.'

Looks promising, in fact everything we ask for gets the same response, 'Milega.'

From then on we christen his establishment the *Sab Kuch Milega* café (the everything is possible café).

After eating our first satisfactory meal in twenty-four hours, we wander around Gangotri. We cross a small bridge that spans the river. Here the water is icy cold and moves quickly, churning and gushing over rocks, spraying mist into the air. Beneath us, the river's power is condensed by a constricted passage. Hypnotised by the swirling aqua-green water, we watch a red sari spinning and turning in the current, temporarily caught in an eddy below us, before it is sucked under. Gazing down the river that falls steeply away over large rocks shouldered by the village, I can see why the place is regarded as a divine point of pilgrimage.

We continue in mute awe. It's a beautiful day. We reach the point where a small tributary converges with the Bhagirathi river. Dividing the tributaries is a small hill some ten metres high. There's a narrow set of stairs that climb the slope. At the top of the stairs is a stone wall with an old wooden door in its centre. Near the base of the stairs an old man squats, wrapped in a grey woollen blanket. Smoking a pipe, he silently nods hello to us. The stairway and the secret doorway tantalise us, and with curiosity we ascend. The door has Hindu scripture painted across it in red. My heart thumps with anticipation as I twist the rusty door handle and push, but nothing happens. Then Dahlia reaches for the handle. 'Let me try.'

Turning, she pushes, giving it a little nudge with her shoulder. The door creaks open revealing a small clearing in the centre of which stands a banyan tree. Under its canopy is a red effigy standing maybe a metre high. Flickering candles placed around its feet dance light across its face. Turning back to the old man at the base of the stairs, I shrug my shoulders, 'What is this Ji?'

Smiling, the old man removes his pipe and cackles, 'Vishnu, temple to Vishnu. It is stairs to Vishnu.'

I look at Dahlia and Mary. 'Stairway to heaven hey?'

Dahlia, with her hands on her hips says, 'Right then.'

With that she steps through the opening and walks over to the centre of the clearing. Turning back to us, 'You guys coming in or what?'

I smile. 'Think I'll pass thanks, not quite ready to pass through the pearly gates just yet.'

Mary giggles. 'Hmm, me too. Too much for a mere mortal like myself, especially before lunch.'

Deadpan and determined not to give us the satisfaction of laughing, Dahlia looks past us and down to the old man. 'So what now, what happens now?'

The old man rocks back and forth smiling. Stopping he points up to Dahlia, framed by the doorway. 'You. You go up.'

He then points up to the sky directly above his head. 'You go up now, to Vishnu.'

Laughing, he rocks back and forth again. We're silent – it doesn't seem so funny anymore.

* * *

Back at our hotel the mid-morning sun has stretched across our balcony and it's bright and warm. Warm enough to strip down to T-shirts and soak up some high altitude rays. Nimrod and Rianne are sprawled out across the floor, gazing up at the sky. Alexander sits on a wooden chair, leaning heavily on the railing, his breath strained and his white embroidery cotton shirt dark with perspiration. His eyes are bloodshot. 'Damn altitude, makes everything an effort, feel like I've just run a bloody marathon.'

He doesn't look so good. Originally we planned to start the two-day trek up to Gaumukh in the morning. Gaumukh, the glacial source of the Bhagirathi river is 1000 metres higher. However, deciding an extra day to acclimatise would be prudent, we laze in the sun for the remainder of the day. Slowly Dahlia's icy demeanour begins to thaw. In the evening over dinner at the Sab Kuch Milega café, I ask Alexander about his shamanic experience in South America that apparently cured him of HIV.

Realising he has a captive audience, Alexander pushes away his plate, lights a cigarette, leans back in his chair and starts twirling the end of his moustache. 'Ah, yes. An intriguing tale it is indeed. Let me start by firstly talking about the concept of disease. In the West we're obsessed with focusing on the detail of an illness. The problem is we forget to look at the bigger picture, the reason behind the malady. However, here in the East and in other far-flung cultures around the globe, illness is approached more holistically. There is a clue to this in the etymology of the very word *disease*. Break the word down, *dis*, meaning absence or opposite of, and *ease*, meaning freedom from concern and anxiety. So to cure a *dis*-ease the application of western medicine is only addressing the symptom and not the underlying root cause. It's considered by many alternative cultures that the actual problem is one of spiritual imbalance.

'This was certainly the case in my situation. My *dis*-ease was the result of years of heroin abuse, self-destruction and perpetuating unhappiness through my contraband distribution. You could say my contracting HIV was a major spiritual shakedown. Not that I thought that at first though. No, in the beginning I turned to conventional western medicine. But it didn't help and my condition deteriorated, I was dying. Desperate, I sought more obscure paths, which lead me to the depths of the Amazon jungle in Brazil. I was seeking a substance called Ayahuasca, which means vine of the dead and has been used for thousands of years by Indian shamans.

'It's concocted by the mixing of the vine of one plant with the leaf of another. The psychoactive ingredient is DMT or

208

dimethyltryptamine – a psychedelic chemical similar to the neurotransmitter, serotonin. DMT is also produced naturally by the body, at birth and at death. Ingesting it creates a cathartic and purgatory experience. It opens your crown and third eye chakras, illuminating you to the divine. It is like dying and being reborn.'

Nimrod finishes rolling a joint, lighting it, he passes it to Alexander, 'So what happens when you drink this stuff?'

Alexander switches his cigarette for the joint and draws in a lungful. 'Ah. The effect is different for everyone – some people feel nothing, some feel like they meet God, some are nauseous and some break down and cry. If you're very lucky, the Queen of the Forest will appear before you, the apparition of Mother Nature herself. The first time I drank it I was sick for hours, all very purgatory. Visions and flashbacks of my life, I wept like a baby. In the second ceremony my spirit was lifted into the cosmos where I flew through the galaxies. Then the third time I explored the inner universe, adrift in a glory of colour until I finally appeared before the Queen of the Forest. I was staring at a tree and she just stepped out of it. She touched my forehead.

'After that my health rapidly improved. I stopped taking my medication, and to the amazement of my doctors back home, I made a complete recovery. Although I'm still HIV positive, my immune system today is fighting fit. Never felt better. I've since heard of another remote tribe of Indians in the Amazon that has a ritual of licking the back of a certain species of frog that is supposed to strengthen the immune system. I'm very interested to investigate this further in my psychoactive explorations in the near future.'

Sharing the story of my own rites of passage, when I met my spirit guide, the cockatoo, I talk of the lucid dream where

I flew through the valleys of my childhood with my old friend.

The conversation steers towards the importance of dreams and signs provided by nature in the form of animals. Alexander asks me, 'The aborigines in Australia, they think animals are symbolic of the spirit world, the Dreamtime I think they call it. They believe in a mythical beast called the Rainbow Serpent do they not?'

'Yeah, the Rainbow Serpent is meant to live in the land, it's kinda the land itself.'

Stroking his moustache, Alexander continues, 'Interesting. The mythological significance of serpents seems to reoccur in many ancient cultures. The Rainbow Serpent also occurs in some African and Amazonian Indian cultures too you know. A very powerful symbol is the snake. All over the world in ancient history there are mythologies of snakes. From Babylon and Egypt, to the pagan religions of the Celts, from the Greeks, Romans, Hebrews to all across Asia, not to mention the Americas.'

Alexander turns to Dahlia who avoids eye contact while twisting a dreadlock with her fingers. 'Even your neighbours, the Vikings believed a giant serpent circled the entire earth under the sea.' He then looks at Nimrod. 'The Hebrews also believed in Leviathan, another monster from the deep.'

Alexander passes me the joint and continues, 'Christians, Buddhists, Muslims, Hindus, Confucians and Taoists all have myths regarding snakes. Many saw snakes as representative of the underworld, as well as birth and death, the sun and the moon. Here in India snakes have many meanings. Vishnu, the god of protection, sleeps on the coils of a giant serpent *Ananta*, who has 1000 hooded heads. Ananta represents the cosmic ocean, the divine sleep and the divine awakening. The snakes often depicted wrapped around Shiva's neck, however, have a different meaning. They represent death itself.'

There's a silence. Dahlia who has been quiet for some time, tearing shreds off her paper napkin, looks up. 'I hate snakes. I have never seen one, like a real snake, but I have had nightmares about snakes. I hate them.'

An uneasy tension falls over the group. Mary attempts to lighten the mood, smiling at Dahlia. '*Vakta ute för ormen*, that's Swedish for watch out for snakes isn't it? Funny, it's the only words I know in Swedish. I don't know why I know that.'

* * *

During breakfast the following morning at the Sab Kuch Milega café, we watch the first of the season's pilgrims bathe themselves in the freezing cold river. Nimrod addresses the group with a mouthful of muesli, pointing at us with his spoon. 'We have a serious problem people.'

Slurping my morning chai, 'What's wrong Ji?'

Nimrod raises his eyebrows. 'We are almost out of charas. We must find supplies before leaving tomorrow.'

After breakfast Nimrod and I try to score. We begin by hanging with a group of sadhus sitting in the street, smoking chillums and exchanging spiritual anecdotes. A sadhu dressed in black robes, introducing himself as the Black Baba, leads us to a small encampment just outside the village. He tells us we must wait for another baba to arrive. A bit over an hour later a new baba arrives. He hobbles along with a crutch and only has one leg. He has a long beard, dreadlocks and an intense gaze that makes us feel like he's staring straight into our souls; he does have a nice smile though. Black Baba introduces him as 'Mr. Baba Santos'.

He's a man of few words, well, no words in fact. Black Baba

does all the talking. Baba Santos just stares at us unnervingly, with his nice smile. His charas is the best quality we have yet smoked in India, so after I agree to buy a *tolla* (ten grams), I let Nimrod work his Israeli magic and secure us the best possible price. Looking at Baba Santos's appearance in closer detail, I notice he wears a bone necklace of small carvings, hundreds of miniature skulls. I saw similar designs in Rishikesh carved from yak bones. Making idle conversation as I pass him the chillum, 'Nice necklace, it's made from yak bone yeah?'

Smiling at me, while staring deep into my soul, Baba Santos takes the chillum and holds onto my hand. He emits the only words I ever hear him say, 'No, it human bone.'

I shudder. Black Baba leans towards me. 'Mr. Baba Santos is Aghori baba.'

A cold chill runs down the back of my spine as I recall Jimmy the Ambassador of the Sunrise's definition of Aghori sadhus back in Varanasi. The babas that eat human flesh, who live in graveyards and speak to demons and spirits. Looking down at Baba Santos's missing leg I wonder if he chewed it off in hunger, maybe there is a shortage of corpses in the area. With that we leave Santos, the one legged Aghori baba with the nice smile, and head back to the Sab Kuch Milega café where we reconvene with the others for dinner. Alexander returns from a day of strolling; he's rosy cheeked and now looks well acclimatised. 'Ah, I had the most amazing day. I walked up into the hills and met a sadhu who lived in a cave. We talked all afternoon. He told me that this place is very powerful and that Shiva watches everything. He said we must have reverence for everything we do here, otherwise he can be merciless in his recrimination.'

During dinner a young Spanish guy, Rodriguez, joins us – in his mid to late twenties, he's tall and gangly, with short-cropped black hair and a patchy, baby fluff beard. A nurse from Madrid, he's on his way to Australia to work for one year and this is his first time out of Europe. He wears mismatched hiking clothes and a South American-styled rainbow-coloured beanie with a pom-pom on the end. He stares at Dahlia. 'Are you people going to go to de source tomorrow?'

Bristling, I sense competition for Dahlia's limited attention. Alexander smiles, 'Why, yes we are, would you care to join the family? Come sit, eat, drink, smoke and be merry.'

Of course, he accepts the invitation. Alexander pats him on the shoulder and proclaims loudly, 'So it is done, a party of seven, very auspicious number is seven. Let us raise our chais in cheers rainbow people, for tomorrow begins a great adventure of the highest spiritual calibre.'

CHAPTER 11

Passing the Point of No Return

Rising early the next morning, there's a bite in the air. Removing the bandage from my injured foot reveals an angry sore – it's not healing and looks infected. Dousing it in iodine I wrap it up in a new bandage donated to me by Mary. She dotes on me a little and I enjoy the first attention I've had from a girl in some time. Wincing, I put on my shoe. We meet Rodriguez at the Sab Kuch Milega café – grinning, he's still wearing the ridiculous multicoloured beanie. All of us stamp our feet, rub our arms and blow warm air into our palms. The party of seven leaves with trepidation, heading out of Gangotri and begins the steep ascent up a set of stairs to the gravel mountain path. Dahlia is the last one to complete the climb. Blushing and panting she slumps down onto a rock. 'I'm not sure I can do this.'

I look at her. 'Well this is your last chance to turn back, after this it's an eight hour walk to the Bhojbasa ashram where we'll sleep tonight. There is no other civilisation up there.'

She picks herself up and brushes herself down. 'Right then.'

She marches off in front of the group, leading the way and setting a brisk pace. The rest of us all look at each other; Alexander raises one eyebrow. 'Right then it is!'

The steady uphill climb, following the course of the river soon stifles all conversation as we struggle to breathe. The scarcity of the oxygen in the air makes my mouth dry and breath rasp the back of my throat. We fall into single file and ultimately walk alone, separated by our varying levels of fitness. Dahlia adamantly maintains a healthy lead while Alexander brings up the rear. I'm a bit concerned at Alexander's ability to complete the hike, being the oldest and in the worst physical condition. Also, he is hardly appropriately dressed. White flared slacks and matching top with embroidered designs, white-leather disco loafers and a white feather woven into his hair. A bamboo cane walking stick completes his dapper appearance. Freshly waxed moustache and always smoking a cigarette with a defined elegance, he certainly has style but it's nowhere near as practical as the hiking boots and denim the rest of us wear.

As we slowly ascend the narrow path the peak of Shivling mountain comes into view. It's the mountain that Gaumukh's glacier emerges from. Shivling is shouldered by two other mountain peaks that all loom higher with each passing hour. These triple peaks represent the three spikes of Shiva's trident. Passing through a forested area of alpine beech and pine trees, the air here is cool and sweet – its late morning now. Dahlia, Mary and Rodriguez all sit at a small chai stand quietly sipping on cups of the wallah's brew. Four tired doe-eyed donkeys look up at me from their breakfast of alpine thicket. They're tethered together and straddled with ornate saddles. They represent the only form of transport for the wealthy pilgrims unable or unwilling to make the journey under their own steam. I join our party. Sitting behind us is a rich Indian family from Delhi, all smiling and jovial and of rotund proportions, clad in bright blue, pink and yellow silk saris; they are obviously the donkeys' cargo. Within twenty minutes, Rianne, Nimrod and finally Alexander join us. Alexander removes his chillum pipe from his rainbow-coloured many-pocketed sadhu bag. 'Chai chillum then *chello?*'

Nimrod mixes, packs and ignites, Alexander recites the smoking mantra and the chillum is passed around. Dahlia shakes her head in refusal. 'No. I'm not smoking here. Actually, I'm not sure if I am smoking at all anymore.'

With that she stands up, brushes herself off and again takes the lead. Reluctantly the rest of us stand and trudge along behind her. The midday sun is hot and as we edge higher in altitude the landscape becomes increasingly barren. The patches of alpine forest give way to the occasional stunted shrub until there is nothing but boulders and dirt. The path thins to no more than a goat track only a couple of feet wide. The hills grow steeper, nothing protects us from slipping and falling to the rocky ravines far below. In places, the loose earth path has disintegrated and eroded away. The edges crumble and fall down the near vertical drop under each footstep. Small landslides have taken out sections of the path completely. Clinging to the dirt sides we scramble onwards and upwards. Occasionally orange-robed smiling sadhus, returning from Gaumukh, carefully shuffle past each of us.

The valley through which we climb is shouldered by the mountains of the Himalaya. Standing beneath them now it's easy to see why they are revered as gods. Towering high above us, their snowy peaks knife through the clouds. Outlines so sharp against the blue sky they almost look fake, like two-dimensional board cutouts from some grandiose Bollywood film set. By the afternoon, I'm parched, having drunk all my water hours earlier. Grateful when the path crosses a mountain brook, I gulp mouthfuls of the icy water, quenching my thirst. So cold it numbs my fingers. By late afternoon, the shadows draw into dusk and I'm relieved to see Bhojbasa ashram from the crest of yet another incline. Although I'm still warm, the sweat on my back starts to chill and I can see that before too long the elements out here will be harsh and unforgiving. One by one the rest of our party reaches Bhojbasa, each falling into the dust exhausted.

The ashram is simple and we sit on a cold concrete floor with the sadhus also on pilgrimage. We all join in singing mantras before eating dhal and rice with our hands. After dinner we watch the remaining light give way to night. The three mountain peaks towering over Gaumukh transform through varying hues of purple then blue to an ominous dark. Standing next to Dahlia, as the air chills, I sense she's beginning to warm to me. Staring up at the mountain I murmur, 'Wow, it's amazing huh, feels so powerful.'

Without looking at me Dahlia responds, 'It looks scary to me.'

'Yeah, it looks like death.'

I don't know why I say that – Dahlia turns to me. 'Don't say that, it scares me.'

'Sorry.'

I feel stupid for saying something so mindless. Dahlia looks troubled. 'You know what you were saying yesterday about animals being signs, do you believe that's true?'

'Yeah, it's like ancient knowledge we've somehow lost along the way, but yeah I believe seeing animals can represent some sort of message.'

'And snakes, all that stuff Alexander was saying about snakes, he speaks some rubbish sometimes.'

'Well it's true that snakes are revered in heaps of cultures. Why?'

Dahlia afraid now, stares at the ground, kicking stones with her feet. 'I saw a snake today. It slithered across the path. It was quick but it was definitely a snake. I've never seen a snake before. Is it a sign? It's a bad sign isn't it?'

Back-pedalling I stammer a response. 'Well not necessarily, not all animals have to be a sign, and anyway snakes can be a good omen, all depends on your perspective.'

Dahlia is quiet. I'm not sure I've quelled her fears. Nearby a group of sadhus ignite a pile of rubbish into a bonfire to abate the biting cold; they laugh and banter as noxious smoke permeates the crisp air. Tired, we all retire early in preparation for the big day ahead. Our sleeping area consists of a pile of mattresses on the floor. All seven of us squeeze onto them. I'm pleased Dahlia chooses to lie next to me. Falling asleep with the scent of patchouli oil from her dreadlocks, I'm happy.

* * *

Rising at first light, we're all quiet as we finish our chai and leave. It's four more hours to Gaumukh and then we have to come back here before nightfall, as there is nowhere to stay up there. It's the seventh of May at seven am as seven people march out of Bhojbasa ashram to begin the final ascent to arguably the most holy place in all of India. Again Dahlia takes the lead, walking faster than yesterday; she has a sense of urgency.

The terrain transforms again as the path pulls away from the river. We climb over piles of boulders, long since discarded by the receding glacier. The larger ones are jagged and splintered from the ice while the smaller ones have been polished smooth by the glacier's abrasion. These moraines, or rivers of rock, are the aftermath of the glacier's retreat into the bosom of the mountains. Scientists say that in another few years there will be nothing left of Gaumukh's glacier, because of greenhouse warming. Sadhus say that Shiva's mightily pissed at this and retribution will be severe.

It's hard going – only a quarter of the distance we covered yesterday, but climbing another 500 metres. Reaching a small plateau, the river is nowhere in sight but is easily defined by its roar. The sound of the water resonates as a rumble. It breathes and growls like a sleeping dragon. The terrain looks alien, like the surface of the moon. Dahlia sits at the final chai stand before ground zero – in time the rest of the party arrives. It's surreal, like the restaurant at the end of the universe out of *The Hitchhikers Guide to the Galaxy*. Sitting there, all seven of us fall into a deep philosophical discussion as Nimrod prepares one last chillum.

Alexander contemplates. 'Every day we're alive is really a blessing, take it from me, I came close enough to death to learn to appreciate each and every beautiful day.'

Rianne smiles. 'It's a new one out of the box right?'

'Exactly.'

Rodriguez pipes up, pointing a finger in the air like an exclamation mark. 'Seize de day.'

Passing the chillum to me, Nimrod lights it. 'Yes after being made to fight in a war I didn't believe in I've also learnt to enjoy every moment. I make sure to watch every sunset like it is my last.'

Rianne interrupts, 'Yeah we know, and never eat standing up, never run when you can walk, and um …'

I cut in, 'Never sleep in a tent right.'

Nimrod nods his head and we all laugh. I pass the pipe to Dahlia, she shakes her head. 'No, I'm giving up smoking.'

Raising an eyebrow I pass it to Rianne instead. I continue, 'Life's fleeting, it's over in a heartbeat, no point obsessing about the future or regretting the past at the expense of the *now* guys. The *now*, this split second is all there really is. We have to learn to die to each passing moment to let go and always be in the present. Here and now, everything else is an illusion.'

Alexander beams. 'Exactly, smoke and mirrors.'

Mary looks thoughtful. 'Hmm. Yeah. My, my – that is interesting. I think it's why I keep travelling and delaying going back to Canada. Mum wants me to do a law degree. She's always saying it's time for me to knuckle down and plan my future. But I'm more interested in making jewellry and studying shamanic practices and stuff. That's what I love about travelling I guess, always experiencing new things and meeting cool people.'

Alexander scoffs, 'Planning for the future? Poppycock! You just keep doing your own thing my girl, don't let mother bully you. Sounds to me like she needs a good dose of LSD to sort her out, and if I hear you've succumbed to her will when you return, and join the legions of the other soulless planet-raping corporate fuckers, be warned, I'll be forced to send in the psychonauts to rescue you from yourself.'

We all laugh. I imagine Alexander flying into rural Canada in a chopper painted with flowers, like some hippy SWAT team, dropping love bombs of acid in the reservoirs. The Doors would be playing, like some bizarre scene out of *Apocalypse Now*.

Dahlia stands up. 'Basically what we're all saying is that life is too short and you never know when you are going to die. So you had better make the most of it and just do whatever you want, whatever makes you happy. Never put off anything you want from life, when you can do it now.'

Alexander raises his chai glass. 'Touché my dear.'

Dahlia picks up her bag. 'OK then, I'm going, now. I'm going to the source.'

Spinning on her heels she marches defiantly down the track. Nimrod calls out, 'Hey, what's the hurry, it's not like you have an appointment or something. We are on top of a mountain.'

She doesn't respond. Getting up I follow. Dahlia walks quickly and gets ahead of me, disappearing over a mound of boulders. By the time I reach the crest of the same moraine, I can see her below. Kneeling in a tiny open-air temple to Shiva, she prays. It strikes me as a little strange and for some reason I'm surprised to see her paying homage so seriously. For the first time in four hours, the river is in view. I'm shocked. I thought it would be a quaint, clear, babbling brook, surrounded by mountain flowers. It is nothing of the sort. Flowing fiercely, the water is black with sediment, angry, turbulent, hissing and foaming, like lava spewing from the surface of Mars. A premonition of death fills my mind.

Rumbling like thunder, the river is ungodly and deafening. The sound of water smashing against rock washes out all other sound, like white noise on a television. The awesome destructive power of Shiva and his tempestuous wife Ganga is all apparent now. Sliding down the loose stone slope, I catch up with Dahlia as she stands up and heads along the track again. I quickly squat in front of the Shiva temple, touching my forehead before running to join her at her side. We walk in silence up to the top of another mound, and there it is, no more than a hundred metres further up the river in front of us. The glacier, the source of the Ganges, a formidable wall of ice some thirty metres high and forty metres wide, with black angry water churning out from its base. The birth of the river, it's called the 'cow's mouth' as it emerges from the mountain. The glacier, a dirty grey colour, at first it looks like crags of stone, but then we realise it's a cliff face of ice. It is magnificent and terrifying all at the same time.

Sliding down the slope, loose scree falls with us as we

reach the base of the moraine and a thin mudflat that follows the river's edge, which Dahlia continues along towards the base of the glacier. It's easier going than scrambling over the moraine ridge that shoulders the river. I'm about to follow but something catches my eye in the rubble at my feet. Glistening in the morning sun, I bend down and pick up a stone, a small piece of white quartz that's perfectly shaped like the map of India.

Transfixed by the stone I don't even notice Mary skid down the slope and walk past me, following Dahlia. By the time I look up, Dahlia is some hundred metres in front, standing on a large boulder that juts out into the river. The end of the road, she's as close as is possible to the glacier, almost directly beneath it. She's dwarfed by the enormity of the ice looming above her. I begin to walk towards her. Rianne and Rodriguez continue along the ridge top above the mudflat, clambering over stones towards the glacier's face, while Alexander and Nimrod stay atop the crest of the moraine, spellbound by the sight, standing where Dahlia and I were only moments earlier. Alexander focuses his camera.

Suddenly a huge piece of ice, massive, monolithic, breaks from the glacier's face and falls into the river. It disappears, consumed by the livid water. It's like a silent movie, in slow motion. Only the continuous roar of the river can be heard, that and my heartbeat as it pulses through my temples. All other sound is blanketed out. The black water splashes up into a huge wave. From where I stand it looks like it engulfs Dahlia and the boulder on which she stands like a giant hand. Hurrying along the mud flat, I want to warn her that it may not be safe where she is. We're all getting too close. Stopping for a moment I turn to my right and look out to the centre of the swirling river. A large boulder cleaves the water. On top of it sits a rock the size of a coconut. As I begin to wonder who could have placed it there I notice the water creeping up the boulder slowly swallowing it. Looking down at my feet, water spreads over the mudflat and I have to scramble up the loose gravel slope to escape. Maybe the fallen chunk of ice caused the water to rise or maybe it's Ganga's fingers reaching out to grab me.

Looking back to Nimrod and Alexander, they're yelling at me but I can't hear a thing. Desperately they signal for me to return. Panic rises – adrenaline surges as my heart pounds. Dahlia, where is Dahlia? From where I am now the boulder she was standing on is obscured from sight by a slight meander in the river. Madly, I dash towards where I last saw her. The rumble of the river is deafening the closer I get to the glacier's face. I see Mary in front of me. Screaming till my voice is hoarse she hears and comes back towards me. Seeing the fear in my face, Mary instantly knows something is amiss. I shout, 'Have you seen Dahlia?'

Mary's lips quiver and she looks scared, 'No.'

'Shit. Go back to the others.'

As she rushes past me she slips, falling towards the water. I manage to grab her arm in the nick of time and throw her back against the slope of the moraine. She looks at me and our gaze connects. We both know she was almost a goner. I continue to where I last saw Dahlia. The rock where she stood has disappeared. On the ridge above me I see Rianne and Rodriguez. Rianne's crying and Rodriguez looks ashen faced. I scream out, 'Where the fuck is Dahlia?'

But the river is too loud – we can't hear each other. Signalling to them to head back, I turn around. The water already starting to recede, reveals the mudflat that now shimmers like chrome, our footsteps of seconds earlier, polished off. I look out to the boulder in the middle of the river that is again exposed, but the rock that sat on top a moment ago is gone, washed away. I run across the mudflat to the base of the moraine that moments earlier, Dahlia and I had descended. Sitting there, reflecting in the sun is a chunk of ice the size of a house brick. Clawing my way back up the slope, my heart beats so hard it feels like it will explode, my legs feel weak and I'm light-headed. I meet up with Rianne and Rodriguez. Rianne is hysterical. 'She's gone, she's gone – Dahlia drowned. The river took her.'

Time stops still, like somebody just pressed a pause button. We're all in shock. Time starts again. Nimrod rushes to Rianne to comfort her. I look to Mary, she's about to breakdown and cry. I yell at her, 'Don't you fucking dare cry Mary – I need you to keep it together. You and Rodriguez are our fastest walkers. I need you guys to go back to the ashram to raise the alarm.'

Turning to Rodriguez. 'Stick together guys.'

They dash off down the track. Rianne is a mess. 'I saw her go, I was right behind her. I was going to go to the rock too but the water came up so fast. She looked so scared. The river just took her.'

She collapses, weeping uncontrollably. I look at Nimrod, he understands the gravity of the situation. 'I will take her back to the chai shop. Then help you look.'

We both know that in this freezing water we don't have long to find her, hypothermia would be swift. Her chances of survival are slim at best. The icy water is like concrete slurry, the current strong enough to carry chunks of ice and rock. It would be like trying to swim in a blender. Looking around for Alexander, he's nowhere in sight. I turn to Nimrod, 'Where's Alexander, does he know?'

Nimrod shrugs his shoulders as he leads Rianne away. I call out, 'Let's search and meet back at the chai shop in an hour, OK.'

Much of the river's edge is impossible to reach with steep ravines masking large sections. Searching futilely where I can, in my heart I know she's gone. Walking back to the chai shop I see Alexander sitting on top of a moraine with a view of the river. He knows what happened, I can see from his face. Shaking his head as he climbs down, he holds back the tears. 'I saw her go man. I just took a photograph of her the moment before it happened. She floated for a second then she disappeared under the water.' Braving a smile, he fumbles in his bag for a cigarette. 'I'm sure she will be OK though, probably washed up downstream.' His hands shake as he lights his smoke. 'I have no doubt she has found some sadhu and is sitting by a nice warm fire, drinking chai and bossing the poor sod about.'

Alexander is obviously in shock. Back at the chai shop Nimrod sits with Rianne, he too shakes his head. Moving close to Nimrod I whisper in his ear, 'I reckon she's gone mate, but Alexander is in complete denial. You get these two back to the ashram. I'm going to run ahead to catch up with the others to see if they have managed to organise a chopper to search the river.'

I get back to Bhojbasa ashram by late afternoon. Mary is arguing with the local policeman. He is also the chaiwallah, donkeywallah and thali cook. She looks frustrated. 'Rodriguez is searching up the river with some locals and I've been trying to get through to somebody, anybody, to try and get a helicopter up here. All we have is this CB radio and nobody speaks English and nobody wants to help. They seem to think it's a fucking joke. Nobody's taking me seriously because I'm a woman.'

Over the ensuing hour we manage to get through to Delhi. They say they can send a chopper, but only by tomorrow morning. Not long after, Alexander, Rianne and Nimrod return, followed shortly by Rodriguez, his search also futile. We sit there in the fading sun of the late afternoon feeling completely useless, wondering what to do. Alexander is still convinced she will be fine. But then the bearer of bad news arrives in the form of a small Indian boy wet with sweat from running down the path. 'Ji, Ji, there is a body in the river, it is a girl.'

Our hearts sink as he explains how a hiker found Dahlia's body wedged between two rocks, revealed only when the water subsided. I turn to the policeman. 'We must go and get her, now.'

He looks at me. 'But it is nearly night, ve can be fetching her in the morning.'

Glaring, I tower over him. 'No damn it, we go now.'

'Who vill go, hmm, who?'

Realising he's a one-man show, I look around at our party. 'We will go.'

He realises we've lost our friend. 'And I vill help, I vill be getting the stretcher.'

The stretcher consists of an old potato sack and two rusty iron bars. With heavy hearts we head back up the path to collect our departed friend. It's dusk when we finally reach her. The rich donkey riding family from Delhi we met yesterday wait on the track offering to help; they point down to the riverbank. The German hiker who found her has already pulled her out of the water and bound her body up in a blanket. It's real, part of me fantasised that we could revive her and everything would be OK. But here she lies before us, dead. Dropping to my knees I place the palm of my hand on her chest. She's stone cold. Feeling her small breasts through the blanket, I recoil. I feel like I have violated her, she never let me touch her there in life so I certainly have no right to do so now. Mary places her hand over her mouth. 'Oh my god, I actually checked this part of the river when I was walking back to the ashram. I must've just missed her.'

Lifting her body together we place her on the stretcher and each with a corner heave her onto our shoulders and begin the slow walk back. The iron bar cuts into the flesh of my shoulder but I don't care, I want the pain. Taking turns bearing the burden of her weight, it's dark by the time we somberly trudge into the ashram. We pass a Frenchman wearing geek chic black-rimmed glasses – dumbstruck by the scene, 'Who is it? What happened?'

I glance at him. 'She is our friend. Ganga took her, but we took her back.'

We place her in an empty hut on a cold concrete slab, usually a washroom, today – a morgue. The German hiker who found her looks at us. 'She vas pretty banged up, it vould be goot to clean her up a bit, yar.'

Tears well up in all our eyes, we're in no state to see the battered corpse of our companion. Rodriguez steps forward, 'I am a nurse, I will do it alone.'

Instantly I've a new found respect for the latest member of the group. Under candlelight and behind closed doors Rodriguez respectfully washes her down and wraps her in her favorite pink poncho. The remaining six, of the party of seven, then file into the room. Alexander, tears streaming down his face, hangs his brass Om near her head and with shaky hands, lights a candle. Nimrod hands out incense sticks and we all circle her body holding hands. We sing hymns and mantras and Alexander gives a moving eulogy. We all touch her feet, light incense off the candle and say our final goodbyes.

One by one everyone files out of the room till I'm alone, kneeling at her feet. Sighing deeply, I stare at the ground, 'I'm sorry Dahlia. I'm sorry you died, I'm sorry I never got to know you better, goodbye beautiful girl.'

I notice one of Dahlia's pink metal bangles on the ground – it must have fallen off her when Rodriguez cleaned her up. Scratched and bent out of shape from the river's battering, the metal is cold. Squeezing my hand through it I place it on my wrist, considering it my penance, my burden of guilt to carry. Everyone returns to our room, crestfallen and stunned. Sitting around together eating out-of-date chocolate, we tell stories about her. Laughing and crying, we're all confused. Alexander pulls out his digital camera and we all look at pictures of her in happier times. The last photo is the one he took seconds before the wave took her. The timer shows the photo was taken at 11:59. Astonished, Alexander's eyes are crimson with tears. 'My god she must have died at exactly high noon. It's like it was destiny. She was always hurrying in front of us. Then standing there beneath the ice that for thousands of years remained intact, only breaking away at that exact moment.'

With that we eventually fall asleep, exhausted.

* * *

Pitch black in the middle of the night, Mary shakes me. Just making out her face, she's terrified as she whispers, 'What's that noise?'

Just outside our hut I can hear an awful racket. It sounds like somebody is throwing the tin plates and cups from the eating area all around the ashram grounds in a fit of rage. I can hear someone in the kitchen slamming doors and smashing glass, like an angry mob is ransacking the place. Listening harder it sounds like whatever it is it's coming closer, till things are thrown against the wall of our hut. Then abruptly it stops and it's dead quiet for a moment. It's eerie. The sound of footsteps breaks the silence, running around and around the hut, faster and faster. The footsteps then sound like they're running up the walls over the roof and down the other side, around the outside of the hut and repeating again and again – each time getting louder and faster.

Mary clutches me now. Both terrified, we look over to everybody else – they all seem to be in a trance-like sleep. How can they not hear all this commotion? Again, the sound just stops. Suddenly the wooden shutters of the window start shaking violently, then simultaneously the window on the opposite wall does the same thing as well as the door – like something is trying to get in. As abruptly as it starts – it stops. A howling wind picks up outside; ungodly, it sounds like a screaming woman. Catatonic, Mary and I lie there in a terrified embrace till morning. There is no sign of the ransacking in the light of the new day and everything appears to be in place. Mary and I mention nothing to the others, everyone has suffered enough already, how would they cope with being told that maybe Dahlia's spirit came back to haunt us last night?

Police from Gangotri arrive with porters that we have to pay to carry her body back. We pass an Italian woman accompanied by a sadhu as we leave the ashram. Stopping us, she looks shocked. 'What happened?'

We explain how exactly at noon yesterday, Dahlia was taken by the river at Gaumukh. Both the woman and the sadhu go pale staring at each other. Going weak at the knees the woman sits heavily on the ground. 'My god. I can't believe it.'

Shaking her head she looks up at us. 'At exactly twelve o'clock yesterday the baba and I were hiking back from Tapovan to Gaumukh, directly above the glacier, when out of nowhere I was blinded by a flash of white light. I couldn't see anything for about ten minutes. The baba here actually started crying tears of blood.'

The last twelve hours of shocking heartbreak, the surreal events of last night's apparent haunting still sinking in, blinking I look at her. 'What?'

'I'm serious, I was blinded and the baba cried tears of blood. At exactly twelve o'clock.'

All of us at a loss for words, they join our funeral procession and we all descend together. The spectacular backdrop of the mountains and valley, today feels completely different. The path is racked with danger. At different points falling rocks and landslides almost take each of us out. Alexander is almost toppled into the abyss when a falling stone smashes into his ankle, leaving him with a nasty gash. A policeman manages to pull Rianne out of the path of another tumbling boulder just in the nick of time, whizzing past missing her head by only inches. The mountain doesn't want us to leave. Reaching Gangotri in the early afternoon we're escorted to the police station. There's much activity – filling forms out in triplicate, which we sign time and time again. We're handballed from officer to officer, each ask us to tell our story, over and over again, repeatedly rewriting the same statement until eventually, we end up with the chief. He looks up at me. 'So please be telling exactly what happened?'

Rolling my eyes I tap my finger on the pile of the statements written out time after time. 'Exactly what is written there, in triplicate and all signed by all of us.'

'Hmm. And what about your names and passport numbers?'

I tap on another pile of notes on his desk. 'Here – as dutifully recorded by your officers again, in triplicate here, here and here.'

The officer starts to blush, realising the abundance of red tape. 'Yes, yes that appears to be all then. You are free to go.'

Rianne enquires, 'What happens to her body now, who will tell her parents?'

'She will be taken down to Uttarkashi for post mortem, but after that it is out of my jurisdiction.'

Nimrod and I look at each other – we've heard that one before. Alexander steps up, 'If it's all the same to you, we would like to accompany her to Uttarkashi, in case the officers there require any further assistance.'

It's agreed and we're all bundled into the back of the ambulance, which seconds as a personnel mover for the army. The officer assigned to drive us stinks of whiskey and is quite obviously drunk – he staggers up to the van, leaning into the back and slurs, 'I am best driver in whole state, have no fear ve vill be arriving in Uttarkashi in no time at all.'

Slamming the door shut he starts to drive us down the mountain. Night falls as we wind our way down the road. Thunder rumbles and a crack of lightning illuminates the sky. A heavy deluge falls on us – the van's windscreen wipers are useless, it's like driving in a fish bowl. We're all quiet in the back, looking at Dahlia's body wrapped in her favourite pink blanket. In death she seems so tiny, like she shrank. The storm worsens, a slew of muddy water gushes over the road. At one point a landslide of boulders rolls across our path. The driver expertly swerves to avoid collision. One even hits the roof of the van smashing down hard and loud as it tumbles across. We're all relieved as we finally arrive in Uttarkashi in one piece.

There is nobody at the hospital, so we carry Dahlia's body into the morgue ourselves. Outside, it's a tin shed with no refrigeration. We place her onto a dirty concrete slab. Our inebriated police escort then drives us to a nearby hotel, loitering in the lobby, swaying on his whiskey sea legs. Smiling and patting us on the back, there's something vaguely threatening about his demeanour. Finally he leaves. We're physically and emotionally exhausted and relieved when we finally close the door on the last twenty-four hours. I look at everyone, 'Man, it was like the mountains didn't want us to leave, the storm – almost not making it down the track. It was like she was meant to stay up there but we stole her back. It was like we had the wrath of Shiva himself upon us.'

Exactly at that moment, lightning flashes just outside the window, startling us, thunder rumbles and the rain again falls heavily. Nimrod looks up, 'Full mountain power.'

* * *

Sleeping late, all passed out together, we don't wake until there is a loud rapping on our door. Dreaming of the tranquility of beach number seven on the Andaman Islands, now awake the awful reality comes flooding back, I open the door. It's the policeman who drove us down the mountain last night. Today, he's not smiling but sweating and looks a little pale, no doubt hung-over. He grumbles, 'You must all be coming down the police station for questioning, now.'

Reluctantly, still wearing the clothes from the last couple of days, we follow the policeman to the station house. There, we again make statements in triplicate, as our passports are passed around and scrutinised by every officer. I sense they're trying to intimidate us, but we aren't buying it. Alexander is resilient. 'What will happen to Dahlia now?'

The police chief, a huge bull of a man, balding with a large moustache, responds without looking at us. He shuffles a pile of papers. 'Ve vill conduct an autopsy today then her body is to be collected.'

Alexander continues questioning, 'By whom? Have the parents been notified? What about the Swedish Embassy?'

'Yes yes, everything is taken care of. You can go now, but please stay in town in case ve need any further information.'

Rodriguez pipes up, 'There is no refrigeration in de morgue and it is very hot today, she will decompose very quickly, she needs to be kept cold.'

The police chief glares. 'Ve are a very poor country, vhat do you suggest?'

I cut in. 'Ice man, put bags of ice on her.'

The officer stands up, leaning over his desk. 'And who vill pay for this ice then?'

Rolling my eyes, I'm about to respond in a barrage of abuse. Alexander gently places his hand on my shoulder. 'We will sir, we will.'

With that we file out of the station house and convene at the nearest chai stand. Rodriguez is irate. 'It is nort right, dey are not having respect for de body.'

Nimrod is calm and practical. 'So, we must find ice.'

Mary rubs her chin. 'Hmm, I wonder if the parents really do know yet?'

It's frustrating as none of us have any contact details for her family; traveller friendships are formed spontaneously and nobody thinks to ask for 'people to contact in case of emergency'. We're unfortunately at the mercy of the powers that be. Rianne chips in, 'I think we should call the Swedish Embassy, make sure they know.'

We're in combat survival mode still, focusing on the problem-solving aspects of the tragedy. The emotional burden is temporarily on hold till will know these necessary things have been taken care of. Nimrod looks puzzled. 'Where will we find ice in this town?'

I have a flash of inspiration. 'The chaiwallah, ask the chaiwallah. If you want anything done in India, ask the chaiwallah.'

Breaking into groups Alexander and Rodriguez are on ice detail, Nimrod and Rianne return to the hotel in case the police need us and Mary and I are to contact the Swedish Embassy. On the phone I'm handballed from person to person till finally I speak to somebody that can confirm that they have been informed and that they've subsequently told the parents. They tell us there is nothing more they can do. By the afternoon Alexander and Rodriguez return to the hotel, they look hot and flustered and Alexander is seething. 'Found an ice maker, eventually, thanks to the chaiwallah. But my god what an ordeal though. Problem is, to make enough ice that Rodriguez calculated we'll need, will take them all bloody night.'

Suddenly there's a knock on the door. It's two police officers who want us to come back to the station immediately. Back at the station house the chief of police waits for us. Gruffly he asks for our passports again. 'Ve need to take a photograph of you.'

Lined up in a row, a young police officer takes a group photo of us all together. From behind the camera he calls out, 'Smile.'

I'm not sure if it's like a mug shot or some bizarre photo for posterity. As we're herded back into the station house, I'm a little nervous, they have our passports and have told us not to leave town. Are they going to say we're somehow responsible for her death? Maybe they suspect us of murder – maybe we'll never leave this town. Suppressing a welling up of guilt, I'm not ready to deal with the emotional burden of blame just yet. After all it was me that first suggested the tragic journey to

Dahlia. Grinning smugly, the police chief returns. 'Ve have finished the autopsy and ve conclude that the girl drowned.'

Looking around at us all as if he expects us to be impressed, he continues as he passes back our passports. 'Ve have now finished vith the body, and I plead to your humanity, take it back vith you.'

Alexander looks up at him in horror. 'What?'

'Yes you can take your friend back now.'

I'm confused. 'Take her where exactly?'

'Back to your hotel, or as you like.'

We're dumbstruck. He's pleading to *our* humanity? What he's proposing is inhuman, for us to take back the no doubt decomposing body of our friend, and sit there with her in our hotel in the sweltering heat, for an undetermined period of time. We all refuse, marching out of his office in disgust. We go to the phone again to call the Swedish Embassy. Mary explains to them, 'They want us to collect the body that is rotting in a tin shed with no ice. This is a disgrace – one of your citizens is being violated here.'

The embassy tells her that an envoy from the consulate in Delhi has already left to collect her and that we have done everything we can. They advise us to wash our hands of it and leave town. We decide to do just that. Dahlia is gone and there is nothing more that we can do for her. Quietly, the following morning we slip out of town at first light and head south on the first bus, before heading west to Dharamsala, the home of the Dalai Lama and hopefully a place of spiritual refuge and recovery.

The next morning it's, *Chai, chillum, masala, chello to Dharamsala.*

CHAPTER 12

On The Flipside

Even now months later, as I sit here twiddling Baba Krishna's rudra bead necklace between my fingers, I still try and fathom some sense of logic from that fateful day on the seventh of May, nearly one year ago. I shouldered a sense of guilt for a long time for Dahlia's death. All the 'if onlys' would come rushing back, if only she had stayed in Nepal a couple of extra days, if only she had decided to stay in Rishikesh, if only she had stayed next to me whilst I found the piece of white quartz moments before she died. Now I constantly switch from thinking the whole thing was preordained to it being just a crazy, random act of chaos. I guess I'll never completely know.

Is it just my mind trying to justify the tragedy or was the sequence of events actually fate unfolding? Me finding the ace of spades, the symbol of death, in Kolkata at the mouth of the Ganges, then Dahlia finding another one on the bridge over the river the day we left Rishikesh, chance or omen? The rock pools of blood outside our hotel room in Gangotri, the swirling red sari caught in the current, meeting the one-legged Aghori baba and finding the stairs to Vishnu, chance or omen? The door which would only open for Dahlia and the old man laughing at her saying she would go up to Vishnu still sends a chill down my spine today.

Myth states that the Ganges is the melted body of Vishnu

and that Vishnu sleeps on a serpent – a serpent that's the cosmic ocean and Shiva's symbol of death. Then there was Dahlia's fear of snakes, the conversation at the Sab Kuch Milega café about serpents in mythology, then Dahlia subsequently seeing her first snake as it crossed her path the day before she died. Was it symbolic of the death of the body, birth of a new consciousness, the spin of the wheel of life; was it a premonition of Dahlia drowning in the cosmic ocean? I struggle with the philosophical meanings of free will and determinism, trying to decide, as we all do, which is the reality. Maybe the universe is all preordained, at least some of the time. Or maybe it is a malleable thing like clay, it has properties that cannot be changed, but certain aspects of it can be moulded. But how can free will and fate exist together? Maybe for the sake of this story I'll say they just do.

From the moment Dahlia picked up that card on the bridge it was like she was locked into her fate. It had been sealed. The fact that she was always pushing us to keep moving up the track, so she could stand beneath the glacier at exactly twelve o'clock to be washed away, kind of suggests fate. The piece of ice that broke off the glacier and created the deadly surge of water was there for thousands of years, only falling the moment Dahlia arrived. Sheer coincidence? Then the last words she uttered in this world at the chai shop at the end of the universe, talking about how life is too short and you never know when you are going to die and to never delay anything when you can do it now. It was almost like she knew on some deep subconscious level that it was going to happen. Alexander had said, 'It was a glorious death. Trust Dahlia to make such a dramatic exit, and only at the most auspicious place in all of India.'

I don't think she was suicidal though, if she had her time

over again I'm sure she would've not gone to that fateful boulder to be swallowed by the river, but hindsight is always twenty twenty and that's not how the game works.

Sometimes I think that she had been a sacrificial lamb inadvertently brought by us to Gaumukh for slaughter, an offering to Shiva. A god perhaps angry at the receding glacier due to global warming and other blasphemies committed by the world that's long turned its back on the mystical realms. Perhaps we were reprimanded for belittling the sacred pilgrimage to nothing more than a stoners' picnic. Or maybe that's just me trying to find some rationale in a senseless death. Dahlia paying homage to Shiva moments before her demise, my premonition of death upon seeing the river at its source, the flash of white light that blinded the hiker moments after and the baba subsequently crying tears of blood, all suggest the workings of something more than just the sum total of events. Something more than our analytical, logic-obsessed age can explain.

Then there was her ghost that came back the night she died to haunt us. Maybe her spirit was furious that she was dead. I never believed in ghosts before that, but when one comes up and slaps you in the face you tend to reassess your beliefs. I think she died so suddenly that she didn't have time to realise she was gone, perhaps the blinding flash of white light was her soul being thrown out of her battered little body. Or perhaps that was just some bizarre unexplainable microclimatic anomaly that just happened to occur at the very same moment in the very same place. Sometimes the unknown is a more plausible explanation than what the tangible world can provide.

If she was a sacrifice to the mountains, I don't think we were meant to find her and I think that maybe Shiva wanted to keep her there. The Indians seemed nonplussed at our loss, as if it was the will of god. This was apparent in their reluctance to fetch her body from the river. Rodriguez later confessed to us that when he conducted the search party up the river, he'd stumbled across human bones, including a skull. Obviously it was not the first time that this had happened. But we stole her back, snatched her from the icy grip of Ganga and the mountain tried to retrieve its bounty. We almost didn't make it back to Gangotri ourselves, down the narrow goat track that was fraught with danger. Then in the ambulance ride down to Uttarkashi the mountain continued to throw lightning, rain, landslides and boulders at us.

Those of a more cynical nature will probably say that what I'm saying is a load of rubbish. And if I had not been there that day I would say the same thing. However, I was there and it did happen; sometimes fact is stranger than fiction and the bizarre makes more sense than the rational. I could've died alongside Dahlia that fateful day, if I hadn't paused to pick up the piece of white quartz at the base of the final moraine before the glacier wall. A stone perfectly shaped like the continent of India.

A stone I've since fashioned into a pendant that I wear around my neck now, it glistens in the light like it did on that fateful day. It's my lucky charm, my rabbit's foot. It has an unusual quality, its opaque tone sometimes becomes translucent like a piece of ice, almost completely transparent. I kiss it and place it beneath my T-shirt next to my rudra bead Baba Krishna gave me.

In fact we all nearly died up in those mountains, Rodriguez and Rianne trying to get to the rock where moments later Dahlia died, Mary almost slipping into the river, Alexander and Nimrod nearly being knocked off the track and down into the ravine by falling stones. Yes, we all nearly died up there, but we didn't, only Dahlia died. Maybe it just wasn't our time, or maybe we were just plain lucky.

The delayed shock of Dahlia's death slowly surfaced once we escaped Uttarkashi at daybreak and bused south to the next town. We hired a taxi jeep and hauled the red eye all the way the Dharamsala where we sought spiritual refuge. Fragments of memories only remain after Dahlia's death, whereas every second in the mountains has been scored permanently onto my mind. We laughed, sang and smoked chillums as through the canopy of trees dappled sunlight danced on the road. The jeep sped along. We passed field upon field of wild hemp, snaking against the contours at the mountain's feet, until finally ascending into Dharamsala. We stayed huddled together in our little group, our healing circle. We all coped with the tragedy in our own ways. Alexander became roommates with Rodriguez and they spent hours watching old movies on the TV in their room.

Nimrod and Rianne announced they were getting married, ignoring the logistical problem that he was due back in England the following week and Rianne was going to continue travelling throughout Asia. Mary and I shared a room and the subtle signals she had been dropping ever since Gangotri transformed into a passionate embrace. Kissing me deeply, she stared at me. 'I think you may have saved my life up there in the mountains, catching me just before I slipped into the river. So, um, thanks for that.'

We continued to kiss. She then stopped suddenly. 'Look, I just want to make something clear, even though we are sharing a bed I don't want you to get the wrong idea OK. I'm not feeling entirely comfortable with this situation and I just want you to understand that nothing more's going to happen here.'

'Cool, I get it, no funny business. I'll be a good boy and stay on my half of the bed, good night.'

As I rolled over and went to sleep I resigned myself to my plight of continued celibacy. Then in the middle of the night Mary jumped me, tore off my boxer shorts, straddled me, and took me deep inside her. Gyrating her hips until we both came, she then collapsed to her side of the bed. Post coitus and smoking a joint, she confessed – smiling, 'The whole no-sex thing just wasn't working out for me.'

At last, the astrologer's prediction of meeting a lover had finally materialised. We were an unlikely couple, thrown together through tragedy and a genuine need for physical comfort. The sex was an affirmation of life, of needing to feel human, of needing the caress of another person. We spent hours in bed, fucking and talking about of our lives, sharing physical and emotional intimacies.

Later Mary confessed, 'I'm feeling a little disappointed in myself for having slept with you, not because you aren't a nice guy. No, it's just that I only recently broke up with a boyfriend and I promised myself to take some time out from guys. Then you know, like at the first sign of danger, I fall into the arms of another man. Such a girly, girl thing to do – this was meant to be my time to find myself as a woman. My liberation.'

I smiled cheekily. 'Well maybe this is just that, it's all a matter of perspective really. Maybe this is part of your liberation.'

She smirked. 'Steady on cowboy, don't any get delusions of grandeur.'

My final weeks in India slipped away. What felt like an eternity months earlier, a span of time I wasn't sure I could endure then fast ran out. The last days of the party of six evaporated. We ate together, laughed together and prayed together at the Dalai Lama's house. We caught up again with Frida and Carlitos. Carlitos, a sickly deep yellow tone, looked very sorry for himself. 'Hey Australia, I am very sick, I have got hepatitis. I mus' have eaten somefing bad in Laxman Jhula.'

A large whale of a woman supported his weight. She had arms like rolling pins and folds of fat that would fare her well in the worst of winters. She smiled, eying Mary and I up and down suspiciously. Carlitos acknowledged her. 'Gretel here has been looking after me.'

Being polite I smiled. 'Nice to meet you, so where'd you find this big old yellow bear?'

She answered in a booming German accent, 'Ve met on ze Andaman Islands and zen in Kolkata. Zen I find him here all alone, poor baby.'

Turned out it was the same girl he had been courting the whole time, rather than the plethora of different girls he'd insinuated he had seduced. Although he looked weak and feeble, he appeared to take comfort in the matronly bosom of Gretel.

Then like all things the inevitable end arrived, the final disintegration of the group. We all met for a final supper. Frida, Carlitos and Gretel joined us. Although Carlitos was not yet back onto solids, the rest of us feasted on curries, dhal, saffron rice and lassies, finishing with chocolate brownies, chai and, of course, chillums. I passed out gifts for the party of six. Bracelets of little skulls made of bone, I hoped yak, similar to that of Mr. Baba Santos, the one-legged Aghori baba with the nice smile. 'A memento, something to remind us of each other and of Dahlia.'

There were many tears and hugs and kisses. Rianne hugged me and looked into my eyes. 'There is something about you Aaron. Some people have a magic sparkle and some don't. You can see it in the eyes. You seem like a boy that had a sparkle but lost it somewhere in life.' It took me aback. Had I lost my magic sparkle? I didn't know I had one in the first place.

The next day I left on a bus for Delhi with Mary. My flight to Thailand and onwards around the globe was due to depart in a couple of days, and Mary was scheduled to return to Canada not long after. We left the sanctuary of the hills, with its crisp mountain air scented with pine needles and wood smoke, where smiling maroon-clad Buddhist monks appeared and disappeared, like apparitions, down winding narrow lanes into mist. We left this island of tranquility behind to be swallowed back up by the ocean of people and the overwhelming heat of the delta plains below.

Being back in that frenetic commotion and activity of an Indian metropolis didn't bother me anymore. The hustle and bustle of the streets of the Old Bazaar, the blanket of sticky heat, the swarms of crowds and congestion of beeping traffic spewing out noxious exhaust, seemed harmonious as I weaved in and out of it all. I had finally found the rhythm of this place, finally found the beat. You can never walk in a straight line in India; to get from point A to point B you must first go through all the other letters of the alphabet. I would step to one side, instinctively knowing when a bus would hurtle past, only inches from me. Knowing when to stop suddenly to allow a rickshaw to scuttle past, from nowhere and back into nowhere. Everything fits perfectly in India, you just have to find your little spot and work within it, that's all it is, that's the trick.

My last days in India were spent hanging with Mary, lying naked in our hotel room, sex, charas, mangoes, rambutans and reiki. We both knew this was the end of an era – our lives would drift apart. We didn't even kid ourselves and promise to meet up again in the future. We both knew this was the end for us. My last day changed to hours, which changed to minutes before I was due to be picked up by my taxi. Outside it was dark, pre-dawn. Pigeons perched on the opposite building stared at us in our haven. We were both quiet and contemplative – Mary stood naked gazing out of the window. 'Hey Ji, you won't believe it, come and look at this.'

I walked over to the window and looked to the alley below, illuminated by streetlights. There on the ground laying face up was a card – the ace of spades. We looked at each other and laughed meekly, neither of us wanting to ponder the significance of it. We had both had a full quota of messages from the universe for the time being. Did it indicate the end of one adventure or the beginning of the next? Lost in this thought for an eternal moment, I was snapped out of it by the ringing of the telephone in our room. It was the taxi – it was outside. Time to go. I picked up my pack and hauled it onto my shoulders and held Mary in a final embrace, kissing her softly on her forehead, confusing emotions surging through me.

Mary holding back her tears, 'Well Ji, this is it. Thanks for the liberation and all. I'll see ya on the flipside.'

With a clenched fist I gave her a gentle, fake punch on the chin. 'See ya kiddo. Stay true or Alexander and I will be forced to send in the choppers and the psychonaut commandos.'

I turned and walked out of the door without looking back. As the taxi snaked its way through the streets, all was quiet as Delhi still slept. A magical time in a city normally bursting at the seams with people and activity – it was the witching hour. Suddenly, overhead, lightning filled the sky and a downpour of rain like I have never experienced before fell. Within moments the streets transformed into rivers of dirty water. We came to an intersection and my taxiwallah stopped and turned off the engine, I was a little nervous, the clock was ticking – I had a plane to catch. I leaned over to the wallah. 'Hey Ji, lets *chello*, airport, my plane leaves soon.'

He grinned back at me, wobbling his head. 'Monsoon. Monsoon is starting now. Ve must vait till rain is stopping.'

'Dude, *chello, chello*, please.'

'But the vater is very deep.' He pointed to the road in front of me as a torrent of water flowed past. The rain showed no sign of abating and I was fast running out of time.

'No Ji, *chello, chello*. NOW.'

He reluctantly started up the taxi and slowly drove into the flooded street. Halfway across, the engine cut out, he turned to me panicking. 'Please, please sir ve must be pushing taxi out, the vater is coming.'

'Shit.' I opened the door, the water rose alarmingly fast. Stepping out, my feet sank into the filth and disease-ridden stench that rose out of the gutters and open sewers. As we pushed and shoved the taxi, the water continued to rise. Up to my calves, then up to my knees. A wave of fear washed over me. My mind flashed back to Gaumukh and the river. The filthy dark liquid reminded me of the black churning Ganga – maybe she had come back to collect me, maybe I would never leave India. Drenched and exhausted we finally got the taxi out, but he was unable to start the engine again. Desperate, I rustled up rickshawallahs, waking them up in the back of their vehicles till I found one insane enough to try and get me to the airport in the middle of a monsoon. He did a sterling job, driving on footpaths around puddles deeper than Loch Ness, making the airport with only minutes to spare. When I went to pay him I realised to my horror I'd lost my last few rupees. I must have dropped them whilst pushing the taxi. Then for the first time in tourist history a *gora* ripped off an Indian. 'Sorry Ji, but I have lost my money. I am truly sorry, but I'll pay you with my eternal gratitude and a karma blessing.'

He was dumbstruck as I backed away. 'May this act of goodwill be repaid to you a thousand fold in this life and the next.'

I turned and ran. I did the sketchy bail and ran for my life never looking back. As the plane left the tarmac and lifted off the hallowed soil of the subcontinent, I sank back into my seat. As the morning sun broke the curve of the horizon I reflected on my experience and on India. Even though the tapestry of this country's endless history, the very fabric of this society, is worn threadbare, India has a durability, resilience and endurance like no other. In the 'new is best' obsessed West, India would be thrown in the trash, or worse, recycled, rehashed and repackaged. No, everything in India is made of dust, held together with nothing more than faith and belief that it will work, as it always has and always will. There are taxis there older than East European countries, buildings older than the bible and beliefs older than history itself, but your street corner chaiwallah isn't even ten years old.

A country of sublime paradox, where the world's oldest culture of nomadic monks, the sadhus, own nothing other than a chillum and a bowl, but now also a mobile phone and an email address to accompany their sacraments. Vaudeville soapbox sorcerers and snake oil merchants hoodwink dim witted villagers, while overseas throngs of Indian expats excel in all fields at the world's best universities. A country constantly on the brink of ever spiralling environmental collapse, overpopulation, epidemics of everything, revolution and social upheaval from unprecedented economic growth, it weathers its continual exponential transformation with ambivalence. Civilisations come and go, empires rise and crumble, eras wax and wane and India is still India.

Nearly one quarter of the world's population, today it's a country where outsourcing has been adopted as a mantra by the prolific growth of call centres. Bargain basement cosmetic surgery, Bollywood and the new silicon valley of Bangalore, are all giving the very heartlands of capitalism a run for their money. Throughout this immense rebirth into a new century and a new millennium India shrugs her shoulders, wobbles her head and smiles a humble toothy grin. Everything has changed but everything is the same as always. Mother India is certainly bottomless, and I barely scratched her surface.

I had come to India for some sort of enlightenment, to enrich my soul, to ascend to a higher plane of consciousness. I guess in a way, I kind of did, it's just not how I expected it. But that's the beautiful thing about life – it's never how you expect it. I thought I would've done the whole ashram, yoga, guru thing and emerged – what – enlightened? It's funny but much of what I learnt was as much from fellow travellers as it was from India herself.

Nimrod's appreciation of sunsets and Jimmy the Ambassador of the Sunrise's love of embracing each and every dawn. Alexander's seeing each day as being a new one out of the box. Carlitos, Suz the Nip, Dangerous Dave, Ian and the Andaman crew all taught me the value of friendship, however fleeting – as well as the value of a pocket pair of aces in a stacked full house. Dr Mohanti and Victor taught me I didn't need a guru to do yoga, I just needed to do it. Baba Krishna showed me always to look at the world with mystery. Baba Rainbow taught me to look between the cracks and Dylan, to do everything with extra love.

Dahlia taught, through death, that life is fragile and too

short to waste doing things you don't want to – I think she showed us all that. I like to think it was her gift to us all. Dahlia passes my mind every time I cross a river and every time I see a picture of Shiva. His three-pronged trident reminds me of the mountain peaks from which Gaumukh's glacier emerges. The small stream of water emerging from Shiva's head reminds me of that fateful day at the source of the Ganges. Each time I see the scar on my foot I think of India and 'full mountain power'.

Ganga made me face death, mortality and our place in the wheel of life. Almost dying in Varanasi, with the cathartic shedding of kilos, and feverish visions made me realise I had to leave an old way of life I could no longer sustain. A message reaffirmed with the unsolved murder in Rishikesh. Beach number seven on the Andamans gave me a taste of heaven and the stairs to Vishnu in Gangotri a chance to go there. The festival of colours in Kolkata gave me the epiphany that I'm always free if I live in the infinite, glorious, and beautiful NOW.

I often wonder if I'll ever cross paths with my past travelling companions, it's a small world after all. I actually did by chance meet someone from that fateful day in the mountains. It was a couple of months after India. I was in northern Thailand studying silversmithing. I had made a ring from the Shiva's eye Baba Krishna had given me, and a pendant out of my lucky quartz stone that I had found at the source of the Ganges. Over dinner one night, with a group of travellers at the hostel where I stayed, a black-rimmed spectacled, French guy told us all a strange and tragic tale of a girl who had died in the mountains in India. We had been hanging together for a couple of weeks, eating together, drinking together and sharing travel stories. My heart froze as I stared at him as he told the story, my story – Dahlia's story. Finally I recognised him. He was the guy who had asked me what had happened when we walked past carrying Dahlia's body back to the ashram. 'Man that was me you met that day. You spoke to me. That was me carrying the stretcher.'

We both stared at each other in amazement, as we realised the synchronicity of the universe. Or was it just a coincidence? What were the chances of that, is it possible? Of course it is. After all everything is possible, *Sab Kuch Milega.*

EPILOGUE

Back to the Future
(Here now in here and now)

Sitting here, now, I type the closing words of this story on the balcony of our small apartment in Rio de Janeiro. It overlooks a beautiful mountain in the distance. Its proximity to the *favelas* (ghettos) makes it *muito barrato* (cheap). Green humming birds hover at my window and small monkeys clamber in the mango trees above. I contemplate. The evolution I underwent in India still resonates with me today and I suspect it will continue to do so my whole life.

Looking at some photos I developed recently from a disposable camera, found forgotten at the bottom of my pack, they are of the mountains. Strangely all the pictures of Dahlia are darkened with a thick black line across them, whereas all the other pictures are perfectly clear. Her spirit has followed me since the day she died, visiting me in my sleep and occasionally, frequenting the shadows, appearing fleetingly out of the corner of my eye, when I am alone late at night. But I've made my peace with her now. Now this story has been told. Recently, alone on an abandoned beach, I buried her pink metal bangle I had carried until then. A beautiful day, on a beautiful beach, I dug a hole in the sand and buried it. She always liked the sun and beaches and I made my peace with her there, said my final sorry and my final goodbye. I promised myself I'd never return to that beach in my life. It's her beach now.

I never did make it back to Australia. No need, the astrologer's prediction came true. Soon after arriving in Brazil I dreamt of my old friend the cockatoo. He flew back to his tree, scratched an X on his branch and tucked his head under his wing to sleep – he'd come back home to roost. I met my future wife days later and I'm now engaged to be married. Vivi was an apparition of beauty and strength that appeared at just the right place and just the right time – coincidence, irony or the old adage of synchronicity. I was on the last leg of my round the world jaunt, just about to head home to Australia. Amber had emailed me saying she'd dumped the coke dealer and was waiting with open arms, as was my ex-employer in Australia, with only a slight demotion. The same job and the same relationship as when I left, it all seemed too easy, like nothing had happened. So, in the middle of either a panic attack or an epiphany, I decided to do the sketchy bail on myself. I didn't want to pick up from where I left off, slip into my old skin and lose the reality of all those nows. One week before returning home I seriously questioned going back –I just binned my return plane ticket.

That's when I met Vivi, voluptuous, golden-brown skin, blazing dark eyes and long black hair. Not to mention intelligent, educated, razor-sharp wit and no tolerance for my bullshit. She just looked down her nose at my esoteric meandering philosophy and soon whipped me into shape. I was in the process of either getting robbed or maybe even murdered when we first met. I'd wandered away from a samba joint and down a laneway on the wrong side of the tracks in a favela. I was looking for a toilet but instead found a small angry teenage boy with a big gun. I'd inadvertently wandered into gangland and grinned nervously as he told me what I presumed were my last rights in Portuguese. Vivi had noticed me stray from the gaggle of gringos and safety of the street and followed. She chastised the boy, just stopping short of clipping him around the ear before dragging me back to safety. She had scowled, 'Stupid gringo.'

If hell hath no fury like a woman's scorn, then the scorn of Latin woman could freeze it over. I figured she was a keeper, but it took a month to convince her I was the same. Hands on hips, head sliding left and right and cussing in Portuguese and shooting daggers with her eyes she pushed me to finish this book, get a haircut and get a job.

Still a vagabond I'm just no longer jetset. Seems I've parked for a spell, scratched my X in this neck of the woods. Surviving today hand to mouth, I work illegally as an English teacher. I teach corporate executives from planet raping petroleum companies how to spell

G.R.E.E.N.H.O.U.S.E E.F.F.E.C.T

And

C.O.R.P.O.R.A.T.E. C.O.N.S.C.I.O.U.S.N.E.S.S.

A first world drop out and illegal immigrant, my employer, a mulatto Brazilian, calls me his *little white slave* and *gringo Mexican*. The trip may be over but the journey has only just begun. A gecko runs across my foot. I grin. I like living where geckos reside. I'm on a new mission now, to find my lost magic sparkle. I suspect it could be in the heart of the Amazon jungle. I'm planning an expedition to meet an Indian shaman and drink a potion made from the Vine of the Dead. But that's a whole different story. In case you were wondering here's what happened to my old *comprades*:

Dangerous Dave was never heard of again, but there was a rumour he ended up becoming a professional poker player in Los Vegas.

Ian changed his name to Munty, never to return to the

IT industry, instead he bought a Royal Enfield and moved to the south of France. Last I heard he was trying to set up his own version of the Shiva Riders, the 'Shanti Shanti Riders', at present he's the sole member of the gang. His bike is currently broken down and he is waiting for parts to be sent from India.

Suz the Nip ended up hooking up with a Kiwi lad and is living in a kombi van in New Zealand. They survive by fleecing backpackers at poker. They intend to move back to India in the near future.

Carlitos recovered from his bout of hepatitis and now works as a tour guide in India. He is still looking for any volunteers to bear his children.

Jimmy, Ambassador of the Sunrise, Bacon slipped into a nasty heroin habit back in England. He has since moved back to his bamboo hut on the Andamans and is clean again. He passes his days counting coconuts. His crystal chillum is still in operation.

Nimrod never married Rianne – he went back to England to sell children's painting kits in shopping malls. He intends to go to film school in New York next year and fulfill his dream of becoming a filmmaker.

Dylan finally made it back to the States where he worked briefly as a plumber for the family business. But he decided it wasn't for him and ran away to join the circus where he performs with fire poi. He still wears his lungi and still practices reiki, sending extra love vibrations around the world.

Victor opened his own yoga school in Manhattan where he teaches stressed out, high-flying executives how to relax and be shanti shanti. He misses his roof top yoga class in Laxman Jhula and intends to return soon.

Frida went back to Wales where she did an exhibition of her photographs of India. Her controversial photo of a headless corpse titled 'Jane Doe of the Ganges' caused quite a stir.

Rianne is still travelling. After horseriding through Mongolia with Rodriguez and working on a kibbutz in Israel, she's now somewhere in South America with a bunch of Israelis.

Rodriguez finally made it to my home town in Melbourne. He embraced the Australian culture with gusto. He grew a handlebar moustache for a charity event, 'Movember'. He liked it so much he still dons it today and refers to himself as the Dirty Sanchez, oblivious to its connotations.

Alexander hitched a ride with the Shiva Riders from Dharamsala to Manali where he assisted with the new season's harvest and charas production. He intends to make a pilgrimage back to Gaumukh soon. He eventually intends to go back to the Amazon to lick the back of a certain species of frog and hopefully transcend the material plane.

Mary never went to law school. She changed her name to Xela, after a Guatemalan town where she met a shaman who convinced her she was meant to be a witch. Today she's studying silversmithing and practices reiki. The Psychonaut Commandos are on permanent standby.

Frankie finally made it out of Nepal and back to India, the day after I left. Still riding the wave of Kobra power, he worked briefly as a volunteer saving Sun Bears in Borneo, but didn't get along with the organisers. He was last seen heading into the jungle. He now refers to himself as the 'Wild Man of Borneo'. He is apparently developing the power of levitation from his meditative powers. He has vowed to deny himself pleasures of the flesh and has proclaimed himself to be a monk. He has renounced sex as an evil distraction, shelving the Kobra indefinitely.

Acknowledgements

Barry Scott and Transit Lounge for giving this book a home, Matt Wagner for helping me murder my darlings, Mrs Moneypenny Mum for proofreading, printing and generally keeping my affairs in order, Dad for pointing out the clanger on the first page, Maus for his words of encouragement and bailing me out, Herbs for trying to get me an agent, Gonzo for threatening to kick me out of the country, Caine for his couch in Barcelona and Buenos Aires, Euclydes and Celeste for taking me into their home, Nélio for employing me as his white Mexican, the full mountain power crew (you know who you are), the Andaman poker crew, Frankie, Scottie Boy and Kingfisher Beer, Brahma Beer and Cachaça 51 for greasing the wheels. But most importantly I want to thank my muse, my best friend - my no bullshit Brazillian wife for wrangling me into writing this, and as I promised, giving her the last word.

Aaron Smith is an ex-punk rocker and one-time policeman on the Australian television series *Blue Heelers*, a theatre and script writer, and ex-first world drop out who lived in the favelas of Rio di Janeiro. He works as a freelance journalist writing for a number of Australian and international publications, including most recently *Australian Geographic*, *AG Outdoor*, *Australian Traveller*, *Forty Degrees South* and *The Mercury*. Aaron also appears regularly on ABC Radio 936 to talk about travel. He is completing a Masters in Journalism at the University of Tasmania where he lives with his hard-headed no-nonsense Brazilian wife.

More at www.jetsetvagabond.com